M000278600

EAR CANDY

The Inside Story of America's #1 Cover Band, Foxes & Fossils

Paul F. Caranci & Sammie Purcell

1 2 3 4 5 6 7 8 9 10
Written by Paul F. Caranci & Sammie Purcell.
Cover and interior design by Elisha Gillette.
Published by Stillwater River Publications, Pawtucket, RI, USA.

Names: Caranci, Paul F., author. | Purcell, Sammie, author.
Title: Ear candy : the inside story of America's #1 cover band, Foxes & Fossils /
    Paul F. Caranci & Sammie Purcell.
Description: First Stillwater River Publications edition. | Pawtucket, RI, USA :
    Stillwater River Publications, [2022] | Includes bibliographical references.
Identifiers: ISBN: 978-1-958217-56-6
Subjects: LCSH: Foxes and Fossils (Musical group) | Rock groups--United
    States--History. | Rock musicians--United States--History. | Older musi-
    cians--United States. | Music and the Internet.
Classification: LCC: ML421.F7 C37 2022 | DDC: 782.421660922--dc23

In Loving Memory of Scott King, a good and decent person who gave so much of himself to others. Though taken too soon, his talent will forever be showcased through his music and will live on through Foxes and Fossils.

TABLE OF CONTENTS

Part III
Odds and Ends

Appendices

Ear Candy

AUTHOR'S PREFACES

Paul F. Caranci

Neither the band nor its individual members have a star on the Hollywood Walk of Fame. They don't have a platinum or gold record. They don't have a big-name producer, or a manager and you have never heard their music on the radio. But *Foxes and Fossils* have become an overnight YouTube sensation, and their wave of success seems to have no crest.

Residing in Georgia, Virginia, and Tennessee, the band members include very seasoned and talented musicians, ranging in age from sixty-one (drummer Johnny Pike) to seventy-three (guitarist Toby Ruckert). Sixty-one-year-old bassist Scott King, band leader, sixty-five-year-old Tim Purcell, and his sixty-four-year-old childhood friend Darwin Conort, round out the players. They have had remarkable musical careers and, as younger individuals playing in various other bands, they have opened for the likes of Ray Charles, The Turtles, The Dave Clarke Five, The Who, Peter and Gordon, The Allman Brothers, and many other mega superstars.

While all five 'Fossils' sing, the primary vocals are provided by a trio of 'Foxes'. Sammie Purcell, Tim's youngest daughter, Maggie Adams and Chase Truran are young, talented, and beautiful women who each began singing with the band when they were only about fifteen years old. Their harmonic blend is absolutely stunning and can bring a tear to even the most critical eye.

As a multi-generational band, they are quite versatile, too. They have covered a variety of songs ranging from the 1950's to the 2020's. They have a unique and uncanny ability to take the most beautiful song and make it just a little bit better.

Some allege that their success is simply a product of lucky timing. It is true that their music hit record heights during the pandemic lockdown of 2020 when many more people than usual discovered music on YouTube. But the straightforward truth is that they are simply that good. Their songs have been viewed on YouTube over eighty-one million times and they have been named by several YouTube critics as the number one YouTube cover band in the world.

They have had a stunning impact on the YouTube music world, and their story is a truly amazing one. And now, meet the *Foxes and Fossils*.

Sammie Purcell

When we were first approached about the prospect of writing a book, I honestly didn't think much would come of it. Even when I started running through edits, it still sort of felt a little fake—a little out of body, like something like this should not be happening to me, you know? But now that you're presumably reading this in an actual book that you can hold in your hands, I guess I'll have to come to terms with the fact that this book is, in fact, real—a wild thought!

Editing and running through this book over and over has been an interesting experience, but I think what I've enjoyed the most has been reliving the formation of the *Foxes and Fossils,* and learning so much about the early lives and careers of the band members I've basically known my entire life. So many new stories have leapt out at me from these pages—including a few I didn't even know about my own dad—that have made me laugh, tear up, and maybe even cringe a little bit, in equal measure. I hope they do the same for you.

Thanks for reading, and thanks for being a fan.

ACKNOWLEDGEMENTS

Historical and biographical works of non-fiction are completed only with the help and support of a great many people working toward a common goal. Completing this book was no different and the authors gratefully acknowledge many people for their effort in bringing this project to fruition. These include band members Tim Purcell, Darwin Conort, Toby Ruckert, Scott King, Johnny Pike, Sammie Purcell, Maggie Adams, and Chase Truran, as well as family and friends of the band, Scott and Karon Truran, Larry and Ellen Adams, Mike and Mary Thomas, Ross King, Scott Kale, Fontaine Nimmo, Billy Parks, Jill Ewing and Bruce Johnson, all of whom provided countless hours for interviews and/or dredged up the many photographs that appear in this book.

In addition, we are thankful to the amazing fans of Foxes and Fossils who took the time to provide information helpful and critical in the preparation of the book. These include Brad Burns, Christopher Ketchum, David Weaver, Terry Heinlein, Paul Giammarco, Kevin Burns, Linda and Bob LaFrenierre, Mike Frey, Gary Tupholme, Monique Kooij, and Steve Poegl for providing charts that have taken untold hours of research to compile, as well as much of the content that appears in chapter 12 of the book.

Finally, a special thank you to Bruce Johnson and Steve Becket for their work in creating and sharpening the many versions of the front cover image of this book. We are grateful for your thoughtful work, the extra effort and the quick turn-a-round on that project.

INTRODUCTION

January 2010: From Boredom Comes Opportunity

Tim Purcell has spent his entire life making music. An extraordinarily talented man, Tim is an accomplished musician, vocalist, songwriter, and a gifted athlete—a Renaissance man of sorts. In his career, he's had the good fortune to make music with several successful bands. His goal was to be in a band where he would be the weakest link—if that were the case, he reasoned, the band ought to be pretty good.

Tim's career began when he was just a teenager, and by 2010 he had basically done it all. He'd performed in high school talent shows, he'd sung the National Anthem for the Atlanta Braves, and even opened for Ray Charles at the inauguration of Georgia Gov. Sonny Perdue in 2003. Over the span of 40 years, Tim had realized all of his musical goals—well, almost.

There was one elusive target that he just never seemed to hit—making it. Getting that record deal, getting his songs on the radio, becoming a household name—who knows, maybe even a legend. But no matter how hard he worked or how well received his music was in his circles, he was never able to catch a big break or build the momentum that would push his career to the next level. Not as a young man in The Bret

Hartley Band, his first all original group, nor his first professional group, Lou's Blues Revue. Not with his personal favorite original band, Perfect World, and not even with The Riley Hawkins Band, the house band at Mama's Country Showcase who performed for over 2,000 people every weekend night for two and a half years.

Though he may have wanted—or thought he wanted—to be a rockstar in his younger years, in 2010, Tim was 53 and in a different place. He no longer had the desire for fame. Perhaps he never really did. What he did long for—all he ever really wanted to do—was to make good music. That was when he was happiest.

On a particularly wet and chilly day in early January 2010, Tim wasn't thinking about record deals, or even about making good music—he was just plain bored. His wife Terri, a corporate attorney for Coca-Cola, was at work, and his two oldest daughters were off at college. He sat on the couch in the den of his home in Smyrna, Georgia, wearing sweatpants and a t-shirt, strumming his guitar and feeling kind of blue.

He began to fool around with the Simon & Garfunkel classic song *America,* a "wistful and optimistic, personal and universal and most of all, uniquely American"[1] masterpiece.

"Let us be lovers, we'll marry our fortunes together," he sang softly as he played the classic melody on his six-string.

"I got some real estate here in my bag...,"

As he sang, he couldn't help but think about the very disappointing holiday season his band had just experienced.

Tim's band at the time, The Mustangs, had achieved a decent level of local success over the years. They worked a

---

1   Wikipedia Encyclopedia, America (Simon and Garfunkel song), Recorded in Columbia Studio, New York City on February 1, 1968. Release on April 3, 1968, from the album Bookends. https://en.wikipedia.org/wiki/America_(Simon_%26_Garfunkel_song).

large number of gigs, including appearances at local fairs and festivals as well as some very high-paying private functions for major corporations in and around Georgia. They entertained at parties for giants such as Coca-Cola Enterprises, Price Oil, and Alabama Power, just to name a few. Despite their local festival network and their extensive web of corporate connections, at the end of 2009, The Mustangs had just experienced one of the worst holiday seasons they had ever known.

In their wildest dreams, The Mustangs couldn't have predicted that all their prior success would come to a sudden and screeching halt because of political reckonings coming to fruition in the nation's capital. Public outrage at major American auto makers and big business in general was at a fever pitch after executives from Ford, Chevrolet and Dodge/Chrysler flew their private planes to Washington to ask Congress for a financial bailout. With the eye of the public focused on corporate excess, holiday parties and corporate shindigs quickly became a thing of the past. For the past several years, the band had earned a significant portion of its income during the winter holiday season. In 2009, The Mustangs only worked two holiday gigs and were idle on New Year's Eve for the first time in memory. There was nothing the band could do about this turn of events, and the future did not look good.

Singing and fiddling around with his guitar generally helped Tim relax. It put him at ease even in the most stressful situations, and it was a good cure for boredom. He sure needed a distraction on that bleak wintry day, so he continued to play *America:*

> *"...Toss me a cigarette, I think there's one in my raincoat.*
> *We smoked the last one an hour ago, ooh, ooh, ooh, ooh.*
> *So, I looked at the scenery, she read her magazine,*
> *and the moon rose over an open field.*

Kathy, I'm lost I said—though I know she was sleeping.
I'm empty and I'm aching, and I don't know why, ooh,
ooh, ooh, ooh..."

It sounded good, but this solo rendition rang hollow in his ears. While the lyrics are great on their own, it's the harmony that makes *America* such a beautiful song. He could hear the harmony in his head, and an idea took root. Tim called out to his daughter Sammie, who was seated at the computer in another room, and issued a challenge.

Sammie was only 15, but had already displayed an unusual capacity for music. She had a strong voice of remarkable range and unassailable quality, and was a quick study when it came to learning songs. She had already performed with The Mustangs, filling in when lead female vocalist Judy Browne was absent from a gig, and she had a great ear for harmony.

Tim had always been amazed at Sammie's talent. Before she could even really talk, she would sing along to the radio whenever she was in the car with him. She would really open up her pipes when her favorite song, the Trisha Yearwood standard *How Do I Live*, came on, belting along with gusto while strapped in her carseat in Tim's 1997 Chevy Cargo van.

He had purchased that van especially for gigs and had it customized with removable back seats, enabling him to transport The Mustangs' sound system from job to job with relative ease. He used that same vehicle for the next 18 years until a rear end collision totaled it, and was heartbroken when he had to let it go. During an interview, Tim fondly remembered teaching all three of his daughters to drive in that van. "If they could drive it, they could drive anything," he reasoned. He remembered driving around with Sammie in her front seat carseat (that was legal back then), hearing her sing and witnessing her ability to switch from melody to harmony and back again. "She could do it flawlessly," he recalled.

Tim frequently captured Sammie's voice on tape in his home studio. "For kicks, I recorded all my girls," he said. By the luck of the draw, Sammie got to take advantage of the home studio the most. She was younger than her next oldest sister by six years, so from the time she was 12 until she went off to college, she was the only child at home. This and the fact that Tim's studio ability and equipment continued to improve over the years really helped Sammie as her voice matured.

"Have you ever heard the song *America* by Simon & Garfunkel?" Tim asked Sammie on that dreary January day. She had not, so Tim had Sammie listen to it a few times, asking her to pay particular attention to Art Garfunkel's exquisite harmony. As she listened, Tim slipped down to his basement studio and recorded a rhythm track and lead vocal, laying the basics down for Sammie to put on a harmony

Joining her dad in the studio a short while later, she added the finishing touch; a harmony so pure and effortless, that it got Tim to wondering...what if...?

Part I
THE PLAYERS
The Early Years Through The Mustang Era

Chapter 1

TIM PURCELL

The Early Years

Timothy Porter Purcell was born at Crawford Long Hospital in Atlanta, Georgia on February 22, 1956, the third child of Captain Donald Eugene and Dorothy McCrary Purcell. Before Tim's birth, the couple had put down roots in the Atlanta suburb of Hapeville, a city located just south of downtown adjacent to what is now known as the Hartsfield-Jackson International Airport. Tim's parents hailed from two small towns in Alabama that were only four miles apart, but didn't meet until after World War II. Donald's sister introduced them, and they hit it off—they dated for a short while before marrying in 1946.

Don, as he was called, enlisted in the United States Army Air Corps just a few months after Japan attacked the United States at Pearl Harbor. He piloted a B-24 Liberator nicknamed SNAFU—a bit ironic, Tim said, as his father (to his knowledge) never said the word represented by the fourth letter of that acronym. Don successfully completed some 30 bombing missions over Europe and was highly decorated

Don Purcell in an early 1940's U.S. Air Corp photo.
(Photo courtesy of Tim Purcell)

before being honorably discharged from active service near the war's end.

On June 30, 1945, Captain Purcell married Dorothy McCrary. The newlyweds lived in New York City for five months while Don trained for a pilot job with Eastern Airlines, and then moved to Jacksonville, Florida, where they lived for three years. While living in Florida, their first child Steve was born. About two years later, the couple moved to Hapeville. The town's proximity to the airport was convenient for Don, who was now flying for Eastern—a job he would hold for the next 35 years.

Tim's sister Donna was born five years before Tim in 1951. His brother Steve was nine years his senior and already away at college by the time Tim was eight. Despite Steve's long absences in Tim's youth, the younger brother has vivid recollections of both Steve and Donna's record collections, first 45 singles and later albums. Those records had a huge influence on Tim and his interest in music. During the late 1960s, Tim recalled that Steve would always return home from college in the summers with more albums. "I devoured them,"[2] he said.

The Purcells lived in a nice, modest home, nestled into the predominantly blue-collar town where many residents found employment at either the airport or the Ford Automobile facility located in Hapeville. Dorothy, known to her family and friends as Dot, was a very talented pianist and organist with a beautiful voice. The family attended Sunday services at the Methodist church, though Dot occasionally played the organ at the Baptist church which, as is typical in the south, sat catty corner across the street—kind of like CVS and Walgreens or McDonald's and Burger King. To Tim's recollection, his parents had no vices, and neither ever touched alcohol. Later in life, Dot would buy a bottle of wine for her adult children to enjoy at holiday gatherings, but she never poured a glass for herself or had a single sip. The Purcells were a hard-working couple who saved their money all of their lives. As parents they were strict, but loving.

Pranks and Other Mischief

Tim had a mischievous side as a child, something he apparently inherited from his father. In late 1942 while flying a plane from his training base in Oklahoma on the long route to England, Don decided to take a detour. Ignoring orders to remain at 9,000 feet, he "buzzed" his parents' Alabama home in the small town of Bessemer. "We went over [the house] about

---

2   Ibid. Page 3.

six or eight times, I guess, at an altitude of 200 or 300 feet," Donald recalled in an interview with his grandson, David. "We had to pull up to miss the smokestacks at the Pullman plant. During this time, the RPM's on the airplane engines were being run up and back by the co-pilot. My dad had a lot of chickens and when we left, he had a lot of broken eggs."[3]

The entire interview can be accessed online at the American Air Museum website (see link in footnote).

Like his dad, Tim had a prankster's mind. When he was about seven years old, he enjoyed playing with an authentic army shovel his dad had given him. "It had a changeable spade on a short handle, [so you] could use it as a shovel or a pick,"[4] Tim said. One day, he decided the shovel would be the perfect tool to build a trap into which he could lure his father. Tim intercepted his dad, who was dressed in his Eastern Airlines uniform "fixing to go on a flight," Tim said. "I told him there was something he had to see across the street in the wooded lot. I had carefully camouflaged a three-foot-deep hole with sticks and leaves. I asked him to wait on the edge of the woods while I got my 'surprise' ready. I went and stood on the other side of the hole and beckoned him forward. He fell in, injured his already terribly compromised left knee (a high school football injury) and sullied his uniform to the point where he had to limp home and change before he could go to work."[5] Tim doesn't recall if his father whipped him for staging the prank, but to this day he admits freely, "I've never been more ashamed about anything I've done."[6]

---

3   American Air Museum in Britain, 2006 as written by David Purcell. Page 2. http://www.americanairmuseum.com/person/43919
4   Tim Purcell in a written response to interview questions asked by the author. July 28, 2021. Page 2.
5   Ibid.
6   Ibid.

Dorothy McCrary became Mrs. Donald Purcell in 1945
(Photo courtesy of Tim Purcell)

The Hills Are Alive...

When Tim was eight years old, his mom strongly encouraged him to audition for the high school's 1964 production of *The Sound of Music*. Though he was resistant to the idea at first, he ended up really enjoying it. "Maybe it was being around high school girls," he joked. Whatever the reason, Tim really relished it. "Later in life, I became a huge fan of musical theater," he said. "All of my daughters participated in drama throughout their school careers. I really think I missed my calling."[7]

At the same time Tim was enjoying playing Kurt in *The Sound of Music*, the family experienced a life-changing event. Dot was pregnant with a fourth child due that fall,

---

7   Ibid. Pages 1-2

5

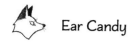
CHRISTMAS

Bapeville Junior Service League
December 13, 1961

Narrator - - - - - Helen Stephens

Accompanists - - - June Clemans

Written By - - - - Gerry Wells

PROGRAM

It's Beginning to
Look Like Christmas - - - - Willson
Lucille Leathers

I Saw Mommy Kissing
Santa Claus - - - - - - - - - Conner
Carole Clemans & Tim Purcell

The Christmas Song - - - - Torme'-Wells
Gerry Wells

Gesu Bambino - - - - - - - - Yon
Dot Purcell

Sweet Little Jesus Boy - - Mac Gimsey
Betty Drukenmiller

A 1961 program from Tim's first performance before a live audience.
Note that the program also included Tim's mom.
(Image courtesy of Tim Purcell)

and the family was overjoyed when she went into labor in early November. Don walked his wife to the car carrying her small overnight bag, and the couple took the relatively short drive to Atlanta's Crawford Long Memorial – the same hospital where Donna and Tim were born some years earlier. On November 5, 1964, Dot delivered a baby girl who the couple named Amy. But shortly afterwards, the doctors told Dot and Don that Amy had Downs Syndrome. The couple made the difficult decision to not take Amy home, opting to place her in a group home where they could visit her and she could get the care she needed.

When his dad told him that his baby sister would not be coming home, Tim's excitement turned to shock and sorrow. He retreated to his room where he began to pray. "I thought if I prayed hard enough, God would fix it," he recalled years later. That didn't happen, and the experience shook Tim's faith, souring his attitude toward religion.

Tim was not the only member of the Purcell family who had difficulty adjusting after Amy's birth. Dot was understandably distraught after making the difficult choice to institutionalize her baby. The weight of that decision caused her to retreat to the security of her bed where she remained for about two months in a state of deep depression. At the time, Dot's faith wouldn't allow her to get past the feeling that Amy's diagnosis was a punishment from God, and she couldn't understand how she might have offended him so egregiously.

Eventually the family adjusted to their new normal, loving Amy for the blessing she was. Though she never lived at the family home, she was close by and visited her family as much as possible, particularly on holidays and birthdays. When she would see Tim, she would without fail clap her hands together and shout, "That's my brother!" Her unbridled happiness always brought a smile to his face.

Tim's mother was a strong woman of undeterred faith. This helped her navigate what was a most difficult time in her life, and after considerable thought—and perhaps as a means of distraction—she decided to enroll at Georgia State University. She earned a bachelor's degree in elementary education and accepted a teaching position at Meadows Elementary School, where she taught the middle grades and earned a "teacher of the year" award. But she grew restless after a couple of years as a teacher and turned her attention to real estate sales. She did very well in that profession, achieving more than $1 million in sales in a single year at a time when the average home sold for only about $60,000.

Donald was also upset over the fact that his youngest daughter couldn't live at home with the family. As the primary breadwinner, he focused on his work. His job often kept him away from home for two or three days at a time, and Don's airline schedule combined with Dot's teaching and subsequent real estate dealings, sometimes left young Tim home alone after school. Sometimes Marie, the ironing and cleaning lady who came once a week, would double as a babysitter, or Donna would keep him company on the rare day she was free from after school extracurriculars. At times, however, Tim would come home from school to an empty house. Despite the lack of round-the-clock supervision, he can't recall ever feeling neglected. Times were simply different back then, he said. Besides, he had a strong constitution, and his penchant for keeping himself busy kept him out of trouble despite the large degree of independence that was given to him.

Tim and Darwin both played on Hapeville's 8th grade basketball team. After a slow start, the team finished with a 7-8 record. Darwin, #44, is standing on the left while Tim, #42, is standing second from the right. (Image Source: Page 111 of the 1974 Hapeville High School Yearbook)

Growing Up in Hapeville

Looking back, growing up in Hapeville seemed idyllic. There were many similarly aged children living in Tim's neighborhood, and he would frequently join them in games of street baseball or hide-and-go-seek. He recalls engaging in such activities until the streetlights lit up the darkening roads. In the 1960s, long before the advent of cell phones, the illumination of streetlights was the universal signal that playtime was over. That's when most children knew that it was time to get home.

Tim's parents strongly encouraged his siblings to take piano lessons in their youth, but Don and Dot never pushed Tim in that direction. To this day Tim isn't sure why, but

suspects it has to do with Amy's birth and his mother's need to expend her energy elsewhere. He likely would have resisted those attempts anyway, as he preferred sports.

Tim did, however, take guitar lessons when he was about seven or eight years old at a little building in Hapeville called The Band Box. The lessons were classical, which was not what Tim had in mind. "I wanted to play rock-n-roll, and my father wanted me to play like Chet Atkins," he said. "I didn't see those lessons leading to either of those."[8] The lessons lasted only a few weeks before Tim grew bored with the tedium of learning scales, when what he really wanted to do was play and sing songs. Luckily, that opportunity presented itself when his church's youth minister began offering group guitar lessons. Finally, Tim had a chance to learn a few chord positions, which enabled him to play more than a few songs. "That might be where I first met Darwin [Conort]," Tim recalled, noting that Darwin has similar memories. If the two did meet during those group lessons, they didn't develop a close friendship—that would come years later.

Hapeville High School

After seven years at the Josephine Wells Elementary School, Tim embarked on a new academic venture. In the Fulton County School District at the time, eighth-grade classes were held in high schools, where students had their own lockers and changed rooms for the start of each new class. Tim was 13 years old in 1969 when he found himself wandering the halls of Hapeville High School as an eighth grader. The experience was very different from elementary

---

8   Author Interview with Tim Purcell. December 31, 2021.

school, and he found the whole thing pretty intimidating at first, but adapted rather quickly. The eighth-grade lockers were located in the same hall as those of some pretty cute ninth and tenth grade girls. Tim, who was smart, athletic and charming, was okay with that—to say the least.

Tim quickly learned how to finesse his way around high school girls. He quickly became friends with a pretty girl named Pam Cook, and though she was a year ahead of him in school, a mutual attraction began to develop. By the time they actually began dating, Pam was a 17-year-old junior whose father just happened to be an Atlanta Falcons season ticket holder. More than once, Pam was able to snag her father's tickets, complete with a parking pass for the lot under the stadium right next to the players' lot.

"Pam taught me to whistle," Tim recalled fondly. "And not the purse your lips and blow type of whistle. I mean the two fingers in the mouth, loud-ass whistle. It doesn't speak well of me and it probably led to some hearing loss, but Pam and I discovered that if we both whistled as loudly as we could at the same time, the resulting overtones were quite obnoxious and painful to anyone near us. Those people in front of us at the [Falcons] games were quite perturbed (much to our impish delight) when we practiced our skill after a good play. To this day, I think about Pam anytime I use the two fingered whistle technique."

Star of Court and Field

Throughout his five years as a Hapeville High Hornet, Tim established himself as both an outstanding student and a three-sport star. He was the quarterback on the football team, forward on the basketball team, and pitcher/outfielder on the

baseball team. Unfortunately, a series of injuries would derail his athletic ambitions.

Ironically, Tim recalls one of his concussions (perhaps his fourth) among the most memorable (pardon the pun) injuries he suffered on the gridiron. "We were playing a game against St. Joseph's that had regional playoff implications," he said. "We only had 18 players on the team, so everybody who could actually play played both ways [offense and defense]. I was doubling up as a defensive back and intercepted a pass over the middle with about two minutes to go in the first quarter. It was a rainy night and a muddy field. There was no one in front of me and if I could just make the corner, I would score a touchdown. Little did I know a speedy wide receiver had the angle on me and was closing fast over my left shoulder. As I was about to start making my way to the goal line, he reached out and horse-collared me from behind. You could see on the film that my feet went straight out from under me and flew up in the air while the back of my head bounced very hard on the ground. I remember hearing a loud whistling noise and the lights being very bright. We took over possession and huddled up. It was obvious to the players in the huddle that I was concussed. The back-up QB, also the starting running back, asked me (at least that's what he told me later—I don't recollect) if I could just take the snap and toss him the ball. Apparently, I could and did so despite the coaches signaling, from the sideline, other plays to run. We ran maybe three plays and were actually moving the ball when the quarter ended. I staggered over to the sideline where our medic (the local fire chief) was stationed and he asked me if I knew where I was and what day of the week it was. While I knew the day, I had no idea where I was because we were playing on a neutral field not typically used by the teams. He looked into my eyes and called the ambulance. I ended up in the hospital and we ended up losing the game...."[9]

That's not the only amusing story Tim can tell about his football years at Hapeville High. By the time he was a junior, Tim had been the starting quarterback on the football team for two years. That's when he got to know a boy who, as it turned out, would become one of the school's most successful and famous graduates. But at the time, Jeff Foxworthy was just a skinny little tenth-grader on the B-team who practiced with the varsity. For reasons unknown to Tim at the time, Jeff really didn't like him. "We ran the wishbone, and Jeff played defensive end," Tim said. "With only 18 varsity players available to practice, we had to do half-line scrimmages and the B-team often participated. Defending the wishbone requires the defensive end (Jeff) to tackle the quarterback on virtually every play. He would literally try to kill me! The reason for his animosity, I think, was that I was dating a girl that he had a big crush on; the very beautiful Denise Ivie. Fast forward to the year 2000 when my friend and former college roommate, John Huie, a highly successful entertainment agent with Creative Artists, calls me from Nashville. 'You're never gonna guess who I just signed,' he said to me in a rather excited voice. 'Jeff Foxworthy,' he added before I could venture a guess. I said, 'Yeah, I know Jeff. I grew up with him.' To which Huie responded, 'I know. I asked him if he knew you and he said, 'Tim Purcell, he got all the 'ladies.'" (What he actually said can't be printed in a family book.)

---

9   Ibid.

The Intellectual and The Musician

For Tim, high school was easy. He had both a strong intellect and an innate athletic ability that set him apart from most other students. The classwork was instinctive for him and he didn't need to study very hard to achieve the status of class salutatorian. The time he didn't devote to studying gave him extra time to concentrate on his other interests—sports, girls, and music.

Aside from establishing himself as a top-notch student and an all-state athlete, Tim's years at Hapeville High School would prove important for another reason. That is where he became friends with Darwin Conort, an extraordinary guitarist and singer who could harmonize better than most, matching Tim note for note. He had known Darwin for some time—they attended the same church, they were in the same Cub Scout Pack for at least a year, and they played on the same eighth-grade basketball team. But they did not become close friends until Tim joined American Apple, a band of teenaged wannabes that tried to cover a variety of 1960s bands from Grand Funk Railroad to the Zombies. The name—American Apple—was a reference to the Beatles Apple record label.

Tim was surprised when he received a phone call from Johnny Chappell, the bass guitarist with the band. "I heard you can sing, and we need a keyboard player," Chappell told him. American Apple's original keyboard player had gotten into some trouble at school and his parents grounded him, but he was willing to let the band use his keyboard if they could find someone to play it. Chappell wanted to know if Tim was interested.[10] Tim didn't let the little fact that he didn't actually know how to play the keyboard keep him from

10   Author interview with Tim Purcell. November 29, 2021.

taking on the opportunity. Sensing the chance for fame, fortune and chicks[11], he had Chappell tell him what songs they'd be going over and agreed to audition. He immediately sat down at his mom's piano to teach himself the few chords necessary to play those particular songs, and learned enough to bluff his way through a rehearsal in Johnny's garage. After that, he officially became a member of American Apple. "We didn't last too long," Tim said. "We practiced a lot and I think we may have performed in a high school talent show once, maybe a party or two…but it definitely put the performing bug in me. I liked it."[12]

Band members included Chappell (bass), Doug Mazur (drums), Darwin Conort (guitar/vocals), and Tim (organ/vocals). But American Apple didn't provide much competition for the other local band from those high school days, a group called The Fabulous Us. Tim envied that group, who actually performed at some high school dances and had a pretty good sound. "We (American Apple) were limited by the fact that the only ones who could play their instrument well at all were Darwin, and to some degree, Doug," Tim recalled.

Despite their lack of success and longevity, American Apple brought Tim and Darwin together in a friendship that has now spanned almost 50 years. "I think the thing, at least for me, that drew us together was the fact that we both could sing harmony," Tim said. "A lot of our friends could kind of do it, but none like we could. In a weird way it kind of made us want to be together."[13]

While Tim spent most of his time in high school concentrating on girls and sports, Darwin devoted himself to

11   Purcell, Tim, A Brief Look at Tim's Performance History.
12   Tim Purcell in a written response to interview questions asked by the author. July 28, 2021. Page 3.
13   Ibid.

music and playing in bands. Beyond the eighth-grade basketball team, Darwin didn't show much interest in sports,
Tim recalled. "I was a three-sport athlete and was busy year-
round with games and practices, so my involvement in bands
was limited," he said.[14]

At first, Tim's parents encouraged his musical ambition
and even purchased a used Farfisa Combo Compact organ
for him to use in American Apple when the original keyboard player wanted his organ back. But despite that initial
support, Tim's mother was not all that fond of Darwin, referring to him disdainfully as *"that Darwin"* whenever his name
came up. Like most parents of the baby-boom generation,
Dot and Don were becoming more and more convinced that
rock and roll was "the devil incarnate and that the children of
the 1960s were all on the verge of becoming heroin addicts,"
Tim said. "As time went on, I basically had to sneak around
them to do the rock band thing."[15]

While Tim focused on sports and potential athletic scholarships, Darwin became part of a real working band called
Mantra. The drinking age was 18 at time, so Mantra was
able to play at a couple of clubs in the Underground Atlanta
entertainment district and on the Stewart Avenue Strip, as
well as community events around the city.

A High School Injury
Impacts Tim's College Choices

With his graduation in sight, Tim found himself in the
enviable position of having potential athletic scholarship
offers from several colleges. But a second sports-related

---

14   Ibid.
15   Ibid.

Caution — Seniors at Work

Dale R. Pearce   Samuel Plant   J. Timothy Powell

Timothy P. Purcell   Judy Ray   Peter R. Rintye

109

*Page 109 from the 1974 Hapeville High School Yearbook showing
Tim's senior photo. Is that Tim hanging from the driver's side of the
Volkswagen Beetle in the photo at the top of the page?
(Photo from the 1974 Hapeville High School Yearbook)*

17

injury—a complete ligament tear on his left ankle sustained while playing basketball in February of his senior year—signaled the end of most of those offers. Unlike the concussions that left Tim confused and not immediately knowing that he was hurt, this injury left no doubt. It was devastating and caused him to miss his entire senior baseball season. This really stung, as the prior year's team had gone all the way to the state semi-finals and most of the players were returning for their senior year with hopes of a state championship. What's more, Tim had been the star pitcher and batted third in the line-up, making his chances of being a senior year star even more assured. Unfortunately, he never took the field that year.

Even though Tim rehabbed all summer in preparation for the upcoming college football season, he was simply not the player he once was. After the ankle injury, Davidson College was the only school to offer him a scholarship, and even that offer was rescinded when the school's football program was de-emphasized in May of 1974. Private scholarships based on financial need were still offered to incoming football players by Davidson, but the Purcells did not fall within the qualifying income guidelines.

Football and the Search for Girls
at Davidson College

As if graduating second in his class wasn't achievement enough, Tim was named as a first alternate to the Air Force Academy. Tim admired his dad and thought seriously about following in his footsteps toward an aviation career, but reconsidered after his ankle injury. Plus, the idea of the regimented lifestyle didn't really appeal to him. In any case, he had already given a verbal commitment to Davidson to attend in the fall semester and play football. Davidson also allowed football players to play other sports, meaning Tim could play baseball thus further tipping the scales in Davidson's favor. He opted out of the service academy in favor of Davidson, a fortuitous decision as his eyesight began to fail shortly thereafter which would have disqualified him for flight training.

Davidson College is a small, private liberal arts college in the town of Davidson, North Carolina. Tim—still more interested in sports, girls, and music than academics—majored in psychology (one of the least difficult majors offered), and earned his degree four years later. But despite the relative ease of the major, college wasn't a slam dunk for Tim like high school had been. He really had to apply himself. He managed to play football in his freshman year, but decided to leave the team when he re-injured his ankle playing in the spring game. The injury prevented Tim from playing baseball for the second season in a row, but he was able to play his final three years at Davidson and was named co-captain his senior year.

As a college freshman in the fall of 1974, Tim still had feelings for Denise, his old high school flame. Denise was now a high school senior, and Tim's feelings had only grown in intensity—so much so, in fact, that he was considering transferring to Valdosta State, Denise's college of choice. But when he returned home for summer following his freshman year, he learned that Denise had been seeing a friend of his for almost a year. "That blindsided me and broke my heart," Tim recalled. "But thank God she did what she did, [or] I wouldn't have met the real love of my life."[16]

---

16   Ibid.

He spotted that true love one lucky day during his fresh-man year at Davidson when he and his buddy Kenny Bell were on their way to math class. That's when Tim was struck by Cupid's arrow. "Wow, who is that?" he recalled asking Kenny about a very beautiful girl who had just passed them on the path. "That's Terri Peat," Kenny responded. He seemed to know a great deal about her. Kenny told Tim that Terri was in her second year at Davidson and had always dated upperclassmen. With a ratio of 1,200 men to only 100 women on campus, upperclassmen always seemed to snag the pretty ones. There was certainly no shortage of David-son men showing an interest in Terri, and Tim very quickly joined their ranks.

Tim realized it would be difficult to attract her attention, but he just knew that he was meant to be with her. "I'm going to marry her," Tim said to Ken as they walked. It would take two more years before Terri even noticed Tim.

It was on September 9, 1976 when Terri, now a senior at Davidson, was attending an off-campus party with some friends just across from Martin Manor, an older house on Main Street where she was living that year. Tim, who was now a junior and had the reputation in Terri's circle of friends of being just another dumb jock, was also attending the party. He was very surprised when Terri joined him and a group of students around the keg as they were getting some beers. "I offered her one and as I was pouring it she says, 'So how do you know Rod?' referring to the guy I happened to walk in with," Tim said. "Seems she was wanting to meet him."[17] Tim wasn't going to allow that little detail to spoil his chances. "I brushed it off and turned on the charm," he said. "We talked for a while and then mingled separately, but I kept my eye on

---

17   Ibid. 4

her, and as she was preparing to leave, I asked if I could walk her back to campus. She said sure, and as we were walking, the conversation turned to music. I told her I could sing and play. She was doubtful, given my reputation among her peers, but I told her I would show her if she'd let me."[18]

Tim's Most Consequential Concert

The two walked to Chambers, the building that housed the school's large auditorium and theater. The auditorium was locked, but Tim had long ago figured out a way to slip the lock and gain entry to play the beautiful Steinway grand piano that was on the stage. Before Terri could figure out what was happening, he broke in and escorted her to the stage where the piano was located behind a closed curtain. Like a seasoned maestro, he took his seat on the piano bench and proceeded to play for her. His weapons of choice were songs from Graham Nash's wonderful solo album *Songs for Beginners*. "I don't know if I won her heart then or just shared a secret side of me that piqued her curiosity, but I will always remember the name of that building," Tim said. "It was called Love Auditorium."[19]

Following the impromptu concert, Tim walked Terri home and then returned to his own off-campus house that he shared with four other guys. Terri Peat never did ask Tim about Rod Young again, although Tim points out that Rod would have been a good catch for her as he went on to become a renowned plastic surgeon in Charlotte.

Although they dated frequently throughout the fall and winter of 1976, the relationship was not exclusive. But by spring of 1977, they were spending as much time as they could

18   Ibid. Pages 4-5.
19   Ibid. Page 5.

together. After graduating, Terri attended Emory Law School in Atlanta, but made it clear to Tim that her choice of an Atlanta-based law school had absolutely nothing to do with it being near his hometown. "She wanted to make sure I understood that,"[20] Tim said. Somehow, he doubted that was the whole truth.

Despite being in different cities Tim's senior year, the two continued to see each other as often as possible. Tim graduated in 1978 and moved back to Atlanta, where the couple dated for three more years before exchanging vows in October 1981.

Moving Back to Atlanta

Not many of Davidson's roughly 1,300 students knew that Tim could sing and play, but that changed when he entered a campus talent contest his senior year. Tim's performance was sterling, but it didn't earn him first place. That award went to a student who, the faculty judges would later say, simply "needed it more than I did".[21] Despite the hard-luck loss, Tim's talent was now apparent to the Davidson student body, so when he and a friend decided to perform at the student union on campus, the place was packed.

After graduation from Davidson, Tim began looking for a place to live that would keep him from moving back to his parents' home. Darwin and some of his musician friends were living in College Park, Georgia—an Atlanta suburb that abutted Hapeville—in a stone house just off the road in a wooded area with a creek running in front of it. The house, according to Tim, could be described as nothing less

---

20   Author interview with Tim Purcell. October 4, 2021.
21   Author interview with Tim Purcell. November 28, 2021.

than gross. It was so damp and humid that there were literally mushrooms growing in the main room's yellow and orange shag carpet. Despite the obvious flaws, and against his mother's advice—she begged him not to go live with "that Darwin!"—Tim moved his twin bed from his parents' home into the stone house. "I only lived there for about two months until my brother-in-law got me an interview for a job in the credit department at Lowe's," Tim said. "When I was hired by Lowe's I figured I needed to move closer to Decatur where I'd be working, so I left the stone house. Even in that short period of time, the mold that got on my bed frame was so bad that I had to throw it away."[22]

The Spread Eagle Band

While living together at the stone house, Tim and Darwin performed together in a duo called The Spread Eagle Band. The name was a crude attempt to cash in on name association with The Eagles, who basically ruled the roost in pop music at the time. The pair worked up about a 20-song playlist, but played only two gigs together before moving on.

Their first performance was in the fall of 1978 at the now defunct Little Five Points Pub, an Atlanta club known for its live music. With their friends from Hapeville and Tim's friends from college who lived in the Atlanta area, they drew a very large crowd and had a great time. The show was even broadcast on WRAS, Georgia State University's FM radio station.

The second show Tim booked was for a Saturday night at Davidson College, thinking they would draw a crowd equal to or even larger than the one that attended Tim's show while

---

22   Ibid.

still a student there. Like the first show Tim did, this one was held in the student union in a room that held about 200 people. To Tim's surprise, at showtime it was only about half full. After the success of the Little Five Points Pub performance, playing to a half full room was pretty discouraging. The wind left their sails, and the Spread Eagle Band was no more.

Tim still has a recording of two of the songs they played; *Autumn* (Edgar Winter) and *Had I Known You Better Then* (Hall and Oates) that were taped from the WRAS radio broadcast.

The Brett Hartley Band aka Traveler

Darwin and Tim moved on from the now defunct duo, and along with fellow Hapeville High graduate Marty Bone formed The Brett Hartley Band, named—with some poetic license—after the author of so many great stories of the American west. Tim, Darwin, and Marty were the band's core members, but plenty of others came and went. The band played all original music and Marty was the leader. He was an accomplished songwriter and guitarist who played a big part in Tim's development as a songwriter and producer.

A couple of years Tim's senior, Marty had the good fortune of hooking up with some terrific players right out of high school. Together, they formed a band called Carrie Nation. The band was named after a radical member of the pre-Prohibition temperance movement who was famous for attacking taverns with a hatchet.

Carrie Nation became the house band at The Bistro, a legendary now defunct club that was located on West Peachtree Street in Atlanta. As the house band, they were given living accommodations on the second floor of the building and performed almost every night on the first floor, which had

Vocalist Tim Purcell (left) performing with Mantra in Hapeville. That is Paul O'Daniel on drums and Darwin Conort at right on guitar.
(Photo courtesy of Jill Ewing)

been renovated into a bar with a stage. Along with Carrie Nation, other house bands at The Bistro over the years included Jimmy Buffet, The Teddy Baker Band (in which Toby Ruckert played), and White Face. Carrie Nation got great reviews when they played there, and patrons would arrive early and stand in a line that wrapped around the block for a chance to get in. The band moved on to California and eventually disbanded.

Marty, who had been back in Atlanta for a few months after Carrie Nation's demise, didn't initially warm up to the idea of playing in a band with Tim and Darwin, thinking they weren't up to his standards. But then, he heard a four-track version of the *M.A.S.H.* theme song on which Tim played guitar and synthesizer. He apparently liked what he heard, realizing that Tim might actually have some talent. That was the impetus he needed to give it a go.

When a band that plays all-original music has to find players, the same issue always arises. It is one of those immutable facts of band life—in order to attract decent players, you have to offer them an incentive. More often than not, that would be money. "To make money, the band has to play paying gigs, and that usually means playing cover music,"[23] Tim said. That is what The Brett Hartley Band ended up doing. However, they didn't want people to confuse The Brett Hartley Band, which played original music, with a cover band. So, they named the cover band Traveler. Working the local clubs Traveler would still sneak in an original song or two in a typical three-set gig.

Traveler never made it big, but they came close. In 1981, the Atlanta radio station 94Q (WQXI-FM, now STAR94) sponsored a statewide talent contest with a grand prize that included recording time at a major studio and a guest spot on a live television broadcast. Traveler submitted *You're the One,* an original song written by Marty and sung by Tim. The band won first place, but ironically had split up two weeks before they learned of their success. In order to take advantage of the prize package, they regrouped one last time, and in 1982 recorded *Gimme Your Love* and *Guess I Lost Again* at Master Trax Studio in downtown Atlanta, and also made an appearance on the Georgia Public Broadcasting Television network performing the contest winning song.

The band had some pretty good original music, including

---

23   Purcell, Tim, A Brief Look at Tim's Performance History. Pages 1 & 2, and author interview with Tim Purcell. October 4, 2021.

Promotional photo for Traveler includes from left to right, Tim Purcell,
Steve Phillips, Andrew Miller, Marty Bone, Darwin Conort
(Photo courtesy of Tim Purcell)

Cry No Tears (1979), the first song Tim ever wrote; *Love's an Old Fool* (1981), the first song he ever recorded; and *Only Make Believe*, another Marty composition that became the title cut for an album by Atlanta legend Tommy Strain and his band Magic Cat. Despite winning the contest, Traveler's reunion was short lived.

The Nelsons

Though Tim felt disappointment over Traveler's end, it seems that all things happen for a reason. As it turned out,

Tim's next stop would be another Atlanta-based original band, The Nelsons, featuring Garry Limuti, his then wife Patti Ray, and an on-again off-again dynamic female vocalist, Rose Robinson. Tim described The Nelsons as his "first venture into hipness."[24]

The band had been playing in some of the coolest clubs in town and were looking for a male lead singer to complement Rose. Tim believes Limuti to be one of the most talented guys he has ever worked with. "His guitar playing and songwriting are superb, second only to his artistic (drawing) ability… He is wickedly smart," Tim said. "As an artist, he specializes in photo realism. You can't tell the difference between a photo and one of Garry's paintings. He is a good-looking guy who wanted to be a rock star so bad. He could shred on the guitar and wrote the coolest songs."[25]

Marty Bone had auditioned for The Nelsons after Traveler's break up, but it wasn't a good fit. Tim had heard a couple of The Nelsons recordings through Marty, and thought they were great. When he found out The Nelsons were looking for a male singer, he called Limuti to see if they would let him audition for the spot. It helped Tim's odds of landing the job that he not only could sing, but by this time was a more than adequate keyboardist. That was enough to get Tim the audition. But at the audition, Tim had the distinct impression that Rose didn't like him because he didn't have the right look for the band. "This was an era that saw the rise of 'punk,' asymmetrical big hair and studded clothes," he recalled. "Not a look that went well with being a credit manager at Lowe's."[26]

Rose's opinion notwithstanding, Garry was impressed with Tim's audition and wanted him in the band. Rose on

---

24   Purcell, Tim, A Brief Look at Tim's Performance History. Pages 2 & 3.
25   Ibid. Page 3, and Interview author with Tim Purcell. October 4, 2021.
26   Ibid.

Tim playing keys with Traveler after a win in the
94Q radio contest forced them to regroup.
(Photo courtesy of Tim Purcell)

the other hand—not so much. She made it clear that if Tim joined the band, she would walk. Garry's wife played a little keyboard and could also sing, so Garry figured that Rose was expendable and hired Tim. True to her word, Rose did not remain with the band.

The Big Break?

Of all the bands Tim played with over the years, The Nelsons probably provided him with the best opportunity at getting a record deal. In 1980, John Huie, Tim's good friend and former college roommate, along with Ian Copeland,

started Frontier Booking International (FBI) in New York
City. The booking agency was formed primarily to book
Ian's brother Stewart Copeland's band, The Police. FBI han-
dled some other major acts as well, including The Go-Gos,
Iggy Pop, and Squeeze.

"In 1984, I visited New York and played The Nelsons
new demo (*I Imagine You [The Innocent]*) for John and Ian,"
Tim said. "Ian listened to a short piece of the song and apparently took a big liking to it. He popped the recording into a
tape player that piped music over the entire office proceed-
ing to cart me around, pulling me into each individual office
saying over the music, 'This is our next star, right here, listen
to this! Can you believe this? This is Huie's friend that he has
been talking about. This is going to be big!!'"

*Garry Limuti (pictured here) would
play a part in the lives of two Fossils: Tim Purcell and Scott King.
(Courtesy Garry Limuti)*

Tim was overwhelmed, sure that this was The Nelsons' big break. He called Garry, who was equally thrilled about Ian's reaction to their music. That night, John and Tim had dinner with some guys who were in from San Francisco. For Tim, that dinner would be an education about life in the fast lane. The two dinner guests were none other than lead guitarist Neal Schon and keyboardist Jonathan Cain, from the American rock band Journey.

"Neal, Jonathan, and Steve Perry, Journey's lead singer, had rented a hotel suite in New York for the purpose of writing a new album," Tim said. "It turned out to be *Escape*, the band's seventh and most popular, containing Journey's monster hit song *Don't Stop Believing*. So, I'm sitting at the restaurant next to perhaps the prettiest girl I'd ever seen in my life. She starts talking to me and before I know it, her hand's on my crotch and I'm like, 'God, here I am, this is the big time. What the hell,' and I'm just freaking out. I was, however, true to my vow with my wife, but it was real hard!"

Tim returned to Atlanta hoping to get the phone call Ian had promised and could hardly contain his excitement. But when the days turned to weeks without a word, Tim called John for an update. That's when he got the bad news. After Tim had left New York, Huie had a falling out with Copeland. John ended up leaving FBI, and joined forces with International Creative Management (ICM) in Los Angeles. Tim never heard back from Ian. For Tim, it was the first of several disappointments. In retrospect, "John opened a lot of doors for me, but it was kind of like the side door," Tim said. "People were seeing me as a favor to John and not on my own merit. At the time it was discouraging, but in retrospect I'm really glad that I didn't end up on some tour bus."[27]

---

27   Author interview with Tim Purcell. October 4, 2021.

Tim and Garry continued to work together and had a few more gigs and recording sessions. After the last recording session, Garry, who was growing impatient and becoming disenchanted with their inability to break through, said, "Well, there's another one (master tape) for the closet shelf." It wasn't long before they both just wanted to move on.

Tim's time with The Nelsons lasted only a year or so. Garry ended up moving to Los Angeles, where he would cross paths with Scott King, someone who would become instrumental to Tim's future success.

Border Patrol

Around that same time, Tim had been playing a lot of golf with a guy named Hugh Pitts. Coincidentally, Hugh had played in Carrie Nation with Marty Bone, and was with the band when they almost made it big in California. Hugh had a connection with a studio owner in Hapeville, and he and Tim did a number of recordings there. The more the two worked together, the more comfortable they grew with each other. Eventually, Hugh invited Tim to jam with him and a couple of his friends, bass guitarist Willie Gentry and drummer Ricky Brunetti. Tim wasn't much of a jammer, but he decided to take his chances. He would not regret it.

That jam session was the first time that Tim ever played with a legitimate rhythm section. "It was like nothing I'd ever experienced," Tim said. "They were playing songs that really weren't my style—light jazz, fusion stuff. I didn't know the chords or anything, but they were so good that I could play a triad or a two-note thing, just find what key they were in and stab chords every now and then. It was the most fun and the best sounding thing I had ever been a part of. It opened my eyes, like I had been blind my whole life. I couldn't believe how good they were, and they all became friends of mine who played in bands with me later on."[28]

That session took place in 1982, and eventually evolved into Border Patrol. Hugh—the erstwhile leader of the band—booked a couple of gigs at a local pizza place. The new band mates recruited guitarist/singer Rick Dupree to round out the ensemble, and started work on a set list for the upcoming dates. About two weeks before the show, Hugh got a call from Tom Johnson, the guitarist/lead singer from The Doobie Brothers. Tom was a friend of Hugh's from his time in California with Carrie Nation, and asked Hugh if he wanted to come out to and join him for a recording session. Hugh jumped at the opportunity and took off for California immediately.

Suddenly, just a week before the gig, the band found itself missing its lead guitarist and band leader. In desperation, Tim turned to his old friend Darwin. Darwin didn't know most of the songs, but agreed to help the band out. Border Patrol hoped that Darwin would also be able to sing five or six songs that he knew thereby lengthening the set list. They played the gig, and Tim thought Darwin did a good job. But as often happens, personalities clashed. Some of the other members didn't get along with Darwin, and shortly thereafter the group disbanded.

Class Act

In 1983, Jim Gentry—a virtuoso guitarist who plays with astonishing accuracy, speed and feel—was approached

---

28   Ibid.

by fellow Georgia State University graduate Diane Durett with the idea of starting a band. Diane was a very attractive and capable female vocalist, and Jim—who was admittedly smitten with her—jumped at the chance. He told Diane that he would get the other players they needed for a band and approached Willie Gentry and Ricky Brunetti. Willie and Ricky recruited Tim, and together they formed Class Act.

Tim was really impressed with Jim. "He could play anything," Tim recalled. "He was vibrant, young, and eager, and he could sing."[29] But Jim's obsession with Diane would in part lead to the band's demise. Jim had a mad crush on Diane, who did not return any of his affections.

Diane was the featured singer in Class Act, and the band's job was to back her up and fill the time before she joined them for her set(s) at gigs. Depending on the size of the crowd, Diane would sing about ten or so songs each night by pop artists like Madonna, while the band would play four 60-minute sets.

"We would begin by playing the dead hour (9-10 p.m.) without Diane," Tim said. "She would come in at the end of the first set to assess the crowd. If it wasn't big enough, then the band would play another set without her. After that set she would check out the crowd again and maybe join in for the third set. If there weren't enough people there, she might not sing at all."[30] Despite a modicum of success, the experience was not a satisfying one for Tim. "It was my first taste of something I never wanted to be," he said. "I never wanted to be somebody else's band."

By the time Class Act had been together for a year, they were really tight. But Jim's frustration at not being able to win Diane's affections was growing almost as fast as the

29   Ibid,
30   Ibid.

number of songs the band played without Diane each night. Not wanting the turmoil from Jim's unrequited crush to spill over, the band decided it might be a good time to part ways with her. No one, however, wanted to be the one to deliver the news. After some debate, the band members flipped a coin, and Tim lost. One Saturday night after load-out, he walked Diane out to the parking lot and told her that things weren't working out. She was very upset, and she made sure Tim knew about it. Tim was fond of Diane and always regretted the way things were left between them.

Many years later, Tim and his wife were attending the 30A Songwriters Festival in the Florida panhandle. They were at a particular venue to see Kim Richey, one of Tim's favorite singer-songwriters. Upon checking the schedule, they discovered that Diane Durett was playing the same venue as Richey one hour earlier. Diane had become a very popular singer-songwriter in Atlanta and was performing in the round that night. While watching her perform, Tim wondered if she would remember him and the parking lot incident that occurred so many years before. When her set was over, Tim found her out front of the venue. "Diane, I don't know if you remember me…" But she recognized him immediately. "Tim Purcell," she said as she walked closer to him. "Come here!" She wrapped her arms around and gave him a big hug. She told him that leaving Class Act was the best thing that could've happened to her. After parting ways with Tim and the boys, she was able to be her true self and had since become a major player in the Atlanta music scene. She harbored no animosity toward him.

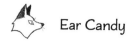

The Limit

After the band and Diane parted ways, Jim and Tim had to decide who between the two of them would become the band's frontman. The only issue was, neither had experience in that role and neither was really very good at it. Enter Marshall Smith. Marshall was one of the original members of the band Wet Willie, but was drafted to serve in Vietnam just as the band was on the cusp of stardom. He was away at war when the band's biggest hit, *Keep On Smilin'* hit the airwaves, and had rejoined them for a limited time as a rhythm guitarist and back-up vocalist when he returned from his service stint just before the band broke up.

With his outgoing personality and club experience, Marshall appeared to be the perfect frontman for the new group, The Limit—a name Marshall came up with. Everyone was excited and looking forward to a fresh start. There was only one problem—and it turned out to be a big one. Marshall had a horrible alcohol problem. He began every day drinking straight vodka from the freezer and would continue drinking all day long. He was good at it and if he was able to get a little nap in the afternoon, you couldn't tell he'd been drinking, but it was habitual and would continue into the evening every day.

The Limit often played at Carlos McGee's, a set of five clubs in and around Atlanta. The main club was located in Buckhead. The Buckhead McGee's had been around for a while, and was the most popular live music club in the city, playing host to elite bands. The success of the Buckhead Club led to the opening of four satellite clubs scattered around the Atlanta perimeter. The Limit played the perimeter clubs on a regular basis and The Buckhead location a few times. The jobs ran from Tuesday through Saturday each week, evolving from small crowds on weekdays to standing room only on the weekends.

But band life isn't always fun and games. Tim described a strange, scary encounter with a girl who was a regular at the College Park McGee's when The Limit performed there. "This girl was a throwback hippie who wore a broad brimmed hat, lacy dresses and long chains like Stevie Nicks," Tim said. "She acted like she was on some type of hallucinogenic, sitting by herself at a table until the music started playing, then doing these crazy interpretive dances, spinning around and putting her face right up against the stage, looking at you and shaking her head while backing up."[31] Tim made the mistake of approaching her during a break and complimenting her dancing. "She just laughed and laughed in response," Tim said. "As the band went back up on stage, a man who had been seated at the bar went over to her table and sat down. He looked just like Charles Manson. He looked crazy. The next night I got to the club early and was sound checking my gear, when I looked up to see this Charlie Manson character walking through the door. He walks toward the stage, stands right in front of me, draws a gun, points it at me and shoots."[32] The gun went off with a loud bang! Fortunately, it was loaded with blanks. The man looked at Tim, laughed, turned and walked away. The club bouncer immediately ran and tackled the shooter and threw him out. He was banned from the club. No charges were filed, but Tim had to run out and buy some new underwear.

It was during his time with The Limit that Tim made a life changing decision. The band was playing in and around Atlanta at least three weeks (and these were five-night weeks) per month, and he was still working at Lowe's. "I was burning

---

31   Author interview with Tim Purcell. November 29, 2021.
32   Ibid.

the candle at both ends," he said. "I remember several mornings when I would come into work and shut my office door to make some 'important phone calls' just to catch an extra 15 minutes of sleep. I would go home at lunch to catch a nap. It was exhausting. I really don't know how I did it."

When Terri became pregnant with their first child, Rachel, in 1986, the couple sat down at the kitchen table and made a list of some of the choices ahead of them. Childcare? Au pair? Terri stay home? There were several possible scenarios, but when it came down to it, the costs involved basically matched or exceeded the salary Tim was making at Lowe's. "We began to consider the idea that I could stay home with Rachel during the day and continue to play music at night," he said. "I could even go 'full time' with the band and earn more money that way." Tim decided to leave Lowe's. It was quite a shock to Tim's parents when they were told of the couple's decision. Tim's mom in particular didn't think it would work. Three daughters and 27 years later, she was proven wrong. Tim takes pride in telling folks that he "retired" in 1986. Truth is, that was when he really started working.

As happens so often in the crazy music world, The Limit found themselves the victim of a raid. Not one where the police barge through the front door with a search warrant, but the kind that finds you losing players to another band.

Starshower was a major band in Atlanta that incorporated all the newest technology—sequencers, automated light shows, and the like—into their act while playing all the biggest clubs. They were the hottest band in the city, they made a lot of money, and they were in need of a bass player. Someone suggested they listen to Willie play. When they heard him, they offered him a job on the spot. Willie was certainly tempted, as this would be a big step up for him both in prestige and money. He told Starshower that he would

Promotional photo of The Limit (left to right) Willie Gentry, Marshall Smith,
Tim Purcell, Ricky Brunetti and Jim Gentry.

accept the offer only if they agreed to take his drummer and best friend Ricky with him. They agreed, and both Willie and Ricky left The Limit.

Tim, Jim, and Marshall were disappointed, but tried to make the best of it. They found a couple of professional players to replace Willie and Ricky for their upcoming gigs and for some scheduled recording sessions, but Marshall continued to struggle with alcohol. On one particular road trip to north Florida, he got embarrassingly drunk on stage. For Tim and Jim, that was the final straw. The two had a long talk that night and decided to fire Marshall and continue as a four piece.

It seemed like things might finally be on track, but once back in Atlanta, Jim called Tim with some more bad news. Starshower had also recruited him, and he had decided to re-join Ricky and Willie.

Lou's Blues Review

Jim's departure was devastating for Tim. What to do now? As he discussed his dismal prospects with his wife, he received a phone call from Lou Van Dora, the leader of Lou's Blues Review (LBR), a very popular band in Atlanta that was equal to Starshower in talent, but played a different style of music. Lou's Blues Review was structured in the style of The Blues Brothers and had a horn section, while Starshower played more funk and arena-style rock. It turned out that one of the founders and frontmen of Lou's Blues Review, was moving on. Lou was holding auditions to find a replacement, and Tim was eager to give it a shot.

Lou's Blues Reviews was performing that week at Timothy John's, a very popular club in the Atlanta area. Instead of a formal audition, Lou asked Tim to come out and sit it on a song or two. When he arrived at the jam-packed, venue he looked over the band's Song List and confidently selected a song he had performed a hundred times over titled *634-5789*. He took the stage knowing he'd make a good impression—but then the band started playing, and Tim realized that he had confused that song with another phone-number hit, *867-5309/Jenny*—a 1982 song popularized by Tommy Tutone. The band was playing the Wilson Picket R & B classic, and Tim didn't even know the words. Being the professionals that they were, LBR didn't miss a beat. Lou took the lead vocals, while Tim just clapped his hands and joined in on the choruses with some occasional ab-libs. Tim thought things were going disastrously, but Lou asked him if he wanted to try another. Lou suggested *My Girl,* a song Tim actually knew, and Tim proceeded to kill it. The crowd loved the performance and immediately after the show, Tim got the job.

If Tim wanted to work, he got what he asked for. After

Lou's Blues Review promotional photo (from left to right) Larue Riccio, Bobby Williams, Lou Van Dora, Donnie Black, Tim Purcell and Andrew Neuhaus

joining LBR, he worked 32 consecutive nights in Atlanta. Tim was now making more money than he had ever made as a professional musician. Lou paid the band with cash on Saturday night, handing each member a sealed envelope with the rule to never tell any other band member how much they were paid. This bred resentment within the band. "Of course the first thing the band members did was compare their pay," Tim said. "I followed the rules, never disclosing my pay, thinking it might be higher than some of the others which made me sort of an outsider. I never really felt comfortable with all that."[33]

Money, however, was never Tim's real motivation for playing music. About a year after Tim joined LBR, Atlanta

---

[33]   Ibid.

club owners started feeling the impact from Georgia's decision to increase the legal drinking age from 18 to 21. Smaller crowds were forcing club owners to cut back on the amount they were paying bands. Lou, however, wouldn't even consider working for less money and started to take Lou's Blues Review on the road much more frequently in search of financially suitable venues.

It was now 1989, and the band was preparing to leave for a gig in Arkansas. Terri was nine months pregnant and almost ready to give birth to Tim's second daughter, Maggie. Tim didn't want to go to Little Rock with the band and miss the birth of his daughter, so he just walked away. He felt very relieved to not have to be on the road with a band that was now traveling a great deal more than he was prepared to do.

Tim described his time with Lou's Blues Review as a real eye opener. "It was the first time I was in a band where everyone wasn't treated equally,"[34] he said. "It's just the way it was, take it or leave it, and after about two and a half years, I left it."[35]

Perfect World

When Tim was still in The Limit with its original five members, he had met a prolific songwriter by the name of Jim Fallon, who—according to Tim—"could write a song a day."[36] The two became friends and began writing together at the end of Tim's time with The Limit and throughout his years with LBR. Nick Jameson of Foghat fame recorded and produced some of Jim and Tim's songs, and at their high point, they were writing two to three songs a week.

---

34 Author interview with Tim Purcell. October 4, 2021.
35 Ibid.
36 Ibid.

Promotional photo for Perfect World. Band members (from left to right) Tim Purcell, Andrew Neuhaus, Jim Gentry, Jim Fallon (in front) Gerry Hansen and John Barrett.

Meanwhile, Starshower relocated to Orlando, Florida and became the house band at a mega club called J.J. Whispers with Jim Gentry as the band leader. But soon after the band took up residence at J.J. Whispers, they met with tragedy when Willie Gentry had a stroke and died. Willie's death was hard for everyone, but especially for his best friend Ricky. Ricky became disillusioned and homesick, and eventually quit the band and returned home to Douglasville, Georgia. That left only Jim Gentry, who wasn't really happy without his longtime band mates. Jim Fallon seeing an opportunity in Gentry's dissatisfaction, travelled down to Orlando and

convinced him to return to Atlanta and form a partnership with him and Tim. That partnership became Perfect World.

"We were quite good," Tim recalled. "We found a wonderful drummer, Gerry Hansen, and Andrew Neuhaus—the now former keyboard player from Lou's Blues Review—agreed to give it a shot. John Barrett joined us on bass and we were all set." Perfect World was all decked out—Tim played a strap-on keyboard and fronted the band. They had sequencers, computers, and mixers with surface board contact technology, providing a level of creativity and versatility unavailable to most bands at that time. And on top of that, they all could play! Sadly, the band lasted only three months and played about eight gigs. But during that time, they competed in a Battle of the Bands sponsored by a local FM rock station called The 96 Rock Off. In a weird twist of fate, Rose Robinson's (from The Nelsons) band—cleverly named Mrs. Robinson's Daughter—took first place with a cover rendition of *To Sir With Love*, while Perfect World finished second. Their runner-up status qualified Perfect World for a spot in a major music showcase being held at clubs all around metro Atlanta. They landed one of the best spots, performing at 9:00 p.m. on a Saturday at "The Avondale Playhouse" one of the hottest clubs in town.

One month prior to their scheduled spot in the showcase, Jim Gentry's girlfriend, who had accompanied him to Atlanta when he moved from Orlando, pressured him into marriage, and they exchanged vows at the Cobb County Courthouse. About a week later, she told him she hated Georgia and was moving back to Florida with or without him. Needless to say, when she left, he left. The band scrambled for a replacement and found one in a really good guitar player and singer by the name of Tony Hill. But even though Tony was a master at his craft, he never really filled the void left by Jim.

The night of the showcase stands out in Tim's memory. "We were at a packed club with a substitute guitar player, performing an original song when someone in the front row yelled, 'Get these grandpas off the damn stage!'"[37] The 30-something "grandpas" were totally demoralized and decided to pack it in.

Buck Shot The Band

While that performance signaled the end for Perfect World, it didn't stop Tim and Jim Fallon from writing more songs. Around this same time, Tim's friend John Huie (FBI and ICM) moved to Nashville to open a country music department for Creative Artists Agency (CAA). John encouraged Tim to take a hard look at the contemporary country music that was rapidly gaining popularity throughout the world. Country music had moved on from the Loretta Lynn era, Huie noted, and new sounds coming from artists like Restless Heart, Hal Ketchum, and Vince Gill harkened back to a time in rock and roll when songwriting and harmony dominated the music scene. John thought Tim's vocals and his ability to write would be a perfect fit—even at Tim's "advanced" age of 36. Tim took John's advice to heart. The more he listened, the more he fell in love with the sounds of Steve Warner, The Judds, and other contemporary country artists.

It was 1992 when Tim got back together with Marty Bone's old friend and his own former bandmate and golfing buddy, Hugh Pitts. At the time, Hugh was playing in a country band with a couple of really good players, bassist/singer Buddy Carvallo and drummer Dennis "Skinny" Anderson. They wanted to add another singer and keyboard player to

37   Ibid.

the group and invited Tim to join their three-piece ensemble. That group became Buck Shot The Band, and Tim welcomed the chance to play country music. He'd been writing a lot of country songs and hoped this would afford him the opportunity to perform some of them.

Buck Shot The Band didn't play any of the big country dance clubs, as most of those had their own house band. But they did perform at little country dives all over town where they were able to feature some of their original songs. And, with only four members, the band could make decent money.

The band got better and tighter with each performance. In early December 1992, the band was performing at Whispers Pub, an establishment that had treated them exceedingly well, and had hired them to perform on the coming New Year's Eve at twice their normal wage. Tim was sitting at the bar during a break when he received a phone call from a gentleman by the name of Bill Gentry (no relation to Jim or Willie). Bill was the co-owner/manager of Mama's Country Showcase, a mega country dance club in east Atlanta. "Hey," Bill said. "We need a lead singer over here. Are you interested?"[38]

Mama's Country Showcase

Mama's Country Showcase was one of those huge dance clubs that had a house band. They also had concerts there almost every weekend, featuring big stars like Tim McGraw, Kenny Chesney, Little Texas, David Allan Coe, and many others. The club had a circular platform suspended high above the stage, out of sight from the audience, that would

[38]   Author interview with Tim Purcell. November 29, 2021.

lower down at the beginning of each set. Sitting or standing on the platform, the house band would play their wireless instruments as the circular platform came to rest on the main stage below. Sometime around October of 1992, one of the cables holding that circular stage broke as it lowered to the ground, causing the stage to crash. The falling stage trapped the legs of some of the band members, causing leg, back, and neck injuries. No one died, thankfully, but the band did lose three or four members to injury. Mama's rushed to replace the injured musicians, but the cobbled-together replacement band never really gelled.

Tim was certainly interested in the offer, until Bill told him that he would be required to start on New Year's Eve. "I can't do that," Tim told Bill. "I'm committed to the people in my band and to the club that has been so good to us. I'm not going to renege on my agreement with them."[39] Bill inquired as to how much Whispers was paying Tim and offered to pay him more, but Tim was true to his word, prompting Bill Gentry to tell him that he was passing up a very good opportunity.

Sometime in mid-January 1993, Bill called Tim again. The club really needed to fix their band situation and he felt Tim was the perfect fit for their club, despite having never heard him sing in person. This time, he offered to make Tim the band leader and to pay him $600 per week (for four nights), which was great money at the time. Tim's response was quite bold, offering to come to Mama's only if they allowed him to bring the other members of Buck Shot The Band with him. Bill agreed to take Tim's band with the exception of the drummer—Bill was pretty fond of the drummer he had and didn't want to replace him.

Tim spoke with the other band members, who agreed to

39   Ibid.

47

come with him despite having to leave Skinny behind. But although he agreed to the move, Buddy had some prescient words of warning for Tim. "If you take a house job, you can just start counting the days till they fire you," he said. "You're on the clock. You don't get to do your own stuff. You gotta do what they say. And I'll tell you what—if the club's successful, you are the last to get credit. If the club fails or is doing badly, you're the first to get blamed." In hindsight, Tim admitted that Buddy was absolutely right.[40] Thus began The Riley Hawkins Band.

Tim recalls one baffling encounter with the owner of Mama's that occurred during a break on a night where the crowd was particularly large. Tim went to get a bite at a little hamburger grille that was operating at a corner of the club when he was confronted by a man who said, "Do you know who I am?"[41] Tim acknowledged that he knew him as Bill, the majority owner of the club (another Bill, not Bill Gentry). Making small talk, Tim asked him how he was doing. Then, out of nowhere, the owner said, "I just want to ask you one thing. Who the hell ever told you that you could sing?"[42] Tim was taken aback and didn't quite know how to answer. Owner Bill started laughing and with a slap on Tim's shoulder, walked away. The bizarre encounter mystified Tim, who to this day still doesn't know if he was joking or not. Regardless, "It did not improve my already low opinion of the guy,"[43] Tim said.

The gig as the house band at Mama's Country Showcase lasted about two and a half years before it came to an abrupt end in the middle of summer 1995. The band was

---

40   Ibid.
41   Ibid.
42   Ibid.
43   Ibid.

unceremoniously fired, presumably due to a declining clientele, and Tim learned of the dismissal from guitar player Hugh Pitts. "I just got a call from Mama's," Hugh said over the phone. "They told us to come pick up all our shit."[44] When Tim and the band arrived at the club, they were met by a security guard with a gun who escorted them through the club to ensure that they took only their own equipment.

A month or two later, Tim and his wife were attending a world series game at Turner Field where their beloved Braves were up on the Cleveland Indians, three games to two. The couple took their seats and were looking forward to an exciting evening, when just before the start of the game, a man and his son walked down Tim's row to find their own seats. Tim and his wife stood to allow them to pass and they sat down next to Tim. To his astonishment, the man was Bill, the owner of Mama's who had cruelly remarked on Tim's singing ability. No words were spoken. Tim isn't sure if Bill recognized him, but the encounter was enough to take off some of the luster from what should have been a great evening—the Braves became Major League Baseball's 1995 world champions that night.

Despite the unpleasant ending and the fulfillment of Buddy's prophetic warning, Tim made many valuable connections during his years at Mama's that would turn out to be instrumental in his future. For example, one night, Rodney Mills stopped by Mama's to speak to Tim. Mills was a renowned recording engineer and producer who had engineered the *Street Survivor* album by Lynyrd Skynyrd. He mixed the album for two solid days following the October 20, 1977 plane crash that took the lives of three band members. There was a huge rush to get the album out after the crash, and Mills finished the whole thing in 48 hours—though he

44   Ibid.

The Purcell family pose for their 2021 Christmas card photo. From L-R Rob Kaercher (holding Tim's grandson Robby), Rachel (Purcell) Kaercher (holding Robby's twin brother Timmy), Tim, Terri, Maggie Purcell, Ian Hopkirk (Maggie's fiancée) and Sammie Purcell. (Photo courtesy of Terri Purcell)

never got official credit. During his Georgia Music Hall of Fame career, Mills produced the Atlanta Rhythm Section, 38 Special and Greg Allman's solo work. The night he visited Mama's, Mills introduced himself to Tim and said he wanted to record him. Tim was ecstatic and asked if he could include the band in the session. Mills was accommodating and they proceeded to record some of his songs. Though not much came of those recordings—Tim found the final product to be pretty mediocre—Rodney and Tim stayed in touch well beyond that date and would eventually work together again.

Another frequent visitor to Mama's who would play a role in Tim's future was a businessman named Mike Huddleston, who eventually became Tim's manager. Though teaming up with Mike seemed like a great idea at the time, hindsight would prove it to be a mistake. It did however lead to the formation of The Mustangs.

Chapter 2

DARWIN "THAT DARWIN" CONORT

The Early Years

William Darwin Conort was born at St. Joseph's Hospital in Atlanta, Georgia on January 21, 1957. He was the last child born to Jack Conort and Dorothy (Sweatman) Conort, whose three children were each born seven years apart.

In the early 1940s, Jack Conort attended night school at Atlanta Technical College, but his education was interrupted by World War II, and he soon enlisted in the army. Stationed in Orange, California during the war years, Jack worked as a flight instructor on the Boeing Stearman Model 75 biplane.

Darwin described his father as "a very smart man who worked the system. He would always get into some kind of trouble, not serious, but just enough to ensure that he wouldn't be deployed into combat and somehow still keep

*Six-year-old Darwin with his parents Jack and Doro-
thy Conort at the Georgia Military Academy
(Photo courtesy of Jill Ewing)*

his job as a flight instructor."[45] He married Dorothy (Dot) in
1942 while still in the military, and their first child, Jackie, was
born on December 3, 1943.

After the war, Jack returned to Atlanta Tech where he
earned a degree in business, and then took a position with the
federal government working as a tax collector. During those
years, the couple was blessed with two additional children,
Noreen on November 9, 1950, and then Darwin in 1957.

When Darwin was five years old in 1962, he entered first
grade at the Georgia Military Academy, a private military

---

45   Author interview with Darwin Conort. December 1, 2021.

school in south Atlanta not too far from his home in Hapeville. One year later, Jack and Dot divorced. "I remember thinking, [without dad home] what will I do? But mom kept me busy,"[46] Darwin said. Of the two parents, Dot had always been the more dominant one in Darwin's life, so while Darwin missed his father, things weren't all that different. Darwin continued to see his dad two weekends per month. He feels today that his parents' divorce "didn't really have a significant impact on me one way or the other."[47]

But for Dot, the divorce was very impactful. She was somewhat desperate and at a loss for what to do after the divorce, "but at the same time," Darwin recalled, "it led to her starting a career working at the State of Georgia's Department of Agriculture that I think gave her a sense of fulfillment."[48]

Music Becomes An Obsession

After his parents' divorce, Darwin completed his elementary school years at North Avenue School in Hapeville. While there, Darwin experienced a life altering moment. During show-and-tell in the fourth grade, another student brought an acoustic guitar to class and tried to play a riff from the song *Secret Agent Man*. Nine-year-old Darwin had a revelation. "That song had a two-string kick ass intro," Darwin said. "I'm watching him try to play it and I'm telling myself, 'I could play that. I know I could.' From that moment, I was hooked. I knew that playing guitar was something I was supposed to do."[49]

46   Ibid.
47   Ibid.
48   Ibid.
49   Ibid.

Darwin hurried home and excitedly told his mother about his epiphany. Within a few weeks, she found a guitar in a pawn shop and bought it for her son. She knew how much he wanted it, and she hoped the gift might help keep his mind off of the divorce. Darwin devoted all his spare time to teaching himself to play. Within a couple of years, he was playing up and down the street, singing to girls while "wearing corduroy slacks with matching shirt and socks, you know, the whole bit, and getting quarters as tips from the girls' dads."[50]

More likely than not, Darwin inherited the music gene from his dad. He recalled stories his dad told him about how he and his two brothers would make music with whatever instruments were available. "Dad dabbled with the mandolin as a youngster and with the guitar as a teenager and a young adult," Darwin said. "But I'm not sure if he ever owned either, as buying an instrument would have been an unheard of luxury during the depression years of the 1930s."[51]

Darwin recalls listening to Chet Atkins, Jim Reeves, and many country stars while riding in the car with his father. "To this day, I love Eddie Arnold, Reeves, Atkins, Hank Williams, it was instilled in me at an early age," Darwin said. "They just kept putting ingredients in the pot for me!"[52] His sister Noreen also played a major role in the evolution of Darwin's musical taste, introducing her little brother to The Beatles, The Dave Clarke Five, and many other British invaders who dominated the charts in the 1960s.

Darwin realized that music and (hopefully) being in a band would be a major part of his life. While still a preteen, he searched the neighborhood for other kids who might have a guitar, hoping that they'd be able to play together.

---

50   Ibid.
51   Written responses to author interview questions. November 8, 2021.
52   Ibid.

Darwin with his sister Jackie Conort posing in front of
the family Christmas tree circa 1987 or 1988
(Photo courtesy of Jill Ewing)

Recognizing her son's obsession with the instrument, Darwin's mother gave him another gift—a Silvertone electric guitar from Sears and Roebuck. Darwin was in love. "It came in a case that had a built in speaker," he remembered. "It was a portable guitar and amplifier. You set the case upright, opened it and plugged right into it. It was amazing. That was NASA to me."[53]

Having a bit of the music gene herself, Darwin's sister

---

53   Ibid.

Noreen played the piano and could read music very well. She was nearly 20 by the time Darwin, then age 12, started to fool around on the ivories. Noreen would play tunes from *Oklahoma!, The Sound of Music,* and other popular musicals. Darwin, blessed with a great ear for music, would listen and watch while she played. When she left the piano bench, he would hop on and easily recreate what she had just played—despite his inability to read music. Noreen was both amazed and annoyed. "I would figure out the top [hand] and then the bottom and play it...badly perhaps, but better than she thought I should have been able to do," Darwin said. "Piano was always my second love."[54]

High School Years

In 1969, Darwin became an eighth grader at Hapeville High School. That's when his friendship with Tim Purcell began to blossom. They knew each other from church but it wasn't until high school that they became really good friends. Darwin said that while the two held a mutual admiration for each other, he also remembers a weird kind of competition that would sometimes arise. "Other than music we didn't have a lot in common, but we were still drawn together. Tim was athletic, and handsome, and had resources, and...I didn't have a lot of that," Darwin said with a laugh. "But we still became good friends. Music was the mediator. High school was fun. We did marching band (eight grade) and chorus (every year) together. Tim came in and out of the rock bands as he was allowed to [by his parents]. He spent a lot of time on sports."[55]

---

54   Ibid.
55   Ibid.

American Apple—Darwin's First Real Band

It was also while in ninth or tenth grade that Darwin participated in his first real band: American Apple. "We had a drum riser with an apple painted on it that had an American flag in it [the apple]," Darwin recalled. "I don't know where that came from—it was kind of odd. But that band actually had a little equipment and a small PA and we did high school parties."[56] The drummer was Doug Mazur, who at 17 was two years older than Darwin. Doug's friend John Chappelle was on bass. "He (Johnny) couldn't play bass and was tone deaf to boot, so I had to teach him all the songs,"[57] said Darwin. "Johnny did, however, have a basement in which the band could practice and that was pretty much as important an attribute as musical ability to a bunch of high schoolers."[58] Phillip Morgan played keys on a Farfisa organ—the most popular keyboard of the bee bop era—and Kenneth Gillespie rocked out on vocals. "Different people came in and out of the band as members graduated or moved on," Darwin said. "Of course, Tim would join in when he got permission from his parents to hang out with 'That Darwin,'" as Tim's mother referred to me."[59] The band remained active for a couple of years.

Mantra

Now 17, Darwin's musical skills had continued to advance. He had moved from pop to southern rock, his true love, and he had started a new band. The name of the band, Mantra,

---

56   Ibid.
57   Ibid.
58   Ibid.
59   Ibid.

*The original members of Mantra from 1974 are
(L-R): Kenneth Gillespie, Darwin Conort, Michael
Randman, Tim Bridges and Paul O'Daniel.
(Photo courtesy of Jill Ewing)*

was derived from a word associated with meditation, and the band members (including Tim) all took classes in meditation from the Maharishi Mahesh Yogi. "I wanted to expand my mind. That was the 70s. The world was changing and there was a lot of information out there. Plus," Darwin added with a chuckle, "if the girls were going to meditate (and several did), yeah, I wanted to meditate."[60]

Despite his interest in girls, Darwin didn't have many steady girlfriends. But he was a popular student in high school, and was elected both student council president and senior class president. "I was a good friend to a lot of people," Darwin said. "I was very social, [but I had] no agenda. It's just what I enjoyed. I wasn't good at school or sports, but I

---

60   Ibid.

Another shot of Mantra performing live. (L-R) Guitarist Steve Coltrain (who replaced Tim Bridges), Michael Randman on bass and vocals, drummer Paul O'Daniel and Darwin Conort on guitar and vocals. (Photo courtesy of Jill Ewing)

could interact with all the various groups—jocks, pot smokers, tough kids, and other groups."[61]

By way of attrition and experience Mantra got better and better. Original member Michael Randman was still on bass, but Tim Bridges had been replaced by a slinging guitarist named Steve Coltrain, who was terrific and taught Darwin a great deal. David Buice had replaced Paul O'Daniel (pictured above) on drums, Tim (when available) played keyboards, and Darwin played guitar. Friends of the band would hang around and serve in various capacities—sound man, roadie, whatever it took to be around the music.

During the approximately five years that Mantra existed, they performed in many bars in Underground Atlanta and at

---

61   Ibid.

1975 photo taken at Atlanta's Fulton County Stadium shows (front row L-R)
Tim Purcell, Brenda Wright, David Buice (Mantra's new drummer), unknown,
Steve Coltrain and his daughter Shanda Coltrain, unknown. (Back row L-R)
Roy Drukenmiller, Eddie Stephenson, unknown, Michael Randman, Carol
Suarez, Billy Bailey, Glenda Rice, Darwin Conort, Chris Padget, Peggy Coltrain.
(Photo courtesy of Jill Ewing)

lots of frat parties. The band even played a post Braves game
concert at Fulton County Stadium in 1975. But bands come
and go, and Mantra was no exception—in 1978, Darwin was
looking for other outlets.

The Stone House

After his 1974 graduation from high school, Darwin
enrolled in Clayton Junior College (CJC), the go-to junior
college for anyone from Atlanta's south side. Darwin isn't
sure why he enrolled, but thinks he was probably just going

through the motions. Deep down, he knew a successful career in music, not a college degree, was his primary goal. His most immediate goal at that point in time was to find a place to live that wasn't his mother's house. George Norman, a friend of his at CJC, told him about a great place that he had found in Red Oak, Georgia, about 10 miles south of the airport. It was referred to as The Stone House, and Darwin quickly moved in. He said that for a bunch of guys in their 20s, The Stone House was indeed the "coolest house in the world".[62]

It was perfect for Darwin, and he remained there for about three years. The Stone House was built by an eccentric airline pilot and was situated in a depression by a creek at the end of a dead-end street. It had a circular floor plan with four bedrooms connected by passageways. The portions of the house that were above grade were constructed with wood. The rooms that descended downward, mirroring the topography of the property, were built of stone. In addition to the bedrooms, the house had a recreation room, a detached rehearsal room (probably originally some sort of workshop), a seldom-used kitchen, and a living room with a working fireplace. There were a few leaks here and there, but it was certainly livable. The "Hobbit House", as Darwin sometimes called it, was nirvana for a musician. He shared the house with anywhere from three to six people at any given time. No one special, just "various people who would come in and pay rent."[63] For about a three month period, one of those renters was his old high school buddy Tim Purcell— who didn't remember the house quite as fondly as Darwin did. Darwin eventually moved away from The Stone House into a secluded farmhouse, and stayed there off and on for five years in the 1980s.

62   Author Interview with Darwin Conort and Jill Ewing. February 10, 2022.
63   Written responses to author interview questions. November 8, 2021.

A January 1990 group photo was taken at Darwin's birthday celebration the year that he and Jill were married. It was taken at the couple's new home in Peachtree City, Ga. (front row L-R) Tina O'Daniel, Jill Ewing, Ashley Allen, Kenneth Gillespie with his arm around Pam Gillespie, Susan Cobb, and James Cobb. (Back row L-R) Paul O'Daniel, Darwin, Terri Purcell (holding daughter Maggie), Tim Purcell. (Photo courtesy of Jill Ewing)

The Spread Eagle Band

During the time that Tim Purcell lived at The Stone House, he and Darwin put together a duo they called The Spread Eagle Band. After developing a setlist of about 20 songs, they performed at the now defunct Little Five Points Pub in the fall of 1978. That gig drew a large, attentive audience, and was aired on the Georgia State College (now University) radio station. All in all not a bad first gig. The pair was feeling pretty good about themselves and booked a second show at Tim's alma matter, Davidson College.

Alas, the success of The Spread Eagle Band's first outing was not to be repeated. Their second performance drew only about 100 less than enthusiastic people, leaving Darwin and Tim feeling rather discouraged. Always having preferred bands to duos or singles, the pair decided to dissolve the duo.

The Brett Hartley Band (AKA Traveler)

Though discouraged, Darwin was not defeated. He quickly regrouped and teamed up with Tim and another Hapeville native, Marty Bone (Darwin's mentor), to form The Brett Hartley Band. Darwin, Tim, and Marty formed the band's nucleus, while bass players and drummers would come and go.

The Brett Hartley Band played all original music, and Marty Bone—the band's leader and a very accomplished musician—was the main influence in the group. "I was always two years behind him in my guitar abilities,"[64] said Darwin, referring to Marty's outstanding musicianship.

The band eventually switched from playing original music to playing cover songs, and to avoid confusion, changed its name to Traveler. Toward the end of the band's time together in late 1981, they entered and won a local radio station talent contest. The band submitted a Marty Bone original song called *You're the One,* but weren't announced as the contest winner until two weeks after they split up. To take advantage of the contest prize—which included a recording session—the band briefly got back together, and in 1982 recorded *Gimme Your Love* and *Guess I Lost Again* at Master Trax Studio in downtown Atlanta.

64   Author interview with Darwin Conort and Jill Ewing, February 8, 2021.

An early 1980's photo of Darwin Conort fronting Traveler.
(Photo courtesy of Jill Ewing)

Getting Acquainted With The "Biz"

Around the time that Traveler won the contest, Darwin began working as an entry-level warehouseman at a film equipment rental facility on the old Lakewood Fairgrounds property just outside of Hapeville. Once there, he discovered that Paul O'Daniel—an old bandmate from both Mantra and Traveler—also worked in the warehouse. Over a period of six years, Darwin learned all that he could about film industry equipment. He began his career by loading trucks, but soon obtained a Class B commercial driver's license so he could make equipment deliveries to actual film sets.

Darwin the Dolly Grip

Darwin moved on from the warehouse and took a day job in the film industry working as a dolly grip for Turner Broadcasting. A dolly grip is the person who operates a camera that is mounted on a dolly and used to film various shots throughout a sequence. Sometimes, Darwin even stepped out from behind the camera and interacted with the stars.

One such opportunity occurred in the mid 1980s. Darwin was working as a dolly grip on a shoot for a Turner Classic Movies (TCM) production of *Cold Sassy Tree*. The movie was set in the late 1800s and starred Faye Dunaway, Richard Widmark, and Neil Patrick Harris. "We were filming a shot where she [Dunaway] was supposed to play the piano," Darwin said. "Somebody called me up and said, 'Darwin, you know how to play piano, show Faye how to fake it for this song.' Next thing I know, I'm sitting on a piano stool next to Faye Dunaway and she says, 'Thank you darling. It's Darwin, darling?' I just said, 'Yes ma'am.'" [65]

Wrestling and Other Stuff

In 1988, Broadcasting mogul Ted Turner purchased Jim Crockett Promotions and renamed it World Championship Wrestling (WCW), presenting Darwin with an opportunity to enter the glitzy world of professional wrestling. He began working as a grip on wrestling telecasts, frequently

---

65   Ibid.

While on set, Darwin was never too far from his dolly. Circa 2010.
(Photo courtesy of Jill Ewing)

interacting with big wrestling stars of the day. By 1991, he had become entrenched in the industry, working in it for eight more years. He even teamed up with his new friend, Michael Seitz—a musician and a professional wrestler for the WCW—to compose wrestling theme music. As a wrestler, Seitz was best known for leading a tag-team called the Fabulous Freebirds. He used the ring name of Michael "P.S." Hayes.

That three-man tag team was the first to enter the arena to the sounds of their own rock and roll theme song. "Michael and I wrote a lot of rock and roll wrestling theme songs. I'd play them and Michael would sing them. He was a very nice man but a very bad singer," Darwin joked. "It was a style of music that I refer to as novelty music. They (the wrestlers) would get very upset when I used that term."[66]

The Stilstone Brothers--The Acoustic Years

While busy with his day job at WCW, Darwin started performing on evenings with Eddie Stephenson, an old friend from the Jonesboro area of Atlanta. They later added multi-instrumentalist and singer Koney Ferrell to their midst and formed a three-piece acoustic act called the Stilstone Brothers. "I was always looking to do something new and an acoustic act sounded like fun," Darwin said. "We had the name on a banner, and because it sounded like a last name, people thought we were brothers. We had no drums and no bass, [just] the three of us playing acoustic instruments and singing."[67]

Darwin discovered that it was much easier to get work as an acoustic trio than as a full-fledged rock band. There were more places to play and the hours weren't nearly as grueling—most of the Stilstone Brothers' jobs at restaurants and pubs were over by the time a rock band would be starting its first set at a club. "We did a lot of songs heavy on vocal harmony," Darwin said. "It was a different style of music than what I'd been playing the last several years and it helped me expand my abilities and [my] approach."[68]

66   Ibid.
67   Ibid.
68   Ibid.

Darwin used this promotional photo in the 1980's to promote his solo acoustic performances. This one hung in Pilgreen's Steak House where Darwin performed off and on from 1980 to 1989.
(Photo courtesy of Jill Ewing)

Darwin and Jill

Like most bands, Darwin's groups had a regular following made up of fans and friends. One such fan who had followed Darwin since the Mantra days was Jan Ewing. Darwin met Jan while attending Clayton Junior College. She would frequently attend Mantra gigs with her sister Jill, a 15-year-old cheerleader at Jonesboro High School with a fake ID that she used to get into the clubs (the legal drinking age was 18 at the time). Jill, who didn't yet drink, would serve as the designated driver so her sister Jan, who was about four years older, could have a few while watching the band. Darwin

Jill and Darwin Conort were married on April 15, 1989. The man standing behind them was the preacher who performed the ceremony.

and Jill were probably introduced around that time, but they really didn't know each other very well.

In 1986, a more mature version of Jan's little sister was eating at the historical Chick-Fil-A Dwarf House restaurant in Hapeville with her brother and some friends when Darwin and Eddie Stephenson walked in. The Dwarf House (formerly The Dwarf Grill) is where the Chick-Fil-A sandwich was invented, and is a Hapeville landmark. The restaurant is also open 24 hours a day, making it a frequent hangout for those in need of a late-night snack. Pointing to Darwin, Jill's brother asked if that was the guy who used to be friends with their sister Jan. Jill acknowledged that Darwin was indeed Jan's friend, but added with a laugh that she didn't want to

The newlyweds cut the cake at the wedding reception.
(Photos courtesy of Jill Ewing)

attract his attention because Darwin had what she thought to be cocaine residue on his nose.

Darwin admitted that he probably looked like trouble, but to his recollection no drugs were involved that night. "I was probably dressed in black leather when I came be-bopping into that Chick-Fil-A," he said. "But that is what we did – we hung-out at the Chick-Fil-A. It was just another place in Hapeville where we had this physical connection. It was the place friends met and hung out until [the restaurant management] ran you off."[69]

Later that year, Jill went to see Stilstone Brothers perform at Mother Shuckers Oyster Bar. Jill, now 26 years old and the divorced mother of two small children, attracted Darwin's attention that night. Something clicked during their conversation and the two began dating. On April 15, 1989, the

---

69   Ibid.

couple were married and started their life together. Darwin not only married Jill, but also became a father to her two daughters; four-year-old Amber and seven-year-old Ashley, helping to raise them as if they were his own.

Darwin continued to play with Stilstone Brothers for a short time after his marriage, but his newfound family responsibilities brought an end to the acoustic band after a five year run. During the band's break-up, Jill earned the title of the "Yoko Ono" of the Stilstone Brothers[70]—a distinction to which she readily admitted during an interview. Darwin, however, quickly came to her defense, adding, "She was always looking out for my best interests and she was usually right."[71] Jill noted that Darwin was most often the "most talented person in the group, but too humble to know it, so he often ended up getting cheated; monetarily and musically."[72]

With Darwin's connections to the wrestling industry, it was only natural for him and Jill to hang out with wrestling families. "During the 1990s, a lot of wrestlers and their families lived in Peachtree City, where Jill and I were living," Darwin said. "There were probably a half a dozen or so. So, not only was my job in wrestling a change in career, but it became part of our domestic life as well...and still is."[73]

Darwin's position at WCW came to an abrupt end when he was unceremoniously fired from Ted Turner's Atlanta operation. Michael Seitz had a contract dispute with WCW and left that organization. He immediately signed a new deal with the Worldwide Wrestling Federation (WWF), a company owned by Vince McMahon and the primary competition for Turner's WCW. Both organizations televised "live"

70   Ibid. (This is a reference to the rumor that Yoko Ono was responsible for the breakup of the Beatles.)
71   Ibid.
72   Ibid.
73   Ibid.

matches on Monday nights. Their rivalry was so intense that it became known in the industry as the Monday Night Wars.

"Darwin and Michael had produced an album, *Slam Jam,* consisting of songs the pair had written for several of the WCW wrestlers," Jill said. "When Michael signed his new contract, he asked Darwin to help him write some songs for the WWF wrestlers."[74] Eric Bischoff, president of WCW in Atlanta, learned of their proposed collaboration and took it as a betrayal. He had Darwin come to his office where he "...hopped up on his desk and told Darwin to get out, he was fired!" Jill said. "It was that competitive. He was so angry."[75]

Darwin maintained that it was his right to continue to write music with Michael because he was a self-employed contractor at WCW, and believes that Bischoff just wanted to make a point. "Bischoff fired me with a lot of fanfare to make an example out of me," he said. "He claimed my collaboration with Michael was a conflict of interest. So, I hired a labor attorney who told me that if [Bischoff] claimed writing songs for WCW was a conflict of interest on my part, it would mean that I was an employee, but for the last eight years I'd been paid as a contractor. If I was an employee, I would be owed 20 hours of overtime per week (plus interest) for the past seven years. I sued WCW and Ted Turner. It took three years, but the week before the scheduled court date, they settled out of court."[76]

Darwin emphasized that though he worked in the wrestling industry, he wasn't a wrestler himself. "I never did wrestle, let's make that clear!"[77] he said. However, there was one time that Darwin got tangled up with the wrestling team,

74   Ibid.
75   Ibid.
76   Ibid.
77   Ibid.

The Nasty Boys, who "bulldozed" him when he was operating a camera during a match. "The announcer shouted, 'Oh my God, he's taken out a cameraman!'" Darwin said. "I felt like I had been hit by a Mack Truck, but I fell over and I sold it baby, because I was on camera. I was rolling over on the ground. It was awesome."[78] Darwin may have thought the experience was fun, but that didn't help ease the pain. "He whined about his bruises for over a week,[79]" Jill said. Darwin humbly concurred.

Though Darwin loved his day job, music was still his passion. He continued to dabble with his guitar when he could, playing New Year's Eve gigs and the like, despite not being part of a steady band. In addition to the success in his work life, Darwin and Jill's personal lives were also developing nicely. The couple had purchased a home together and Darwin took his responsibilities as stepfather to Jill's children very seriously. "It speaks volumes to his character that he raised both girls as his own,"[80] Jill said.

They're Gonna Put Me In The Movies!

For Darwin, whose family obligations caused him to place his music on hold, the 1990s provided him with another opportunity, this time in the film industry. His work at the rental facility in the late 1980s as well as his experience as a grip, dolly grip, and a jib arm operator for the Turner Broadcast Systems (TBS) camera crew, provided Darwin with a marketable set of skills.

The grip department of the film industry is essentially two-fold and supports both camera and lighting crews. Back

78   Ibid.
79   Ibid.
80   Ibid.

in those days, the type of direct lighting available could cause shadows on a set, and a grip's job was to help diffuse the raw lights to soften, shade, and bounce the lighting. Grips were also responsible for everything mechanical—scaffolding, construction, carpentry, rigging, and other related tasks were all in their purview. Darwin originally learned the trade in his 20s. "Back then I was playing [in a band] at night and working a day job learning the raw end of the film and television business, [which included] the equipment, the trucks, the cables and all the labor involved," Darwin said. "It's like being a roadie except it's for a film crew."[81]

By the late 1990s, Darwin had joined the technician's union, IATSE Local 479, and had enough experience to work as a dolly grip full time. "Of course, that appealed to me," Darwin said enthusiastically. "I mean, my God, you're talking the movie business. How can I not be drawn into that? You know, it's like joining the circus and running away."[82]

The End of a 13-Year Union

Throughout the 1990s, things had been going rather well for Darwin. But that all changed in the blink of an eye.

In 2001, Darwin was diagnosed with Hepatitis C. His doctor told Jill that she would need to be vigilant about keeping Darwin on the track to recovery—making sure he didn't drink and that he took his medicine as prescribed. Unfortunately, the treatment for Hepatitis C takes several years and has many unpredictable side effects. For Darwin, those side effects caused a drastic personality change.

"In the 1990s, the Hepatitis C protocol was a cocktail of

81   Ibid.
82   Ibid.

Darwin and Jill remain good friends despite their divorce. Pictured in this July 2020 photo is their extended family (L-R) Granddaughter Riley Harper (16), daughter Amber Tucker-Barrett (Riley's mom), Darwin, eight-year-old grand- daughter Landry (Ashley's daughter), daughter Ashley Allen, grandson Judah Barrett (6) (poking his head out from behind Ashley), granddaughter Austyn Allen (11) (sitting on back right of the couch) and Jill Ewing. (Photo courtesy of Jill Ewing)

interferon and riboviron that had to be both injected and taken orally," Darwin said. "The first month of taking the medicine is like a chemotherapy, and when you start to take that cocktail to lower the Hep C load, it's a lot like going through heroin withdrawal, except you're going into a pro- tocol, not coming out of one. You get the shakes and shivers. Since then, they have improved on the Hep C medication, but I had to take that for a year, and it changed my whole personality."[83] Darwin said this type of behavior change was a very common side effect for Hepatitis C patients, but at the time he felt like he was going insane.

---

83   Ibid.

Jill attested to that personality change. "His emotional issues got really heightened," she said. "Normally, he's a very calm man. My children love him, and he loves them, but he was getting to the point where he was punching walls. He would get so mad at me because I was forcing him to take his medicine and trying to keep him on the straight and narrow until [at one point] he just left."[84]

Around the time Darwin walked out, Jill's daughter Amber also left for college. "It was a tough time of adjustment, and a challenge for all of us,"[85] Darwin said. Unfortunately, the marriage didn't make it. After 13 years, the couple formally divorced in May of 2002.

In late 2003, Darwin met Danita Rhea, an aspiring singer who lived in Peachtree City with her three children. The two dated for a few months and eventually were married in 2004. The union lasted only five years and the two divorced in 2009, but remain friends.

Darwin and Jill also still remain good friends. Darwin is devoted to the girls and to their children, and frequently plays guitar with grandchildren Amber and Riley—the trio even sometimes performs at small venues in and around Hapeville.

Outtakes

In 2002, Darwin received a call from the community events manager for Hapeville asking if he'd be interested in performing at the Happy Days Festival the city was planning for later that year. They were hoping to make the September event an annual celebration and wanted Darwin to organize a reunion band. Darwin did so, and has performed at the

---

84   Ibid.
85   Ibid.

festival in one way or another every year since. "It started as a Saturday festival with music and vendors," Darwin said. "About ten years ago, they gave me a Friday night as a son of Hapeville."[86]

The band he puts together is comprised of a core group of players from various stages of his music life, many of them pictured in the photos throughout this chapter. From year to year, "the reunion band members try to rehearse and form a song list," Darwin said. "But it is like herding cats."[87]

The Toenail Clipping That Binds

Darwin still gets excited when recounting some of his movie experiences. One of his most beloved memories occurred while he was working on the 2011 Hallmark movie called Lost Valentine, starring Betty White and Jennifer Love Hewitt. It was Betty White who caught Darwin's eye. "I hit on her," he said. "She promptly told me that she liked younger men,"[88] Darwin being too old for her.

He also had the opportunity to work with stars Robin Williams and Candace Bergen while filming the comedy Merry Friggin Christmas, which opened in theaters in 2014. "We were shooting a kitchen scene with Robin and Candace [who played Williams' wife] in which Williams, in an effort to aggravate his wife, put his foot up on the kitchen counter to clip his toenails," Darwin said. "I moved the dolly up close to show him clipping the toenail, and when he clipped it, it flipped up and hit me in the eye. I said, 'Ouch,' which busted the take and made the director extremely mad. The

---

86   Ibid.
87   Ibid.
88   Ibid.

(Left) Darwin and Betty White during the 2011 filming of 'Lost Valentine'. (Right) Robin Williams with Darwin in 2013 during the filming of 'Merry Friggin Christmas'. (Both photos courtesy of Jill Ewing)

director said, 'Who the fuck said that?' Robin answered, 'It's my fault, I hit Darwin in the eye with a toenail.' After that, Robin kind of attached himself to me on the set if the situation allowed, because I was the guy whose eye he poked out with his toenail."[89]

Foxes and Fossils

It wasn't until the formation of Foxes and Fossils that Darwin became a member of a band again. He played his first full summer with the band in 2010, but commitments necessitated a change the following year. Years later, he filled in for Toby in the summer of 2018 at some outdoor jobs that Toby couldn't do because of health issues left over

---

89   Ibid.

from his battle with Guillain-Barre syndrome. Darwin had kept up with Foxes and Fossils (and Tim) over the years and was thrilled in 2019 when Tim told him that the band would be doing some recording and videos for YouTube, and they wanted him to be a part of it. Darwin doesn't know how long Foxes and Fossils will be a thing, but if he has his way, he will continue to play with them "until I can't play guitar anymore."[90]

---

90   Ibid.

Chapter 3

SCOTT "THE MANDOLIN" KING

The Early Years

Scott King was born on November 30, 1960 in Alexandria, Virginia to Dennis and Fontaine (Lloyd) King. He was the first of three boys, followed closely by Meade and Ross. By outward appearances, the Kings had a happy marriage. But when Scott was just seven years old, divorce tore the family apart, and Fontaine moved into a small apartment in Alexandria with her three boys. As a child, Scott had a cordial relationship with his father, but didn't see much of him after high school. Eventually, Dennis moved to Maine, and they would only see each other about six more times before Dennis passed away in 2018. Scott doesn't remember the divorce having an adverse effect on him when he was young, but he wondered later if it may have been a factor in the chronic depression that he struggled with for his entire adult life.

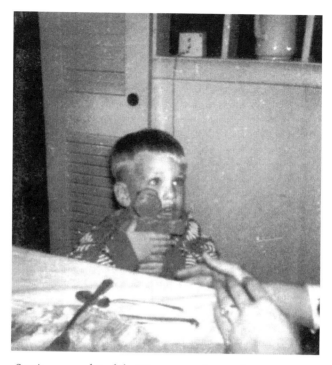

Scott's mom explained that "Scott was so happy when it came time to eat the gingerbread man. This is his reaction when that time came on Thanksgiving Day, circa 1963.
(Photo courtesy of Fontaine Nimmo and Scott Kale)

Scott was 12 years old when the guitar first caught his eye. He had never shown any interest in playing a musical instrument before, but when one of his friends started tinkering around with a cheap electric guitar, that all changed. He thought the guitar seemed pretty awesome, so he asked his mom if she would get him one for Christmas. She complied and in 1972 Scott received his very first musical instrument—a Sears and Roebuck catalogue model electric guitar.

"That was a must have," Scott recalled. "You had to have a bike with the banana seat with the big handlebars (mine was yellow), and you had to have a guitar."[91]

---

91   Author interview with Scott King. October 12, 2021

Though he enjoyed playing, he quickly learned that the guitar was not easy to master. As many budding musicians do, he would listen to records, and later 8-track tapes, for hours trying to learn riffs by listening to the same part of the song over and over again. He found the process easier when he was learning from vinyl, as he could pick the needle up and place it anywhere on the disc. But when he started using 8-track tapes, that all changed. If he needed more than one run through to learn the riff (which he usually did), he could only return to the beginning of the song after listening to the whole thing as there was no rewind button on 8-track players.

In 1974, seven years after her divorce, Scott's mom married Johnny Cassada, a man she met after moving her family to Virginia Beach. Fontaine thought that the boys needed a father, but Scott wasn't particularly fond of Johnny. It was apparent to him that "Johnny really didn't want to have the kids around, he just wanted mom,"[92] Scott said. Johnny and Fontaine were together for about eight years, but the marriage ultimately fell apart. The union did, however, provide Scott and his brothers with a half-sister Warrie and half-brother Jack. About six years after her divorce from Johnny, Fontaine married for a third time. Her marriage to Bill Nimmo is still flourishing after 33 years.

Scott's First Band Experience

The family moved from Alexandria to Virginia Beach in 1974, and eight grader Scott, undeterred by the unfamiliar faces at Virginia Beach Junior High School, was determined to start a band. One of the boys he decided to recruit was Billy Parks. "One day, we just started talking about guitars and he

92   Ibid.

invited me over to his house," Scott said. "He had a guitar that was far cooler than mine. He had a blue Fender Mustang with a matching headstock and racing stripe, and he could play it."[93] Billy also owned a cheap acoustic amp and a Univox 'SuperFuzz' pedal. Scott "was blown away, not by my playing, but at the tone and power I was able to project,"[94] Billy said.

Billy's friend Scooter DeBoxtel played drums and he knew a guy named Bill Hailey who could play guitar. More importantly, Hailey also owned a bass and a bass amp that he never used. Because he wasn't as talented as the other boys on guitar, the group suggested that Scott play Hailey's bass. With the lineup set, they formed the very first band that Scott every belonged to. They didn't have a name, and they never played any gigs—but they did participate in the 1975 Junior High School Talent Show, where they played an original song and several verses of the Chuck Berry classic *Johnny B. Goode*.

"There were no vocals," Scott said. "We didn't know how to end it (the song). So, we simply played it over and over. I'd yell out, Play it four more times!' Then Billy said, 'Play it two more times.'"[95] And on and on it went. "I think we just looked at each other and stopped,"[96] Scott remembered.

While they didn't sound much like Chuck Berry, Scott certainly enjoyed the experience of playing in front of a live audience, catching a bug that would last a lifetime. The talent show was the only time the band played in public.

---

93   Ibid.
94   Written comments submitted by Bill Parks to the author. February 3, 2022.
95   Ibid.
96   Author interview with Scott King, October 26, 2021.

Scott King's high school, First Colonial High School, has not changed since Scott formed his first bands there.
(Photo courtesy of Scott King.)

Horizon

Scott caught wind of a band called Horizon from Virginia Beach's First Colonial High School that was in need of a bass player. He jumped at the chance to join. Horizon's members were all 16 years and older, and Scott—just 14 at the time—was a little bit intimidated by the older boys. But he didn't let that stop him and he got the gig. In addition to Scott on bass, Horizon included Barry Charlton on guitar, David Carter on guitar and lead vocals, Marshall Sands on drums, Mark Whitmire on trumpet, and Ricky Smith on keyboards.

Horizon's repertoire included popular hits of the day by Kool and the Gang, KC and the Sunshine Band, Chicago, and The Eagles. One particularly memorable song that Horizon performed was *Color My World* by Chicago. They didn't have a flute, but Mark was able to recreate the song's signature solo on his trumpet. "It was a very touching and romantic moment when that trumpet started to play,"[97] Scott said.

---

97   Author interview with Scott King. October 12, 2021.

HORIZON, NEPTUNE'S FESTIVAL 1975 Ricky Smith - Piano, David Carter - Guitar & Vocals, Scott King - Bass, Sands Marshall - Drums & Vocals, Mark Wetmore - Trumpet & Vocals, Barry Charlt

*Scott King's (3rd from left) first public performance with his band
Horizon at the Neptune's Festival in 1975. Scott was fourteen.
(Photo courtesy of Scott King.)*

Scott remembered that Ricky had perfect pitch. Some musicians may claim to have that particular gift, but Ricky proved it. "We were playing an outdoor gig someplace and there was a football team that was practicing on a nearby field," Scott said. "One of the guys said, 'Hey Ricky, what's the pitch of the coach's whistle?' Ricky said, 'Let me listen again.'" When the coach blew the whistle again, Ricky—without hesitation—said, "It's between F# and G, depending upon how hard he blows.'"[98] He played those two notes on his keyboard and to everyone's amazement, he was right."[99]

"Perfect pitch, however, is not necessarily a blessing," Scott noted. "Sometimes, it's a curse. Hearing someone play or sing and being able to tell that they were just a little off would drive him (Ricky) nuts."[100]

---

98   Ibid.
99   Ibid.
100   Ibid.

The Cavalier Beach Club

Horizon played a few school dances, performed often at the Cavalier Beach Club, and participated in the Neptune Festival, an annual art festival that took place on the Virginia Beach boardwalk. Because Scott was so much younger than his other bandmates, some of them thought his age might detract from their credibility and encouraged him to lie. In his eagerness to play with the band, he followed orders and pretended to be 16 like all the other members.

Scott vividly recollected his naiveté at his first Beach Club gig. At the end of the performance, the club manager approached him and handed him a $20 bill. Scott was surprised and asked what it was for. The manager told him it was his compensation for the night, something Scott had not anticipated—he played just because he loved playing. The money, however unexpected, was a nice bonus.

By late 1976, Horizon had been together for about 18 months and things appeared to be going well. In addition to multiple paying gigs, they even had the opportunity to perform on a local radio show. But one night while practicing in Scooter's living room, Scott and Scooter got into a little tiff that resulted in the drummer chastising Scott in a rather abrasive way that embarrassed him in front of the others. Without hesitation, Scott packed up his things, called his mother for a ride home, and waited in the driveway until she arrived to pick him up. His tenure with Horizon had officially come to an end.

The North End Band

Later that year, Scott attended a jam session that eventually turned into a band. The jammers decided to call the

Scott hitting the road, probably on his way to a gig.
(Photo courtesy of Fontaine Nimmo and Scott Kale)

group The North End Band. Scott showcased what he called his "limited artistic ability"[101] by developing the band's logo: a compass design with the letters of the word "North" running vertically (north and south) and the words "End" and "Band" positioned horizontally (east to west).

The North End Band recruited a guitar player from Richmond whose name Scott couldn't recall, though he was a talented player. "We started playing backyard beer parties once he was added to the band,"[102] Scott said. The group was more of a neighborhood garage band than a real working band. They played a variety of music including tunes by The Marshall Tucker Band, and the popular song *Sunny* by Bobby Hebb. Their eclectic choice of songs was probably the reason they never had any paying gigs. They mostly played in people's yards or at keg parties where they could score some free beer.

101   Ibid.
102   Ibid.

Scott relaxing before a gig.
(Photo courtesy of Fontaine Nimmo and Scott Kale)

Moontears

Scott remained with The North End Band for about a year before moving on to more professional bands, even though he was still in high school. The names of those bands, as well as the names of many of the musicians he played with, escaped him after all these years, but he maintained that the bands were quite good and the players really talented.

"They were real bands," Scott said. "Most of them had an agent, promo pictures, and matching outfits, the whole bit. The bands would come and go, and the players would move from one to another. I played with Barry Charlton in one of them and with Billy Parks in another."

"While Scott was playing with *Horizon*, I went in a different direction," Billy said. "I experimented with other players and different styles of music, jazz, and other things like that." But in late 1976, the two reunited when Scott recruited

Moontears, featuring (L-R) Andy Kollmorgen, Billy Parks, Sheila,
Tom Stanley, Scott King and Richard Cadorette
(Photo courtesy of Billy Parks)

Billy to play with a disco band that had some older and more experienced players, and was already playing gigs in the area.[103] That band became Moontears.

Billy's memories of playing with Scott in Moontears in 1977 and 1978 are very distinct. "We were both in high

103   Written comments submitted by Bill Parks to the author. February 3, 2022.

school at the time," Billy recalled. "Scott was a junior and I was a senior. We played the disco scene because that was where the money was. We played many clubs in and around the Hampton Roads, Virginia area, including some on the strip in Virginia Beach such as The Cave, Kings Head Inn, and a couple after-hours clubs. Scott played bass, I was on rhythm guitar and classmate, Andy Kollmorgen, was the drummer."[104]

The other three Moontears members were in their mid-20s and had far more experience playing the club scene. "Scott, Andy, and I would play all night sometimes and then drive to school literally still in our stage clothes wreaking of cigarette smoke," Billy said. "I'm surprised any of us graduated. Scott and I had been close friends since junior high school and, though going our separate ways after graduation from high school, remained good friends. It's hard to believe that he actually started playing bass in my bedroom at my parent's house when we were too young to drive. It was a very special time in our lives."[105] Parks left the band after graduating from high school, but Scott stayed with the remaining players of Moontears, who eventually changed the name of the band to Jasmine.

The Snard Brothers

One night in 1979 following a Jasmine gig on the military base in Virginia Beach, Scott stopped at a Crown Filling Station. He had borrowed his stepfather's car, and he needed gas. This was back in the days before self-service gas stations were commonplace, so an attendant pumped gas into

---

104   Interview with Billy Parks. January 29 – 30, 2022.
105   Ibid.

the car. This particular attendant, Bobby Becket, noticed Scott's guitar case lying in the back seat as he pumped. He walked over to the driver's window and, pointing to the back seat, said, "Hey, what you got, man?" "A Fender bass," Scott replied. "Well, I got a guitar. It's really pretty. Pull over and let me show you, it's really pretty,"[106] the attendant repeated.

Scott knew that a serious guitar player would never speak of his guitar using terms like "pretty." He might talk about how great it plays or how nice it sounds, but never how it looked. "Even if it's been run over by three trucks, it doesn't matter as long as it sounds great," Scott insisted. It was late and he felt a bit uneasy, but before he could say anything, Becket walked over to his car and pulled out a blanket. "Strike two," Scott thought. "He doesn't even have a case for this 'pretty' guitar."[107] In an effort to take control of the moment, Scott got out of his car and walked toward Becket. He glanced at the attendant's car and noticed a woman asleep in the front seat—he later learned that she was Becket's girl-friend and they were both living in the car.

"Becket unwrapped the blanket to expose this beautiful Les Paul Custom, cream-colored guitar with gold hardware," Scott remembered. "It was just a fabulous guitar. It turned out that this gas station attendant had a gig up on the Virginia Beach fishing pier in a little place called Ocean Eddy's where fishermen would come after unloading their morning catch, grab a chili dog and a beer, and warm up a little bit before going back out to fish. He asked me to come play with him and I stayed there with him for the next couple of years."[108] Becket suggested they call themselves The Snard Brothers.

---

106   Ibid.
107   Ibid.
108   Ibid.

The duo developed an entire storyline around the origin of their name. Of the 13 Snard children, Becket would say, he was the oldest and Scott was the youngest. All 13 children had presidential middle names—Becket's was "Woodrow" and Scott's was "Quincy." The names became part of their schtick. Together, The Snard Brothers played covers of John Prine, Country Joe McDonald, Willie Nelson, The Eagles, Ricky Nelson, and a slew of others.

Scott loved hamming it up as The Snard Brothers, particularly when he got to sing falsetto. "It all worked really well for us,"[109] he said. Oddly enough, Becket kept his "pretty" Les Paul wrapped up in the blanket, The Snard Brothers only played acoustic music.

They continued to play at Ocean Eddy's all through the summer of 1979, but with the advent of winter the last of the tourists were gone, and the place shut down for the season. During that first winter, the pair searched all over for jobs and took pretty much whatever they could find, including two gigs in upstate New York. "One was on New Year's Eve [and we played] in this structure that was sort of like a castle," Scott said. "As patrons walked through this curved passageway within it, they would come across these two guys playing their guitars."[110]

The other gig was in a restaurant/bar where the actual bar was shaped like an old sailing ship. "We had to carry our gear up the steps behind a wall and put it through a window," Scott said. "We then had to crawl through the window to the stage (platform) where we stood behind a railing like we were on a ship's deck. We were one and a half or two stories up, standing on a stage behind a rail designed to look like the upper deck of this ship. So, we're

---

109   Ibid.
110   Ibid.

way up high above the bar playing to the ceiling in a place where nobody cared!"[111]

Becket also booked another gig at a college bar in Sanford, North Carolina. "We drove back from there in a horrible snowstorm," Scott said. "We were pretty much the only car on the road, and we were moving really slow, white-knuckling the whole way home just hoping we would make it."[112]

The duo made it through that first winter, and when spring rolled around they resumed their steady gig at Ocean Eddy's. They also had an opportunity to open up for a relatively big-name blues band called The Nighthawks at an 800-seat nightclub that was filled to capacity. Beckett was known to horse around on stage, and while his on-stage antics might have been well-received at a tiny bar on a fishing pier, the nightclub crowd didn't take to them so well. Unbeknownst to Scott, prior to taking the stage that night, Beckett had stuffed a big red rubber lobster down his pants. When the mood struck him, "he started screaming, 'I got the crabs, I got the crabs," at which point he reached into his pants and pulled out the rubber lobster that he then tossed into the crowd. Members of The Nighthawks were sitting off stage waiting for their turn to play. "The drummer, who was a big ole' biker-looking guy, got up on stage, unplugged Bobby's guitar, picked him and the guitar up, and carried him off stage," said Scott. "That was the headliner saying we were done. I just stood there and looked around for a second, then unplugged my stuff and carried it out of there. It was a long walk through the crowd that night. That was the only time I ever remember being fired!"

---

111   Ibid.
112   Author interview with Scott King. October 26, 2021 and December 17, 2021.

Ray Griff and Company

On the heels of being fired, Scott picked up a gig out of Nashville, Tennessee. His friend Ray Griff, an accomplished singer/songwriter, was going on a three-month tour of Canada. Ray had his own television show in Alberta and had also written songs for the likes of Jerry Lee Lewis and Dolly Parton. His success must have gone to his head, for he was the epitome of vanity, going so far as to apply makeup to his chest so that when he wore an open shirt it would appear that he had an even tan. Ray had a stutter that at times caused him to almost choke on his words, but like Mel Tillis, as soon as he started singing it would disappear.

Despite Scott eschewing Ray's slick demeanor and leisure suit appearance, the invitation to join him was too good to refuse. "I rode across the country in the chauffeured Ray Griff Tour Bus and toured western Canada with this really cheesy country band for about three months," Scott said. "A tour bus may sound luxurious, but the bus didn't even have a working air conditioner. When the tour was over, I headed back to Virginia Beach."[113]

The Snard Brothers—Redux

While Scott was in Canada, Bobby Becket had teamed up with another guitar player named Teaford Webber. Teaford was a beach bum who was known to spend summer days lounging on the boardwalk, playing his guitar, singing and hustling girls. Scott was surprised that the two had teamed up, but was happy to join them for the rest of the season. But just as the pier was shutting down for the

113   Ibid.

winter, Scott stumbled into another too-good-to-pass-up opportunity.

The Pilots

In late 1981, Scott met a couple of guys out of Richmond and Fredericksburg who were in a band called The Pilots. They were in need of a bass player and had offered the spot to a buddy of Scott's, Sam Erroll. Sam had turned down The Pilots' offer but suggested they contact his friend, Scott King. Members of The Pilots went to see Scott perform at the Hilton lounge with The Snard Brothers and offered him the job on the spot. Even though he hadn't heard The Pilots play, Scott didn't hesitate to throw his lot in with them. He was growing tired of playing in a hotel lounge, and The Pilots were his ticket out. He took the job.

The band had a large PA system and travelled from gig to gig on a tour bus that doubled as their living quarters. They also had a manager, which made the whole thing seem much more serious to Scott. The Pilots played a lot of original music in addition to covers of some new wave artists and prog-rock groups like Styx. For Scott, this seemed like a step in the right direction. But after two years living on a bus with five other guys, the glamor wore off. By 1983 it was time to move on.

Bareback

On what would be Scott's final tour with The Pilots, they had a gig in Greenville, North Carolina. That's where Scott found his next opportunity—the band was called Bareback, and they were based out of Atlanta, Georgia. Like some of the other

THE PILOTS

Scott King, pictured here second from left, with The Pilots—c 1983
(Photo courtesy of Scott King's mom, Fontaine Nimmo and Scott Kale)

opportunities presented to Scott, this too was happenstance—in fact, it was a case of mistaken identity. Scott noticed a promo picture at a club in Greenville near where The Pilots were playing and thought he recognized one of the men in the photo as Bill from a group called Dottie and the Hot Totties. "I went down to see this bass player I knew perform, and it turned out to not be him or his band," Scott said. "But the band that *was* there, Bareback, was just great. I mean, they were so good."[114] After their performance, Scott spoke to the band members for a while and they hit it off. He was thrilled when a few weeks

---

114   Author interview with Scott King. October 12, 2021.

later, Bareback's bass player left the band and Scott got the call to come aboard. He did not hesitate.

In addition to Scott on bass, Bareback consisted of guitarist Tommy Strain, drummer Mac Crawford, and keyboardist Doug Bare. Bare was a rather large man, and when Bareback recorded their first CD they named their record label after him, affectionately calling it RMS Records—Round Mound of Sound Records!

Scott remained with Bareback from 1983 through 1990, playing major clubs and festivals throughout the southeast, 51 weeks a year. With their popularity growing, the bandmates all thought they were on the verge of stardom. Their leader, Doug Bare, was a remarkably talented singer and songwriter and the band was ultra tight. But it was the dawn of MTV and having a large guy like Doug—with his slouch hat, glasses, and a beard—singing lead wasn't what record executives were looking for.

Sometime around 1986, Doug decided to leave the band. He went on to become the key songwriter for the very successful five-man band Blackfoot. Meanwhile, Scott and the others went in search of a vocalist and keyboard player and managed to find both in Atlanta. David Wright was an incredible, leather-lunged screamer, who—despite drinking, taking drugs, keeping late hours, and doing all the other things not recommended for a lead singer—had a simply amazing voice matched only by his stamina. He would remain with the band for four years. But the keyboard player they found, David Manion, lasted only six months. "He just didn't fit into our band," Scott said. "He is a great keyboard player who went on to play with Kansas."[115]

Bareback carried on as a four-man hard rock band, and eventually reinvented themselves as a 1980s "hair band." Over

115   Author interview with Scott King. October 26, 2021.

Images of Scott King performing with Bareback in a
video featuring their original song, 'On The Prowl'.
(Internet Images courtesy of Scott King)

the years, they opened for a great many acts that were either
on their way up or on their way down. By the early 1990s,
however, they realized that the band was really just treading
water, becoming known more for their drinking than their
playing. Tommy Strain, the de-facto band leader, was fed up.

The Derrek St. Holmes Band

Toward the end of 1990, Bareback had only a few gigs
lined up. To supplement his income, Scott took a sales job
in a music store. Around that time, Bareback drummer Mac
Crawford met Derrek St. Holmes, the lead singer and rhythm
guitar player for Ted Nugent's band. Derrek was living
in the Atlanta area and invited Mac to jam with him as an
audition for a new band he was starting. Mac suggested that
Derrek give a listen to some of his bandmates, Tommy and
Scott. Tommy, Scott, and Mac agreed to back up Derrek,

thinking it would be nothing more than a side project, but Bareback vocalist David Wright didn't see it that way. He was insulted and hurt that his bandmates would leave him to go join up with a wannabe rock star. "We went to pick David up for a gig one night and he just wouldn't answer the door," Scott said. "That was officially the end of Bareback."[116] Scott, who had been with Bareback longer than any other band he played with, was quite saddened by its demise.

Scott ended up joining The Derrek St. Holmes Band. While the band was good, Derek himself was a jerk—something he apparently learned from his years with Ted Nugent, Scott said. Derrek paid his backup musicians just $50 per show, which was a very low wage even for the 1990s. He wouldn't allow a per diem unless the show was more than 125 miles from home, and even then, the per diem was only $5 per day. Tommy didn't put up with this for long, and left the band rather early on. Mac and Scott, however, put up with the mistreatment for a couple of years, hoping that Derrek would get a record deal and take them along with him.

Scott did his best to help Derrek. Once while the band was playing a gig in Huntsville, Alabama, Scott reached out to a friend who worked at a recording studio in that city and was able to get the band booked for a free session on a weekend when the studio owner was out of town. They recorded a bunch of demos live, straight to tape. Despite the studio time costing him nothing, Derek didn't offer to compensate the band or anyone at the studio for their time. Even worse, when it came time for Mac and Scott to get a cassette recording of the session, Derrek withheld $5 from each of their salaries to pay for the tape. That insult was the final straw for Scott. On the drive home after a gig in Savannah, "I told

116   Ibid.

102

Mac to pull over and I proceeded to give Derrek a piece of my mind," Scott said. "Later when Derrek complained to his wife about me, she actually took my side! I eventually got my $5 back, but that was the beginning of the end."[117]

With the bad taste of The Derrek St. Holmes Band fresh in his mouth, Scott took some time off. As the Christmas season approached, he took on a few odd jobs to earn a little money, one being a 10-day stint doing the load in/load out for a Richard Petty tribute show in Atlanta. The job was hard work, requiring Scott to carry sheets of plywood and steel used to construct temporary flooring at the Omni.

He also took a job glazing hams at a Honey-Baked Ham store, and continued to work for Celesta—a dog groomer for whom he had started working in the early 1990s. Scott enjoyed the latter job very much. "It was fun," he remembered. "We played a little game I invented called, 'If Your Name Was Blank, What Would You Name Your Dog?' We had a customer with the last name of Mix for example. We would shout the question across the shop. 'If your name was Mix, what would you name your dog?' We came up with Trail Mix, Bloody Mary Mix, [and things like that]. We had a real nice time. Grooming dogs was nasty, tough work, but it was fun."[118]

Heading West to LA

In 1992, Scott got an invitation to come to Los Angeles to be in a band that Garry Limuti (Yes, that Garry Limuti—see the chapter on Tim Purcell) was forming. An interesting aside about Garry, Scott said, is that when he was in junior high and high school, his best friend was Marc David

---

117   Ibid.
118   Ibid.

Chapman, who infamously shot and killed John Lennon in 1980. Chapman had become incensed by Lennon's lifestyle, his song lyrics, and some of his public statements. Garry was heartbroken about it.

Garry had moved to Los Angeles to form a band with Rick Dufay, a guitarist who was one of the original members of Aerosmith. Garry told Scott that Sony Music was behind the project, and their odds of making it big looked pretty good. Sony agreed to pay Scott's expenses, so he flew out to Los Angeles for an audition and got the gig. "Sony flew me back to Atlanta where I packed my stuff and piled it all in my 1976 Chevy Impala and a small trailer and drove across the country," Scott said. However, after only about two or three weeks in LA, Garry abruptly quit the band he had worked so hard to create. "He didn't want to play with another guitarist," Scott said. "So here I was, stranded all the way across the country, sleeping on a twin bed mattress on the floor of a one-bedroom apartment in North Hollywood with this used-to-be-a-junkie, has-been guitarist (Dufay), and without the guy I knew (Garry) and had come to LA to play with."[119]

Without Garry—the songwriter—further attempts to build a band were unsuccessful. With no band and no work, Scott turned once again to Celesta, who just happened to have a friend with a dog grooming business in the Los Angeles area. Scott began to wash dogs for the woman, named Yvonne, six days a week. "Yvonne was very sweet," Scott recalled. "She knew that I was a bass player, so if a dog that was suspected of being a nipper or a biter would come in, she wouldn't let me wash it for fear that it would bite my hand."[120] On Sundays, Scott worked for another dog groomer just down the street,

119   Ibid.
120   Ibid.

104

if only to avoid his apartment. For Scott, the Los Angeles coup de grâce came in late April 1992 when protests and riots arose in response to the acquittal of the four police officers who beat Rodney King. He packed up his Impala and hit the road for Georgia.

Looking back on the LA experience, Scott has no regrets. "It was pretty cool being out there," he said. "Rick Dufay's girlfriend, Marie, did some modeling and appeared in the *Simply Irresistible* video by Robert Palmer. She worked her butt off paying the bills so her boyfriend could pursue his rock star dream. She and I got along great…and I also got to meet some famous people through Rick. He would invite me to his AA [Alcoholics Anonymous] meetings whenever a cool person was expected to be there."[121] At those meetings, held at an old church in North Hollywood, Scott met actor Ed Begley Jr., Steven Tyler, and many other stars.

"As we were leaving a meeting [one night], it started raining," Scott said. "So we [Scott, Rick, and Steven Tyler] ran across the parking lot to get into Rick's car, a little Volkswagen hatchback. Rick turns around and hollers, 'Steven, get in the back, Scott's bigger than you are.' So, here I am standing in the rain, waiting for the lead singer of Aerosmith to wedge himself in the back seat of a two-door car because I'm taller."[122] Rick drove to his little one-bedroom apartment where the three hung out drinking coffee and having an overall great time. "It took everything within me to keep it cool because I was such a big Aerosmith fan,"[123] Scott said.

---

121   Ibid.
122   Ibid.
123   Ibid.

Supporting Roger Ballard

Back home in Atlanta, Scott got a call from Kenny Mims, a guy who had once produced some recordings for Bareback in Nashville. He said that he had just finished an album for Roger Ballard, who had a deal with Atlantic Records and now wanted to put together a six-piece road band. Scott auditioned and got the gig. The band made the rounds of all the Nashville TV shows and performed on the road a bit, but the label couldn't generate a hit for Ballard, so they cut off the money for his road band. After about six months or so, the gig was over.

Highway 101

The Roger Ballard experience led to a couple of additional Nashville gigs, including one with Paulette Carlson, the lead singer of a group called Highway 101. Scott adored her and auditioned for her group, but she had concerns about his commute from Atlanta. He didn't want to move to Nashville, so she didn't hire him. Some time later, she called him up and asked him to go on tour with her to promote her new Christmas record. The six-week stint went through Minnesota, the Dakotas, and "everywhere frozen," according to Scott, around Thanksgiving 1994. "She had this beautiful snow-angel outfit and a Mrs. Santa Clause outfit that she wore," Scott recollected. "It was just a magical time. Snow on the ground everywhere, just riding around playing Christmas music with a bunch of really good people…It was a wonderful experience."[124]

---

124 Ibid.

Scott always had a tremendous love of dogs. He is pictured
with one of his dogs in this circa 2000 photo
(Photo courtesy of Fontaine Nimmo and Scott Kale)

The Daron Norwood Band

Scott's next opportunity was with Daron Norwood, who was being groomed for stardom at an Atlanta club called The Buckboard (Toby played guitar there at the time). Daron would achieve a moderate level of success in the world of country music, even having a few Top 40 hits. His manager owned the club, giving Daron a convenient place to hone his skills nightly. Scott got a call to audition for Daron's upcoming

tour, so he picked up a copy of Daron's newly released debut album and learned all the songs. His over-preparation paid off—he was immediately offered the job. To his delight, he learned that his old drummer friend, Doug Bennett from the Roger Ballard days, had also secured a spot in the band.

Daron was a good-looking, extraordinarily talented singer and musician who played both guitar and piano. The band hit the road, performing mostly in Daron's home state of Texas. But Daron apparently had a hard time coping with success. According to Scott, he was quite full of himself and proceeded to burn many a bridge with radio stations, fans, and other artists. Daron also had a drinking problem, along with some serious character flaws (narcissism among them) that cut his career short. Scott was with Daron for about a year.

In a Country Weekly article, Daron talked more in depth about his drinking problem, which led him to quit the industry in 1995. He later founded Keep It Straight in 1997, an anti-drug, anti-alcohol, and anti-violence program for young people. Unfortunately, he was found dead in his apartment bedroom in 2015 at age 49. No foul play was suspected.

Over the next few years, Scott continued to perform around the Atlanta area with many different acts, and though many of the players he was with were great, none of them had any real ambition other than the occasional club gig. Scott felt as though he was floating through musician limbo.

The Mustangs

In February 2001 Scott received—but didn't return—several phone calls from Tim Purcell, who was looking for a bass player for his country/rock band The Mustangs. Tommy

Strain, Scott's bandmate from the Bareback days, had recommended Scott to Tim. When Tim had no luck contacting Scott, he went back to Tommy to see if he knew of anyone else. Tommy said, "Let me call Scott. I think he would be perfect for you." He did, and asked Scott to call Tim back as a personal favor. Scott obliged, and after talking to Tim agreed to sit in for a weekend with The Mustangs at the Blue Rodeo in Jasper, Georgia on February 12, 2001. Tommy was right. Scott was a perfect fit.

Scott remained a member of The Mustangs until the band's very last performance in 2018. In The Mustangs, Scott finally found a band in which he felt complete. On top of that, he made more money with The Mustangs than he did with any of the touring acts or wannabe rock stars that he had played with before.

Struggles with Depression

"I suffered from depression for years and years, before I even knew it,"[125] Scott said. "I still do."[126] Coping with that depression would be a life long struggle that would lead to substance abuse. Scott was only 12 years old when he began to drink and smoke pot. He finally quit smoking weed completely in 2007. "I finally woke up and realized that I was already stupid and hungry, so I really didn't need to smoke pot,"[127] Scott said with a laugh. But liquor continued to be a tough addiction for him to shake. "My whole life was a binge," he noted. "I would drink every night...My depression, the job I was doing, and the fact that the band [The

---

125   Author interview with Scott King. December 17, 2021.
126   Ibid.
127   Ibid.

The Mustangs perform at Keswick Park in Chamblee, GA on July 4, 2014. (L-R) Toby Ruckert, Tim Purcell, Amy Wallace and Scott King. Scott once referred to The Mustangs as a retirement dance band, a name Tim was not happy with.
(Screenshot by Steve Beckett)

Mustangs] wasn't playing at the time caused me to just drink like crazy."[128]

He said it all came to a head in 2018. "It was Christmas, so I just assumed that we'd take several days off," he said. "At the time, my car was in the shop, which was run by my old friend and Bareback bandmate, Mac Crawford. He gave me the good buddy discount which meant that I [my repair work] was definitely not at the front of the line."[129]

At the time, Scott had been working for Alan Noel, who owned a furniture restoration business in Atlanta. Noel had given up his own ambitions of making it in the music business in 1980 to start a small furniture repair and refinishing

128   Ibid.
129   Ibid.

business in a small space, but by 2018, his business had grown substantially, with warehouse space now measuring the length of about two football fields. The business employed 10 or so people, including Scott, each with their own set of tools and workspace. It was while working there that Scott's alcoholism took its toll.

Scott recalled the events that led up to his hospitalization. "[Without the use of a car] I ended up staying at the shop, an unheated, rat-infested building, sleeping on the floor on an air mattress with my dog over Christmastime," he said. "I was extra miserable, and I just drank and drank and drank, day and night. When I went to pay my rent to my land-lord, Noel's wife, my hand had been shaking so badly when I wrote the check that she couldn't read it. That led to an ultimatum. They told me I could either get treatment or pack my stuff and leave. They threatened to put me and my dog out in the alley that night."[130] At the time, Scott resented Alan for getting involved. Later though, he was thankful for his concern. But despite the warning from Alan, he didn't stop. "I was drinking more than a liter and a half a day and right after Christmas 2018, I wound up in the hospital for 10 days, three of them in intensive care,"[131] he said.

Tim Purcell vividly remembers getting an unsettling email from Toby. "I was in Morocco on vacation with my family when Toby notified me that Scott was found unrespon-sive Monday morning on the floor of the warehouse where he worked," Tim said. While insisting that he didn't drink during work, Scott acknowledged that he would start drink-ing with his coworker and fellow warehouse denizen every weekday immediately following work. They drank all day on Saturdays and Sundays to the point of passing out, and when

---

130   Ibid.
131   Ibid.

they'd come out of it, they'd start all over. Had someone not found him that morning and taken him to the emergency room, it's likely something horrible would have happened.

Tim arrived home from Morocco on January 5, 2019 and went to visit Scott at the hospital. "He was strapped to the bed," Tim recalled. "He couldn't even scratch his face. He remained that way for six or seven days after my return. He was in his bed on his back so long that he required physical therapy to regain his ability to walk."[132] At Scott's request, Tim took Scott's beloved Pit Bull, Ena, back to his own home. When Scott was released, he had no place to go, so both he and his dog temporarily stayed at Tim's house.

Tim's plan was to help Scott pack up his belongings and return to Virginia where he could be cared for by family while getting the treatment he needed. Alan had fired him from his job, so he was unemployed and the heat and electricity in his apartment had been shut off for non-payment. Scott was fortunate that he had yet to be evicted from his condo. Thanks to Alan and his wife's generosity, Scott was given some extra time to pack up and leave.

The apartment, according to Tim, seemed uninhabitable. "He had about 2,000 CDs…well over 60 bass guitars, 30-40 electric guitars, 20 acoustic guitars, 40 ukuleles, 10 mandolins, many not even unpacked from the boxes in which they'd been shipped, stacked all around the place," he said. On top of all that, the place wasn't particularly clean.

Everything had to be sorted and packed, and it had to be done during the day due to the lack of heat and light in the apartment. The sun went down around 4:30 p.m. in the dead of winter and even in Georgia it can get quite cold. But despite the need to get the job done during the daylight hours, Scott's depression caused him to waste most of those

132   Ibid.

hours in bed. "I would be waiting for him to get out of bed so we could go pack and he wouldn't get up until 10:30 or 11:00 a.m.," Tim said. "By the time we got to the apartment, we would get so little done that it seemed like it was going to take months."[133]

Tim stressed the urgency of the situation to Scott. "We had to coordinate getting a truck, loading it, getting his car out of the shop, his license renewed, and a tag," Tim said. "We also had to coordinate the move with his brother Meade, who had agreed to come down to Atlanta and drive the truck full of Scott's belongings back to Virginia. Scott, if we could get all the legalities taken care of, would be driving his own car."[134] Somehow, they got it all done. By the end of March 2019, Scott was back in Virginia.

Scott insisted that his time in the hospital was a wake-up call and that once back home he would get his life back on track. When he got back to Virginia, he found a job working at a nursery/gardening store, but at some point, "everybody who wasn't full time there got furloughed," he said. "The furlough was supposed to be for one month, but it went on for four and a half months, and during that time I started drinking again."[135]

Scott claimed to have gone "back in for treatment" in early 2021, but his brother Ross has no recollection of that.[136] Scott said about the treatment, "I don't know what they did to me, but it seems to have worked."[137] Whether that part of the story is accurate or not, one thing is undeniable; alcoholism and depression can have devastating consequences. Just getting to the next day is a struggle.

---

133   Ibid.
134   Ibid.
135   Ibid.
136   Ibid.
137   Ibid.

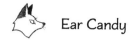

A Different Type of Battle

Once he got the hang of it, Scott really enjoyed making long-distance YouTube videos with Foxes and Fossils. At first, he enlisted Scott Kale—a fellow musician and a superb human being—to help record the audio and video. But Scott eventually ended up doing the audio on his own, and stopped seeing Kale as much. In June of 2021, Kale hadn't seen Scott in a few months, so he stopped by the house to say hello. Afterward, he called Tim to tell him he was worried about Scott. "He's lost a tremendous amount of weight and is deathly pale,"[138] Kale reported. Despite being urged by all who loved him to please go to the doctor, Scott refused. Then in December of 2021, he abruptly told his friends and family that he had terminal cancer.

"The doctors gave me two months to live," Scott said. "I had been feeling bad all year with aches and pains. It got to where I couldn't breathe, so on Monday, December 6, I went to the emergency room."[139] The doctors at the hospital ran a few tests and found that Scott had a lot of fluid in his lungs, and he was diagnosed with heart failure and anemia. His lungs were drained, enabling Scott to breathe freely once again, but the doctors continued to run more tests throughout the day.

At day's end, Scott was informed of the cancer diagnosis. "They couldn't tell me what kind of cancer I had until they conducted more tests which they did the next day," he said. "That's when they told me I had prostate cancer and it had started to spread to the surrounding bones. Later that day they said it had spread to the entire skeleton. That explains the anemia. There isn't enough bone marrow left to produce blood."[140]

---

138   Author interview with Scott Kale. May 3, 2022.
139   Author interview with Scott King. December 17, 2021.
140   Ibid.

The doctors also told Scott that sometime during the past six months, he had suffered a heart attack. "I had been to the doctors for a lot of tests in 2018," he said. "No one told me anything about these issues. Either it wasn't there and had since spread very quickly, or they just missed it."[141]

The cancer doctors suggested that Scott subject himself to rounds of maintenance medication and treatments, but he wouldn't have it. "Look, I know the boat is sinking, I can see the hole in it," he said. "Why do I want to paint the boat? You're wasting my time here. I need something to keep the pain away and something to keep me comfortable. There's no fighting this, you told me that already. There's nothing that can be done about it. So, I just want to get as comfortable as I can and hopefully go peacefully and quietly."[142]

"I had a good life," he added. "You can struggle and kick and scream, do all you want to do, but there's no beating it. So, it's just something I accepted right away."[143]

Following his discharge from the hospital, Scott returned to his mother's house. The three and a half-story duplex has four bedrooms, three and a half baths, a living room, dining room, and kitchen. It also has a half kitchen and entertainment room in the finished basement where Scott lived. That same space was once occupied by Scott's maternal grandfather, who moved in after his wife passed and remained there until about 30 days prior to his own death.

"The first thing I thought when they ran all those tests at the hospital was that it was going to be liver or kidney related or something related to my terrifying amount of liquor consumption," Scott said. "They never brought that up at all. I told the doctors, with a laugh, to take a look at them because

---

141   Ibid.
142   Ibid.
143   Ibid.

neither one of those organs owed me any favors. The cancer is not connected to alcoholism at all and you would think logically that it would be. It's just something that snuck in and got me before I had it looked at."[144]

When Scott informed Tim, Toby, Darwin, and Johnny (his "Fossil" brothers) about his diagnosis, he asked to see them. He said that he wanted to give them some of the many instruments that he has collected over the years.

Johnny and Tim flew to Virginia on Saturday, December 11, 2021. Toby, who was unable to fly due to his own health issues, made the two-day drive to Virginia with Darwin. They coordinated with Johnny and Tim and rendezvoused at the airport to drive together to Scott's house. Though initially apprehensive about the visit, Tim was relieved that Scott looked much better than Tim had anticipated. "He had trimmed his beard and was completely lucid and very conversational," Tim said. "He seemed visibly buoyant that we were there visiting him."[145] Scott described their visit as "a real nice treat for me."[146]

Once past the hellos, the five spoke about Scott's health issues and reminisced a bit. Then, Scott gifted each of them with a special remembrance. "I gave Tim a Les Paul guitar. He's always wanted one," Scott said. "I gave Toby a Ukulele, my current musical passion. I was talking to my brother the next day and I said, 'It's not that I regret giving Toby that Ukulele, it's just that I'm going to have to decide which one I should keep, because I got to get rid of a bunch of them. Then I came to my senses, and thought, you're not going to need any Ukuleles man, so give whatever you want away.' I gave Johnny a bass that [once] belonged to a good friend of his, so that was sentimental to Johnny.

---

144   Ibid.
145   Author interview with Tim Purcell. January 7, 2022
146   Author interview with Scott King. December 12, 2022.

I also gave Toby a Rickenbacker guitar," Scott continued. "Toby is the collector in the band. He once sold a Les Paul for a lot of money. He called it his retirement guitar, so when his wife retired, he sold it. I don't have anything nearly that fancy, but I do have over a hundred instruments."[147] Scott insists, though, that it wasn't a formal collection that he was trying to assemble. "I just found new things to buy and rarely sold anything! The few things I sold I wish I had back,"[148] he said.

Scott's "non-collection" consisted of dozens of guitars, bass guitars, lap steel guitars, mandolins, and ukuleles. "I gave a mandolin to Darwin," Scott said. "I don't know him that well, even though I've known him longer than any of the others. I never played with him until Foxes and Fossils. We had only five or six dates the first year and then he played with us twice the last year and then we started all this remote stuff."[149]

The Long, Hard Road To Goodbye

Scott's health continued to quickly decline and by early January, he required a significant amount of morphine to curb the pain. On Thursday, January 13, 2022, Scott's spirit "slipped the surly bonds of Earth…put out [his] hand and touched the face of God."[150]

Scott's younger brother Ross informed Tim, who shared the news of Scott's passing with his thousands of fans via social media. "We knew this was coming, but the news is

147 Ibid.
148 Ibid.
149 Ibid.
150 High Flight, a poem by John Gillespie Magee. 1941.

no less devastating," Tim wrote. "I got this text from Scott's brother Ross last night. 'Our brother Scott left this world tonight at 7:20 p.m. [His mother] Fontaine and I shared in his last moments. Truly blessed by all the love and support. Scott was calm and in no pain.'"[151]

The same cannot be said of his family, friends, and all those to whom Scott brought joy through his music and throughout his life. True to form, Scott instructed his family to have no service in his memory, but rather to have a quick and simple cremation. The lack of a formal service, however, did not prevent an outpouring of sympathy, offers of prayers and expressions of love from fans across the nation and throughout the world. On behalf of those fans, Rick Silverstein had a tree planted in Scott's memory in the Holy Land on the slopes of the old city of Jerusalem. It will serve as a living tribute to his memory.

---

[151] Facebook message written by Tim Purcell. January 14, 2022.

Chapter 4

TOBY
"THAT REMINDS
ME OF A STORY"
RUCKERT

The Early Years

George Ruckert and Connie Robertson met in New York City in 1937 and got married three years later on July 4, 1940. While living in New York, Connie gave birth to two of the couple's four children: Stuart, born April 4, 1941; and Jeffrey, born July 5, 1944. George worked at the Hoffman Beverage Company until the outbreak of World War II, during which he worked for Grumman Aircraft Engineering Company, providing much needed aircraft for the war effort.

In 1945, the couple moved to West Redding, Connecticut, where their third son, Toby was born on July 1, 1949. Five years later George and Connie welcomed their only daughter, Debbie, on August 6, 1954.

Toby started school in West Redding at the age of six, attending the same school as his brother Jeff. Summers in Connecticut were spent playing sandlot baseball, and games like cops and robbers with other children in the neighborhood. Young Toby loved the snow, and in the cold New England winters you could find him sledding down sloping hillsides, or ice skating on a small pond not far from his home.

George, a true jack of all trades, worked in construction. "He could add a room to your house, install a swimming pool, do plumbing, electrical, you name it," Toby said. "He built the house we lived in while in West Redding. It was a brick ranch with four bedrooms, two baths, and a generous backyard. We had an in-ground pool, a garden, and even a coop with live chickens."[152]

At the time, Fairfield County boasted the highest per capita income in the United States, its relative quiet and proximity to New York City begetting many rich and famous residents. Among those living in West Redding were authors, playwrights, and successful businessmen who had offices in the city, but preferred to live in the quiet serenity of the Connecticut suburb. Hal Foster, author of *The Legend of Prince Valiant,* and Hank Ketcham, the creator of *Dennis the Menace*, were neighbors of the Ruckerts.

Toby's dad strove to instill good manners and social graces into his children, going so far as to travel all the way to a Brooks Brothers in New York City to purchase matching shirts and ties for the three boys. For several months afterward, he required his children—including five-year-old Toby—to eat dinner in their formal attire. These etiquette lessons were not lost on Toby, who would always strive to be diplomatic and polite for the rest of his life.

But things weren't always easy. Death is difficult to understand at any age, but for a seven-year-old, it's nearly

152 Author interview with Toby Ruckert. September 28, 2021.

impossible to comprehend. On September 26, 1956, some neighbors came to pick Toby up early from school. "They didn't say why they had come, only that I had to go home,"[153] he said. Once home, Toby learned that his two-year-old sister Debbie had passed away earlier that day. "I remember wondering why I didn't feel worse about it," Toby said. "I think I just couldn't grasp it."[154]

Soon the Ruckerts found themselves about 1,500 miles south of West Redding in sunny St. Petersburg Beach, Florida. George had some New York friends who had relocated to the Tampa area and had convinced him of the many virtues of southern life. For Connie, the house in Connecticut was a constant reminder of her daughter's death, and a move meant a fresh start. Toby and his brothers may have loved the snow, but George didn't share their enthusiasm. For him, winters in Connecticut meant adding snow chains to the tires of his car and shoveling knee-deep snow. Convinced that a change would be good for the family, George and the Ruckert clan moved down south in 1957.

The Ruckerts rented the first floor of a duplex until 1960 when they purchased a home in St. Pete Beach, just a stone's throw away from the Gulf of Mexico. Years later, Toby's older brother Stuart purchased the home from his parents, and still lives there today.

Toby's dad was an avid fan of crossword puzzles. He would go to bed no later than 8 p.m. every evening and arise early the next morning at around 3 a.m. "He would go to the fridge, get a beer, get his New York Times crossword puzzle book and do one in ink," Toby recalled. "Then he'd put the book away and go back to sleep for another two or three hours before getting up to go to work."[155]

153   Author interview with Toby Ruckert. March 7, 2022.
154   Ibid.
155   Ibid.

Despite missing the snow, the children grew to love living in Florida. After all, living in a place where you could play baseball year round wasn't so bad. George began a job as the service manager for British and Continental Motors, the only import automobile dealership on the west coast of Florida, while Connie continued her work as a stay-at-home mom. But that would all change in 1964. When Toby was 15 years old in high school, his mom got a job as a case manager and supervisor at Florida's Welfare Department.

In high school, Toby began to develop a keen interest in the guitar. His brother Jeff played and had long encouraged Toby to join him. "It would be a lot of fun, especially at parties,"[156] Toby remembers him saying. When Jeff left home to attend the University of Florida, he bought a new guitar as his old one was difficult to play because of its high action[157]. Toby jumped at the chance to take Jeff's old guitar and give playing a try. He started playing, and that was it.

"There was no going back," Toby said. «It really took over my life. When I got home from school, the first thing I wanted to do was take out the guitar and play it. If you really love it, it takes over."[158] And Toby really loved it. He immediately knew that he wanted to play lead. "That was the spotlight,"[159] he noted.

Unlike Jeff and Toby, Stuart never developed an interest in music. Instead, he busied himself with anything electronic, and would spend hours alone in his room building radios and other gadgets. Despite their varying interests and their age differences, the three Ruckert boys were always close.

---

156   Ibid.
157   "Action" refers to the distance between the strings and the fingerboard. The higher the action, the greater the distance. Greater distance requires extra pressure to get a clear note or chord.
158   Ibid.
159   Ibid.

Like most guitarists, Toby was self-taught. "Money was a little tighter [when we lived in Florida] and lessons were out of the question," he said. "While not being mean about it, my parents weren't exactly crazy about me playing music. I learned songs using the 'drop needle' approach."[160] That meant dropping the record-player needle, over and over again, at the spot in the song he wanted to learn until he had it down.

Toby always excelled academically and was an honor student at every level. His parents had high hopes for him, thinking him a potential doctor or lawyer; something that would lead to a more promising future than playing guitar. Eventually, they came to see how deeply Toby cared about music and accepted the fact that their boy was in love.

The Emotions and Painful Loss

Toby's first real opportunity to play with a band came in 1965 when he was just a freshman in high school. He got together with some friends and had a few jam sessions. "At first we enjoyed just playing together, but it [eventually] grew into a band,"[161] Toby recalled. The five-member band that resulted from those jams called themselves The Emotions, featuring Jim Searce on the drums (later replaced by Billy Christian), Mark Benson on rhythm guitar, Mark Bass on lead vocals (replaced for a short time by Charlie Beauchamp before returning), Bob Hohman on bass guitar, and Toby on lead guitar and back-up vocals.

160   Ibid.
*Elementary school included grades 1-6, middle school included grades 7-9 and high school was only three years, grades 10-12. In reality, Toby entered his first year of high school as a traditional sophomore.
161   Ibid.

Music wasn't Toby's only interest during his high school years. At 6'2", the slender guitarist was a natural at basketball, and for a year and a half he played for the Pirates of Boca Ciega High School. However, as soon as Friday night basketball games began to conflict with his band schedule, Toby dropped the basketball team—an easy choice for him.

Compared to other kids his age, Toby was raking in the dough. The Emotions played mostly school dances and alcohol-free teen clubs and by 1966, Toby was making about $70 a week just working on weekends—quite a sum for a high school student. The band was pretty successful as garage bands go, even making a 45-rpm recording. Side A of the 45, produced by J.H. Daniels who ran the Century Records label, featured a cover of The Zombies hit song *Sometimes*. But it was the B Side of the record that proved surreal for the band members. That song, *Why Must It Be*, was written by Toby's brother Jeff, and was laden with "introspective lyrics that were turned into a gem of a ballad."[162]

Though the recording featured Mark Bass as lead vocalist, it was his successor, Charlie Beauchamp, who provided Toby with the bitter taste of tragedy that would turn those lyrics into a prescient glimpse of the future.

Charlie joined the band at the end of 1966 when Mark left to pursue other interests. By all accounts, Charlie was a terrific kid whose interests spread far beyond music. The high school senior was a three-year varsity football halfback, and one of the top second basemen in Pinellas County. He was a national honor student and a member of many school groups, including the school choir, the Letterman's Club and the Exchange Club.

---

162   Lemlick, Jeff, Jeffens 66, Real Teen Tragedies Behind 2 Moody Garage 455. https://savagelost.com/the-real=teen-tragedies-behind-two-moody-garage-455. September 26, 2015.

Members of the Emotions include (L-R) Jim Searce, Mark Benson, Mark Bass,
Bob Hohman and Toby peering out from behind the tree.
(Photo courtesy of Toby Ruckert)

Friday, March 31, 1967, was a particularly exciting day
for Charlie. As he prepared for a baseball game against
Bishop Barry High School, he was notified of his acceptance into Georgia's Mercer University on an academic
scholarship. After the baseball game, he planned to join The
Emotions for the second set of a gig they had booked at the
El Dorado Showcase.

That evening, Toby and his band took the stage at the club
and worked through the first set without Charlie as planned,
but when it was time to start the second set, he still had not
arrived. Just as the band was returning to the stage without
their featured singer, another high school friend entered the

El Dorado and informed the band that Charlie Beauchamp had been injured during his baseball game and was at Mound Park Hospital. Not fully understanding the extent of Charlie's injuries, the band finished the night without him.

While playing second base for Boca Ciega High, Charlie was involved in a collision with another player who was sliding into the bag. He flipped into the air and landed on the back of his head, suffering brain damage that required a tracheotomy and surgery. He died on the morning of Wednesday, April 5, 1967, from a malfunction of the kidneys.

The entire community was devastated. Toby was particularly struck by the tragedy, recalling it as a very sobering moment. "Dealing with the death of a friend is different than losing an aunt or an uncle," he said. "It was such a shock."[163]

Charlie's funeral procession stretched for over a mile, and Toby served as a pall bearer. It took some 30 years for Boca Ciega High School to formally honor Charlie by renaming the football field for him. With the death of his younger sister and now Charlie, Toby had learned that life throws many curves, and things can change in the blink of an eye.

Toby learned to accept change, a coping mechanism that would come in handy over the years. "You have to move forward," Toby would say. "Embrace the change and move forward."[164]

Toby remained the one constant member of The Emotions. Their managers, Paul and Barbara McLoughlin, were able to book the band for some big-time concerts in central Florida. They opened for the likes of The Who, The Turtles, Left Banke, The Dave Clark Five, Peter and Gordon, and The Allman Brothers Band.[165]

163 Author interview with Toby Ruckert. September 28, 2021.
164 Ibid.
165 Lemlich, Jeff, Jeffers 66, Real Teen Tragedies Behind 2 Moody Garage 45s. https://savagelost.com/the-real-teen-tragedies-behind-two-moody-garage-45s. September 26, 2015, and Author interview with Toby Ruckert. September 28, 2021.

(Photo courtesy of Toby Ruckert)

Partial Lyrics of
Why Must It Be

*"This life on earth is hard to bear,
Living with people who just don't care.
Even though I exist today,
If I was to die now, what would they say?
A drop of water I'm meant to be,
Lost in the sea of humanity.
Why must it be? Why must it be?*

Being a musician requires expensive equipment, but Toby found a way to save money by employing some good old fashioned ingenuity. For example, today electronic guitar tuners are a dime a dozen, but in the 1960s, that was not the case. There was only one professional level product on the market; the Strobotuner, made by Conn. Its $300 price tag prevented most young guitarists from owning one, but Toby found a solution. He discovered that the dial tone of the family's telephone, a multiparty land line, was an F# note. He used that tone to tune his guitar. Who needs a Strobotuner when you have a landline?

Toby knew from experience that being flashy does not make you a better player. His philosophy is, and pretty much always has been, "...be supportive. The best thing I can do is to try to support the story of the song. That's my role in the band. To be a team member, not to overplay and get in the way. It's easy to play too much," Toby insists, "it's almost impossible to play too little. I strive to err on the side of playing too little."[166]

As mentioned, The Emotions were managed by the husband-and-wife team, Paul and Barbara McLoughlin. The

---

166   Author interview with Toby Ruckert. September 28, 2021.

*The Emotions during a practice session. Band members are (L-R)
Toby Ruckert, Mark Bass, Jim Searce, Mark Benson and Bob Hohman.
(Photo courtesy of Toby Ruckert)*

couple handled all the band's bookings and, as Toby recalled,
"were just wonderful people. Very generous and caring."[167]
For example, when the band members graduated from high
school in 1967, the McLoughlin's presented them with an
amazing surprise. Using some of her radio contacts in Tennessee, Barbara arranged for The Emotions to spend a week
there where they would open for The Dave Clarke 5 in Chat-
tanooga followed by a couple of nights at a club in Knoxville
and then back across the state for a full night's recording session at a studio in Nashville. In addition, the McLaughlins presented band members with monogrammed Zippo lighters, all
except Toby that is, who didn't smoke. Instead, he was given
a copy of the brand-new Beatles album, 'Sgt. Pepper's Lone-
ly-Hearts Club Band'. "It was the ultra-rare mono version, not

---

167   Ibid.

the stereo album," Toby bragged. "I bet none of them have their lighters anymore, but I still have that album with the cut-out inserts still intact,"[168] Toby said during an interview.

After high school, Toby enrolled at St. Petersburg Junior College and naturally majored in music. After about a year and a half however, he felt the need for a break. The plan was to take some time off and then return to complete his degree. Like most plans of similar design however, this one never came to fruition as Toby became more and more absorbed in his music, and though the members of The Emotions had given it up after high school, Toby played on.

Jimi Hendrix and Other Stuff

In 1969 Toby took a part-time job at a custom tailor shop owned by Michael Braun and Antoinette Ackerman. Toby's job was to show up in the evening, cut clothes from selected patterns, and sew the basic garment together. It was up to Ackerman and Braun to add the finishing touches. One evening, Toby answered the phone. It was Jimi Hendrix, one of the store's clients, asking for the owner. While he never actually physically met Jimi, Toby counts himself in a pre-sumably small number of people who can actually say they spoke to the rock and roll icon on the phone.

The year 1969 will always be associated with two major music festivals. The most well-known of these is, of course, the Woodstock Music and Art Fair—known simply as Woodstock—which took place on Max Yasgur's dairy farm in Bethel, New York. The second one was the Miami Pop Festival, held in Gulfstream Park just outside the south Florida city. Toby attended The Miami Pop Festival and that is

168   Ibid.

where, through mutual friends, he was introduced to Linda Bush. The two felt a mutual attraction and began dating on a regular basis. On October 25, 1970, they tied the knot. Following a small reception, the newlyweds enjoyed a couple of days in Key West, Florida. Unfortunately, "the weather was terrible, and we looked at the inside of a Holiday Inn the whole time,"[169] Toby said.

Mirage

Following his time with The Emotions, Toby had a brief stint with a band called Mirage. He couldn't recall too much about that band, but one incident involving Duane Allman is indelibly seared into his memory.

The incident occurred during a performance where Mirage and The Allman Brothers Band shared twin stages at the same venue. It was the fall of 1969 just before The Allman Brother's Band recorded their premiere album of the same name at Capricorn Studios in Macon, Georgia.

The event that evening was held at a very large national guard armory in Sarasota, Florida. The site hosted a series of teen dances designed to help keep the youngsters off the streets and out of trouble. There was a stage at each end of the building, one for each band. The members of Mirage arrived first, and when The Allman Brothers Band arrived about a half hour later, Toby recognized Barry Oakly, a bass player he had often crossed paths with. The two acquaintances spoke for a while and Barry excitedly told Toby how his band had just signed its first record deal.

On that night, the bands were scheduled to perform in alternating one-hour sets beginning at 8:00 p.m. and ending

169   Ibid.

at midnight. Mirage went first, but when The Allman Brothers Band took the stage at 9:00 p.m., it was obvious to Toby and everyone in attendance that they were something special. Mirage performed their second set and as The Allman Brother's Band prepared to close out the night, the Mirage band members began to pack up their instruments at the other end of the armory. At about 11:45 p.m., a roadie for The Allman Brothers Band frantically hunted Toby down and asked if he had any spare guitar strings because Duane had broken one of his. Toby didn't have the needed string but offered to let Duane use his guitar. The roadie quickly carried it off and gave it to Duane, who strapped it on and finished out the night.

At midnight, the lights were turned up and the kids started leaving. "I waited, but no one was bringing my guitar back," Toby said. "Five minutes, ten minutes, fifteen minutes went by. I thought, 'What the hell?' I walked to the other end of the building and Duane was there talking to two people and holding my guitar. I was getting a little miffed. He saw me, realized it was my guitar, and he handed it to me like it was a dirty diaper, and said, 'Oh yeah, thanks.'"[170] Toby was visibly upset and was about to say something when Duane's brother Gregg jumped into the conversation and gracefully steered Toby away.

"He (Gregg) did the professional thing," Toby said. "He said, 'Boy, you guys were great. We enjoyed working with you. It was a real pleasure, and we hope we get to do it again sometime.' I knew he was trying to diffuse the situation before it escalated, and that was cool,"[171] Toby said.

The guitar in question was a 1950s, highly collectible Les Paul. "Everyone was out there trying to find a used one in a music store or pawn shop," Toby said. "I found this one, but it had been heavily modified, which ruined the value. It had

---

170   Ibid.
171   Ibid.

been repainted and someone changed a bunch of parts on the guitar. From a collectible point of view, it was sacrilege and should have never been done. I didn't do it. I assume, though, that when Duane saw me playing it, he probably figured that I did. He naturally would have been a little pissed that I would take a sacred relic and defile it like that. In actuality, I had purchased it like that and couldn't afford, at that time, to get it restored. But it played great."[172]

Although Toby was initially upset with Duane, he realized down the road that Duane was a sincere and dedicated musician. "When I understood where he was coming from, I couldn't be mad at him," Toby said. "He was a great player and a good guy."[173]

Duckbutter

Earlier in 1969, Toby had been asked to join a Tampa-based band called Duckbutter, whose members played in a little bit of a different, more entertaining style than he was used to. "Some musicians look down on that music," Toby said. "In the late 1960s, it was called underground music*, like [that of] The Grateful Dead and Moby Grape."[174] While one generally didn't hear music from so called underground artists on the radio, they and their style of music did have a considerable following. Playing with Duckbutter taught Toby the

---

172   Ibid.
173   Ibid.
174   Ibid. * **Underground music is music** with practices perceived as outside, or somehow opposed to, mainstream popular **music** culture. **Underground music is** intimately tied to popular **music** culture as a whole, so there are important tensions within **underground music** because it appears to both assimilate and resist the forms and processes of popular **music** culture. (Wikipedia, https://en.wikipedia.org/wiki/Underground_music.)

value of just having fun by being entertaining. "I believe that it's an unwritten contract [that] if someone takes the time and pays the money to come hear me play, then I owe it to them to play something so that at the end of the night they'll be glad that they came and will want to come back," Toby said. "That's important!"[175]

Duckbutter may best be described as a country rock band, and though very accomplished musically, they were all about having fun. The lead singer, for example, would take the stage wearing only boxer shorts and cowboy boots—no shirt, no pants, just boxer shorts and cowboy boots. "He was also an amateur magician, so sometimes, in the middle of a song, he would stop and do magic tricks,"[176] Toby noted.

For the first time in his musical career, Toby had to travel for shows. The Emotions had performed mostly in the central Florida area, but with Duckbutter, he travelled as far south as Miami for gigs, and even performed at The Bistro in Atlanta for six days. The Bistro was a small, Victorian-style house that had been converted into a club. It held only about 80 people, but some very famous acts had come through there. Toby even heard a rumor that Jimmy Buffet actually lived on the upper floor of The Bistro for about a year. Duckbutter's performance there was a revelation for Toby and opened his eyes to the world of musicians outside of the microcosm of central Florida. Unlike Florida, where most bands were starving—especially during the Vietnam War years—Atlanta was exploding. "There was almost more work than musicians,"[177] Toby remembered.

---

175   Ibid.
176   Ibid.
177   Ibid.

Moving On Up To Atlanta

After about a year as the lead guitarist with Duckbutter, Toby decided to move on in 1971. "Band members talk about direction and style of music when they first come together," Toby explained. "Will they do cover material or original music, country or rock? After performing together for a while, a member might decide to change direction. That's what happened here. If a band doesn't have enormous success, they may split up or shuffle members or something."[178] In the case of Duckbutter, Toby said, the work was sporadic. Though the band was fun and very entertaining, Toby wanted to move on to something that provided more steady work. He spoke to his wife about the possibility of moving north to Atlanta. Linda's family was from Tampa, and she hadn't known much of life outside of that area. So while Toby saw unlimited potential in a burgeoning music industry, Linda looked at the move as a way to see other parts of the country that were foreign to her. Consequently, a decision on relocation was made in relatively short order.

A Brief Stint With Forty Fingers

Within a couple of days of their arrival in Atlanta, "Linda had a job in a spa," Toby said. "Two days later, I had a job in a music store and two days after that I was offered a position in a band."[179] The opportunity came via a couple of guys that Toby met at the music store with a band called Forty Fingers. The ensemble played some original music and bounced

---

178   Ibid.
179   Ibid.

around the city for about a year or so. But after that time, they found that they were neither working much nor making a lot of money, so the band just dissolved.

Vintage Guitars and Keith Richards

To earn some extra money in the early 1970s, Toby and a friend named Mike Moffitt, started buying and selling vintage guitars. At that time, the vintage guitar world represented a new and unknown market, so it was fairly easy to purchase some very expensive guitars from pawn shops and from others who had no idea of their real value. By 1972, Toby had acquired about a dozen or so guitars that were nice vintage pieces; very clean and all in original condition. One of those guitars was a Fender Stratocaster made in 1957.

Meanwhile, in late 1971, the home of legendary Rolling Stones guitarist Keith Richards was burglarized, and 11 vintage instruments were stolen. "It was awful," Richards said in an interview. "They're all my babies. Most were vintage Fender Telecasters. They look alike, they sound alike, but they play different."[180] Though it took years, Richards eventually recovered his stolen guitars—he had recorded the serial numbers, a fact of which the thieves were apparently unaware. He also found out who had stolen them. "They turned up on the market...I got the sucker who did it," Richards said. "The guy who pulled the job, he got his. I mean, he's alive, but..."[181]

Until he could locate his own guitars, however, Richards needed to replace them. To make matters worse, The

180   SHEDOOBEE with StonesDoug. May 13, 2010. https://www.tapatalk.
       com/groups/shidoobeewithstonesdoug/keith-talks-about-when-his-gui-
       tars-were-stolen-t23485.html. Tapatalk, Inc. 202 Bicknell Avenue, First
       Floor, Santa Monica, CA 90405
181   Ibid.

Stones were preparing for their 1972 tour of the United States, adding a bit of urgency to that task. Richards' management contacted several vintage guitar dealers, one of whom was George Gruhn of Gruhn Guitars in Nashville, hoping to find the specific guitars Richards needed. Gruhn had some but not all of the requested instruments. He thought of Toby's partner Mike—who lived in Tampa—and called on him for help. Mike had two of the desired guitars, but Richards still needed a certain Fender Stratocaster. Mike suggested that Gruhn, who had traveled to Florida to pick up the guitars, visit Toby in Atlanta on his way back to Nashville to take a look at his 1957 Stratocaster. Gruhn did so, made the purchase, and shipped it and the other guitars to Keith Richards.

In 1972, Toby was reading a Time Magazine article about The Stones' July 25 and 26 performances at Madison Square Garden in New York during their USA tour. Embedded right there in the article was a large photograph of Mick Jagger and Keith Richards singing at the microphone with Richards playing Toby's easily identifiable vintage Stratocaster. "I thought it was pretty cool to see Richards playing my guitar on stage,"[182] Toby said.

Presto

Following the dissolution of Forty Fingers, Toby continued working in the music store where he was approached by three men who were originally from Terra Haute, Indiana but—like Toby—had moved to Atlanta to take advantage of the music scene. They had heard of Toby's skills as a guitarist and wanted to see for themselves. After chatting for a while

---

182   Author interview with Toby Ruckert. September 28, 2021.

and playing some songs together, it seemed to them that Toby would be the perfect fit for their band. They invited him to join Presto.

While Presto played the Atlanta area, they also travelled quite a bit, playing venues in Florida, North and South Carolina, Alabama, and Mississippi. The band was contacted by a booking agent who worked out of the Florida panhandle around Pensacola. The agent had a four-day job for Presto at a club, and when the gig was done asked to meet with the band. According to Toby, the agent told Presto, "You are a good band, but your image isn't good. You don't dress well. None of you have your hair styled, you look pretty sloppy, maybe too casual, but you play well. As you guys are right now, you're like an $800 band for a weekend. But if you dress nicer and get your hair styled, you could be a $1,000 a weekend band. With all that and a female singer, you could be a $1,300 a weekend band. Add a horn-player or two, and you could be a $1,500 a weekend band." And so on.

"He was very nice about it," Toby said. "He basically told us how to make money."[183] But for Toby, none of that stuff was particularly appealing. "I didn't really want to feel like a dancing monkey,"[184] he said. So when the band decided to make those changes, he took a pass and left the band at the end of 1974.

Road Island Red

At the start of 1975, Toby was working in a music store called The Music Mart when a couple of guys from the band Road Island Red dropped in. Drummer Jimmy Garmon and his brother Howard, the lead singer, were looking for a guitar

183   Ibid.
184   Ibid.

player. Road Island Red was the house band at The Nugget, a club on the south side of Atlanta, owned by Sam Tucker. The band's guitar player, Jody Payne, had left to take a job with Willie Nelson and they needed a replacement. In addition to the two Garmon brothers, Road Island Red included a bass player by the name of Bill Benton and a journeyman keyboardist who worked with the band only when he was in town. Don Howard, the owner of The Music Mart, told the two visitors they might want to speak to Toby. The band invited Toby to join up for a week or so until they could find a permanent replacement, and Toby happily accepted. "It was a real good band," he said. "They played hard core country, covering such greats as Merle Haggard and George Jones. It looked like fun."[185]

As Toby was breaking down his equipment at the end of the week, one of the Garmon brothers asked him if he would be willing to stay a week longer. "I said, oh sure," Toby recalled. "Those two weeks turned into 20 years!"[186] During the first couple years of those 20, Toby worked six nights a week, taking only Sundays off.

It was while playing with Road Island Red that Toby began to rethink his decision to collect vintage guitars. He wanted to be known as a player, not just a collector. He took a great deal of pride in his guitar playing and wanted to be one of the best at his craft. Perhaps nothing accentuates that point better than one of Toby's classic stories.

"A guitar player I knew from town came into the club where I was working and introduced me to another guitar player who was with him," Toby said. "They looked at the two or three vintage guitars that I had on stage with me, and one said, 'See, what'd I tell you.' And [it was then that] I realized they had come to see the guitars, not to hear me

185   Ibid.
186   Ibid.

play."[187] That was very disturbing to Toby. Despite the good (and much-needed) money he was making as a collector, he decided then and there to sell his vintage guitars. He wanted to be a guitar player, not a guitar owner. He sold his entire collection to Mike Moffitt. The guitars ranged in value from a couple to several thousand dollars. He kept only one of the lot, an acoustic guitar to play at home. He then went to the music store and purchased a simple used $200 electric guitar to play at work.

For the next several years, Toby continued to improve his playing skills. Before long, he was receiving rave reviews and knew that those who attended his band's performances were there to hear him play, not to see his guitars. But, he also recognized the difference in the sound of his new guitars versus the vintage guitars he previously played. "Vintage guitars just sound different," he explained. "They sound better. And so, I slowly started to acquire vintage guitars once again."[188] His new collection grew in size to about 16 or 17, and one of them was a 1960 Les Paul in great condition. He played it at gigs for a couple of years and then retired it so that it wouldn't get dinged during a performance. Years later, he joked to Scott King that the Les Paul was his "retirement guitar," because of its extraordinary six-figure value.

Fire, Separation And A Road Trip

The latter part of the decade represented a series of tribulations in both Toby's personal and professional life. Most significantly, he had been experiencing some difficulties in his relationship with his wife, Linda. Being a road musician

---

187   Author interview with Toby Ruckert. November 2, 2021.
188   Ibid.

can put a strain on a marriage –prolonged absence is not conducive to a long-term relationship. Toby's marriage to Linda
was unravelling after only eight years, despite being blessed
with a beautiful son, Christian, who was born on March 14,
1978. The couple went their separate ways just a few months
after his birth. "When I was traveling with bands, particularly with Presto, I would be gone all the time, sometimes
a month at a time," Toby said. "It's difficult for a marriage
to survive that kind of thing. You get used to being without one another. We still get along very well. She's a great
person."[189] Today, long after their divorce, Linda and Toby
remain friends and now share three beautiful grandchildren.

Still reeling from the sting of his separation from Linda,
Toby's stress level was about to increase. In1978, over Labor
Day weekend, The Nugget, the club where Road Island Red
was the house band, suffered a devastating fire that burned
the club to the ground. Along with the club itself, all the
band's gear, instruments, amps, and microphones were
destroyed. The only piece of band gear that survived was
Toby's guitar, because he took it home with him every night.
Worse, because bands work as independent contractors, the
equipment loss was not covered by the club's insurance and
represented a total loss for the members of Road Island Red.

Ruckert was at a crossroads. After eight years of marriage
to Linda, he was once again a single man, and following the
club fire, his band had a 10-day hiatus before beginning a
new gig at a different venue. He decided to take a short break
from the struggles of daily life and embarked on a motorcycle road trip that would take him from Atlanta to Montreal, Canada and back. He looked forward to some time for
reflection, and with only a tent, a sleeping bag, some clothes,
maps, and a camera, he began the long trek north.

189   Ibid.

He camped out most of the way. "It was quite an experience," he said. "A road trip is always a real eye-opener and taking one by yourself leaves you with no one to talk to. So, I literally had 10 days to talk to myself and assess my future."[190] Before starting out, he had packed some documents that he thought he might need along the way; a driver's license, a birth certificate, and a copy of the vehicle title were among the items he took with him, hoping to prevent any problems he might encounter at the Canadian border. He took the Blue Ridge Parkway up through Pennsylvania and New York, and when he reached the Canadian border, he had all his papers in order, ready to show the border patrolmen. As he approached the booth, the man asked, "Business or pleasure?" "Pleasure," Toby politely replied. "Well, come on in,"[191] the border agent said without asking for a single document.

After a couple of days in Montreal, Toby headed east for upstate Maine to begin his return journey. Oddly, it was at this checkpoint where Toby experienced his first hiccup on the trip. "When I got to the US Border in Maine, they didn't want to let me out of Canada," he said. "I had real long hair and was riding a motorcycle, and they figured, this guy has to be carrying drugs."[192]

Forcing him to pull his motorcycle to the side of the road, border patrolmen stripped the bike of all his belongings, laying them out on the ground in the parking lot. They searched the bike, lifting the seat to check in the storage compartment beneath. "Clearly, this wasn't their first rodeo,"[193] Toby thought. The border agents found nothing

---

190   Ibid.
191   Ibid.
192   Ibid.
193   Ibid.

suspicious, and they eventually allowed him to cross back into the United States.

By this time the sun had set, Toby entered the total desolation of logging country on a long dirt road. After about 10 or 15 miles, he found a little private campground where he set up for the night. Up until that point, the northeast had been experiencing an unusual warm spell that made Toby's trip a very comfortable experience. Daybreak, however, ushered in some unseasonably cold weather and the 40-degree temperature caused Toby's teeth to chatter and his hands to shake on the handlebars. It was miserable riding his bike, and to make matters worse, he was running out of gas. "I finally coasted into a little town, a little crossroads with about five or six buildings in the whole town," he said. "There was a small restaurant with a bunch of pickup trucks parked around it, and I said, 'That's got to be the place!' I managed to have a great breakfast. There was even a gas station to get some gas and keep moving."[194]

The return trip took him to Boston, then Connecticut to visit his cousin, and then to Richmond, Virginia to visit his brother before heading back to Atlanta. All in all, Toby remembers it fondly. "It was a lot of fun, and it was very insightful," he said. "I would do it again in a heartbeat."[195] The next day, Toby was back at work with Road Island Red. It happened that Sam Tucker, who owned The Nugget, also owned another club a short distance away called The Double Nugget, and he moved Road Island Red into that club as the house band. After about a year, the band left The Double Nugget and began working at various clubs around town until they landed a steady job at a club called Shooters. Toby played with Road Island Red at Shooters for 11 years before moving on.

194   Ibid.
195   Ibid.

Teddy Baker and Friends

In 1978 during one of those short breaks from Road Island Red, Toby met Teddy Baker, a rising star on the music scene who offered to take Toby on the road with him. But the string of bad luck that the 1970s ushered in was not yet over, and the promise offered by this gig proved to be more illusion than reality. The music business can be grueling and frustrating. "The goal of any musician is to get a recording contract and have somebody else paying the bills,"[196] Toby said. Just before the end of 1979, it appeared Toby might have reached that pinnacle of success. He accepted an opportunity to join Teddy Baker and Friends. Teddy had just gotten a record deal with Mercury Records, and the rest of the band was on retainer with the label, meaning that Toby received a check every week. They recorded an album that was very good, but about two weeks before it was scheduled to be released, Mercury was sold to a consortium in Europe. The new owners made a business decision to clean house and start with a fresh slate, essentially shutting down the record label and cancelling the album. Finding success in the music business most often comes down to having both connections and luck. Unfortunately, bad luck just doesn't cut it, and Toby, it seemed, was experiencing a lot of that.

Amidst the string of bad career breaks, Toby's personal life was on the upswing. While working at The Bistro with Teddy Baker in 1979, Toby met a woman named Deborah Levendoski. They talked during a break at a Bistro performance one night and became casual friends. They soon found common ground for discussion—Deborah had also been divorced for about a year or so. "We spent hours talking about what didn't work

196   Ibid.

143

in our previous relationships and what we wanted to do going forward," Toby said. "We were very much on the same page."[197] The two dated for three years and on July 18, 1982, they were married by a justice of the peace in a civil ceremony at the official's home in Acworth, Georgia. Following the ceremony, the couple took a short honeymoon to San Francisco, and one year later, welcomed their first child, Corey, to the world. At the time, Deborah worked at Delta Airlines in its finance division. Toby was back at work at The Music Mart and Corey attended daycare. Corey was often sick with cold-like symptoms, and it didn't take long for Toby and Deborah to realize that the cause of her illness was exposure to other sick children at the daycare center. That prompted Toby to leave his day job at the music store so he could be with Corey during the day. Deborah continued to work at Delta by day and was home to care for Corey at night while Toby played the clubs. The instant they stopped sending their child to daycare, Corey stopped getting sick. Deborah and Toby got to see each other for only a couple of hours each day, but the decision was worth it as Corey was seldom sick again.

Road Island Red--Redux

The demise of the Mercury Record deal in 1980 also ended Toby's involvement with Teddy Baker and Friends. He called his bandmates from Road Island Red to see if they still had a spot for him. Of course, they did, and he was welcomed back to the country band, still playing at Shooters.

197   Ibid.

Country music artist Mark Wills
(Photo by Rudi Williams)

Back with Road Island Red, Toby had a steady schedule performing five nights per week.

The Buckboard Bandits

Toby continued to perform with Road Island Red until the mid-1990s when he was offered a gig backing up a singer named Mark Wills at The Buckboard, a club on the north side of Atlanta (Smyrna -Tim's hometown) owned by John Gallichio. Daren Norwood, who had been the lead singer at the club for the past couple of years, left to go on tour (with Scott King playing bass) after getting a record deal. With Norwood on the road, Wills, a very good young singer, was promoted to the front of the stage. Gallichio, who was also Mark's manager, was putting together a band of veteran players to help Mark learn the ropes about performing.

When Toby was hired, Gallichio told him it would be the most work intensive position he would ever have, and he wasn't kidding. The Buckboard Bandits played from Tuesday through Saturday from 9:00 p.m. until 2:00 a.m. They rehearsed on Tuesday and Wednesday nights after the club was closed. On Monday nights, the band played a talent contest backing up customers who thought they could sing (Tim participated in this several times), and on Saturdays they performed at promotional events for WKHX, the same radio station that would later use The Mustangs. In essence, the band "played six nights a week, plus extra rehearsals, plus showcases, plus talent nights, plus radio show events," said Toby with a laugh. "We were busy."[198] With that workload, Toby was earning as much as $1,000 a week, which was a lot of money for a local musician in those days.

The money, however, was not the biggest attraction for Toby. "The great thing about it was that we got to work with a lot of different artists," he said. "The Buckboard brought artists in for concerts about twice a month. The club held around 400 people, so when a new artist came out, the first time they played the Atlanta area was often at The Buckboard because they weren't yet big enough to play an arena. The acts we worked with included [artists such as] The Dixie Chicks, [now The Chicks], Kenny Chesney, and other soon to be household names."[199]

Once a month, the Buckboard hosted a showcase where major record labels would come out to view talent. The Buckboard Bandits would play a set with Mark Wills as a means of showcasing his talents to the producers. He eventually got a record deal. He was spotted by Carson Chamberlain and Keith Stegall, from the Mercury Nashville label. Chamberlain and Stegall produced Wills' eponymous debut album, which was released in the fall of 1996. The record

---

198   Ibid.
199   Ibid.

The Ruckerts at home (L-R) Kelsey, Toby, Deborah and Corey
(Photo courtesy of Toby Ruckert)

became a moderate hit, peaking at number 38 on the country charts. Wills followed up that album with *Wish You Were Here* in 1998 and *Permanently* in early 2000. Both albums went platinum.

By this time, Toby and Deborah had already welcomed their second daughter, Kelsey, to the world, and Toby wanted to be there for her rather than spend his time on a tour bus. Therefore, he decided not to tour with Mark. Instead, he took a part-time office job managing Mark's affairs. He worked in the morning four days a week while still playing guitar at the club at night. During that time, he was able to learn a great deal about the management side of the business doing Mark's promotional work for radio stations. Meanwhile, Mark's star continued to rise, culminating in his induction into the Grand Ole Opry on January 11, 2019.

Without Mark at The Buckboard, the approximately 25-year-old club started to decline. In an attempt to revive

his business, the club owner hired a five-piece band called Peach Tree Station, who took over the position of house band from The Buckboard Bandits. As a result, Toby found himself, at the end of 1998, without a music gig for the first time in a long time.

Tim Purcell And The Mustangs

That's when Toby met Tim Purcell. Tim's British guitar player, Duncan James, had just left Tim's band, Tim Purcell and the Mustangs, and Tim needed to fill the void. Tim had heard that The Buckboard Bandits were dissolving and invited Toby to his home for dinner and a discussion. Before meeting with Tim, Toby called Duncan to get his impression of Tim and the band. Duncan had nothing but good things to say, so following a pleasant evening and a good talk with Tim, Toby decided to give it a go. "My first job with the band was on New Year's Eve, 1998,"[200] Toby said. He continued to play with The Mustangs and later became the lead guitarist with an offshoot band called Foxes and Fossils.

Utobya

For many years, Toby had longed to have a recording studio in his home, but never had the proper space. That changed in 1985 when Toby and Deborah purchased a new home allowing Toby to realize his dream. «I now have a full-blown professional recording studio in my home," Toby said. "I can record entire bands at one time, recording on up

200   Author interview with Toby Ruckert. November 2, 2021.

Utobya—Toby's personal recording studio—is his 'perfect place'.
(Photo courtesy of Toby Ruckert)

to 48 tracks. For the first time, I actually have a room where I can set up a studio and leave it without taking it down at the end of each session. I call it Utobya"[201] With this ideally perfect place, his Utopia, Toby was able to make good money recording demos for singers and songwriters.

Before long, Toby had acquired several pieces of vintage studio gear, enabling him to create high quality recordings. "When I met Tim, we were able to record some of The Mustangs CDs here at the studio," Toby said. "We used them mostly for promotional purposes." The CDs were a valuable promotional tool that got the band a lot of work. "To avoid any legal issues, we put a disclaimer on the label of the CD that read, 'promotional use only, not for sale,'" Toby said. "But as the band gained popularity, we had so many requests

201   Author interview with Toby Ruckert. March 7, 2022.

for CDs that we started selling them at shows. Sometimes we would make $400 or $500 in an afternoon just selling the CDs and tee shirts."[202]

The Mustangs produced eight CDs: a live CD was recorded at a performance at the Cadillac Ranch, a club just north of Atlanta in 2000; In 2002, the band produced CDs of two live performances, one recorded at an ABC Radio Christmas party, and the other at an Apple Realty party; they made yet another in 2003 at the Rusty Rooster, a mega club south of Atlanta; their one and only Christmas CD was recorded at Utobya in 2006; the following year, they produced another CD compiled of several live recordings; and finally, their last studio CD came out in 2009.

Toby used his studio in 2011 to record *A Curious Mix,* the first album from Foxes and Fossils. While the instruments and most of the vocals on this production were recorded at Toby's studio, some of the vocal parts and all of the vocal editing was done at Tim Purcell's digital studio.

Where Has The Time Gone?

Toby, now 73 years of age, had always been in remarkably good health. He even had stretches in his life where he went 20 years without seeing a doctor. But once again, his luck changed.

On June 3, 2016, as the world learned that 73-year-old sports legend Muhammad Ali had lost his 32-year battle with Parkinson's, Toby's neurologist gave him a formal diagnosis of the same disease. Today, he experiences noticeable tremors in his left arm and occasionally in his left foot but is quick to point out that it does not adversely impact his ability to

---

202   Ibid.

play guitar. "It only becomes problematic if my hand is in one position on the fret board for a prolonged time,"[203] he said. He is on medication to slow the progression of the disease and takes each day in stride.

In January of 2018, he was prescribed an antibiotic by his physician that triggered an episode later diagnosed as Guillan-Barre Syndrome, a very rare condition affecting the immune system characterized by rapid-onset muscle weakness that damages the peripheral nervous system. "Within twenty-four hours, I was paralyzed from the neck down, on a ventilator and in a coma," Toby said. "My wife was absolutely beyond angelic during that time. She sat in the hospital 22 hours a day. She would go home to change clothes and then return to the hospital."[204] The comatose state lasted about a month and the doctors expressed concern that the prolonged exposure to a breathing tube might do permanent damage to his vocal cords—which it did. Toby was hospitalized for about three months. Today, he needs to take necessary precautions and is not permitted to be vaccinated from any disease, including COVID-19 or even the annual flu.

From 2011 up until the pandemic, Toby was doing a considerable amount of recording at his studio. He was working with many songwriters who were sending him material to be demoed. "In a five-year period, I probably did the equivalent of twenty albums," Toby said. "I was pretty busy all the time and it was a nice source of extra income. It was perfect for me. It was nice to do something at home where I could enjoy the creative aspect and learn something at the same time."[205]

Today, Toby still uses his recording studio to record his own musical contributions to Foxes and Fossils releases even

---

203   Author interview with Toby Ruckert. November 2, 2021.
204   Author interview with Toby Ruckert. September 28, 2021.
205   Author interview with Toby Ruckert. March 7, 2022.

as he continues to demo singers and songwriters. While the pandemic has put a slight damper on his ability to interact with people in person, the value of his studio has grown, and now includes about 50 microphones, many of the high-end variety. For the last five years or so, he has used Johnny Pike to provide the drum tracks for the recordings.

Despite his recent health issues and the solitude created by the pandemic, Toby remains upbeat. In fact, it is difficult to have a conversation that doesn't find him flashing a robust smile. He recollects both his music career and his family with pride and never seems to tire of the fun and the pleasure he derives from both. He recalls with great affection all the memories connected to that very special Atlanta club known as The Bistro. It was there that he performed with Duckbutter, opening his eyes to the many opportunities for musicians in Georgia and prompting his move to Atlanta; it was at The Bistro that he connected with Teddy Baker and Friends, the band that presented him with his first real possibility of success in the music business; and most importantly, it was at The Bistro that Toby met Deborah, the love of his life.

Chapter 5

JOHNNY
"HELP ME, HELP ME"
PIKE

The Early Years

Theodore Franklin Pike—known simply as Frank—grew up in Manchester, a small town in Georgia where he met and fell in love with Denyse Dorothy Kendrick. The couple married on September 5, 1953, in a Methodist church ceremony and honeymooned in Callaway Gardens, a working man's resort just a short drive from their hometown. On April 2, 1958, Denyse gave birth to the first of the couple's four children, Julie Diane, at Georgia Baptist Hospital in Atlanta. A short time later, Frank joined the U.S. Coast Guard, and the couple moved to the small town of Homestead, Florida, just south of Miami. The couple's second daughter, Cathy Gail, was born on December 23, 1959, and their first son, John David, arrived about a year later on December 16, 1960.

After Frank's honorable discharge in 1961, the Pikes moved to Marietta, Georgia—a suburb of Atlanta about 75 miles north

The Pikes—from left to right, sisters Tracie, Cathy,
Julie and Johnny—July 2015
(Photo courtesy of John Pike)

of Manchester. Frank took a job at the Lockheed Company, where he would work for more than 30 years.[206] During his time with the aeronautics giant, Frank built military aircraft and ultimately found himself managing the quality control department. Denyse Pike also worked at Lockheed for a short while, until she became pregnant with the couple's fourth child. She gave birth to Tracie Lynn on September 30, 1962.

Frank and Denyse were hard workers—with four children under four years old, they needed to be. The couple, offering their children a sterling example of what was required for a successful life, provided for all their wants and needs. The children were raised in the Methodist faith, and Johnny vividly recalls walking to church as a family every Sunday morning.

In the fall of 1971, Denyse decided to enroll at Kennesaw

---

206   The Lockheed Company, a major manufacturer in American aerospace, was founded by Alan Lockheed in 1926. In 1995 the company merged with Marietta Martin and became known as the Lockheed Martin Company.

Junior College (now Kennesaw State University) located in a small town of the same name just minutes from their home. She had decided to become a nurse, and the school offered a great program. Johnny recalled the incident he thinks may have led Denyse to that profession. One day, Johnny, his mom, his sister Tracie, and a family friend, Lisa, were at a local shopping center. While walking outside, Lisa hit her head on a large metal support pole, resulting in a scary-looking wound above her eye. There was a lot of blood, and Denyse didn't know what to do or how to treat the injury. She quickly gathered the group together and drove to the emergency room where Lisa could be stitched up. "That incident, along with the yen to start a career, is what brought mom to the world of nursing,"[207] Johnny said.

Following her graduation from nursing school, Denyse accepted a position as an emergency room nurse at Kennestone Hospital in Marietta. For the next 35 years, the hospital was like a second home to her. She ultimately became the director for oversight of emergency operations and administration before retiring in 1997. Over the course of her long career, she developed a reputation as an amazing nurse and top-notch administrator. Her staff and the emergency room doctors loved and respected her, and friends of the Pike family counted themselves lucky if they were ever in need of emergency care. "They all knew to ask for Denyse Pike if they were unfortunate enough to make a trip to the ER," Johnny said. "They knew mom would take care of them. She truly was a legend!"[208]

Johnny's fondest memory of his early years centers around

---

207   Johnny Pike's written comments provided to the Author on February 7, 2022.

208   Johnny Pike in a written response to interview questions asked by the author. August 25, 2021. Page 1.

family gatherings, especially trips to his parents' hometown of Manchester on the weekends. "That is where my grandmother and lots of aunts and uncles and cousins lived," he said. "We made this trip quite often. We'd have these huge gatherings at my grandmother's house where the kids played, and the parents hung out and did what parents did in the 60s and 70s."[209] Life for Johnny was all about family. In that regard little has changed, though mom, dad, and most of those aunts and uncles are gone. As John so eloquently put it, "We kids are now those parents with families of our own."[210]

10-Year-Old Johnny Develops a New Love Interest

Sometime around the fourth grade, Johnny developed a love and a passion for music that would last a lifetime. For reasons he didn't yet understand, certain songs on the radio would affect him, causing a surge of emotion that lasted long after the songs ended. Along with that passion for music, Johnny displayed an intrinsic rhythmic ability. "I could hear a song and tap out the various snare, kick, and hi hat patterns by hand,"[211] he said. It was a talent that must have been obvious to his parents, as they decided to invest in drum lessons for their son. While he doesn't remember much about those lessons, he does remember where they were held. "[I remember] going into Johnny Carlton Music, a little music store close to our house, and seeing all those instruments hanging on the walls and just loving it,"[212] Johnny said. At home, he would tap on anything

---

209   Ibid. Page 2.
210   Ibid.
211   Ibid.
212   Ibid.

that made noise; pots, pans, the table, whatever was within reach. "[I had] one of those (made out of paper basically) drum sets you'd see in the Sears catalog toy section,"[213] he said. Johnny's constant pounding tore it to pieces, but he didn't have to do without drums for long. One day, his parents surprised him with a "spectacular sparkle-red set of Stewarts." That little drum set remained in his bedroom for years until he was able to save enough money to purchase "a better, more adult kit."[214] Those little red Stewarts helped spark "a lifelong passion for playing drums and an incredibly strong love of music that has never left me,"[215] Johnny recalled. Looking back, Johnny wishes that he had taken advantage of music lessons, both private and in school. "By not doing high school band, I missed an opportunity for a musical education—learning and practicing rudiments, reading music, all of it,"[216] he lamented.

As a youngster, Johnny was content to play along with records on the stereo or copy the drum part from TV show theme songs, such as the great drum solo from the *Hawaii Five-O* theme. "I mastered that one pretty well and my dad would have me play [it] for anyone that could tolerate it,"[217] Johnny said. Copying the sound on records is how Johnny learned to play the drums and is still his method of choice. The only difference between then and now is the improved technology at his disposal, making the process a bit less tedious.

While Johnny's sister Julie didn't play a musical instrument, she was very much into the incredible rock and roll music of the 1970s and remains just as passionate today. Her love of music was a benefit to Johnny. "She had a killer stereo with speakers that lit up with the beat and these great albums that

213   Ibid. Page 3.
214   Ibid.
215   Ibid.
216   Ibid.
217   Ibid.

I couldn't get enough of," he said. "I would go into her room and listen whenever possible, look through all the liner notes and pictures: Led Zeppelin; Humble Pie; David Bowie; Joe Walsh; Beatles; Stones. I was, and still am, fascinated with all of it. I may have liked music early on, but when I discovered this stuff, it went to a whole new level, and I thank Julie for it."[218]

Johnny And His Sisters

Johnny and his sisters had a great childhood. The four siblings were very close as children, and being the only boy in a family of four kids had its perks. While the three girls had to share a single bedroom, young Johnny enjoyed the splendor of his own private bedroom, complete with that red sparkly drum-kit in the corner!

Johnny remembers one special Christmas when "Santa" delivered a burgundy, 75cc Indian motorcycle. "[That motorcycle] became my best friend for the next couple of years until I finally blew it up trying to keep up with all the other neighborhood kids who also had dirt bikes," Johnny said. "With all the woods and trails close by, once you outgrew the bicycle, a dirt bike was a must."[219]

Johnny freely admits that he might have been a bit spoiled as the only son, acknowledging that all of his sisters considered him to be mom's favorite. But Johnny had no favorite when it came to his sisters. "I honestly was close with all three sisters growing up,"[220] Johnny recalled. "At various times I might have hung around with one more than

158

the others, maybe at parties or school related events."[221] His sisters' friends were another one of the many advantages of being a young boy with older sisters. There were pretty girls everywhere! All of his sisters were popular and attractive, often leading friends to joke, "What happened to Johnny?"

Johnny and his sisters got along well and were happy. But life is full of twists and turns that are often beyond one's control.

Frank and Denyse Call It Quits...

Perhaps it was the strain of raising four teenaged children, or the difficulty of nursing school. Maybe it was the pressures of work, or fatigue from their daily routine. Whatever the reason, Frank and Denyse divorced while Johnny was in middle school. He never did learn the reason for the divorce, and Denyse never remarried. "She was completely content with raising my sisters and me and immersing herself in her career,"[222] Johnny said.

According to Johnny, the divorce "rocked the boat for us a bit." It's difficult for any kid to grow up without a full-time father, and it was difficult for Denyse as well. She now had to deal with a job and the additional challenge of raising four children as a single mom. It was a weird time for the kids, living full time with mom and spending every other weekend with dad. But as usual, Denyse was up for the challenge. Despite the hardship, neither parent ever spoke a negative word about the other. The children, too, adjusted to the new normal as best they could.

---

221   Ibid.
222   Johnny Pike's written comments provided to the author on February 7, 2022

Johnny Pike and Denyse, his mom and hero.
Circa early 1990's (Photo courtesy of John Pike.)

...And Mom Takes Charge

During the years following the divorce, "mom truly became the center of our world," said Johnny. "Here she was, a single mom with four young kids [in] elementary, middle and high school...no easy task, but mom was up to it and then some."[223] All four Pike children agree that mom was "our hero for so many reasons."[224]

Denyse and her children lived in a modest brick house on Cason Drive in a wonderful neighborhood called Kingswood Estates. The unfinished basement had been partially framed by Johnny's dad, who had hopes of adding some additional rooms to the home. Denyse had a washer and dryer down there and the kids considered it a cool place to hang out—think, *That*

223   Ibid. Page 2
224   Ibid.

'70s Show. Outside, there was a carport and a big fenced-in yard that was ideal for the children as they grew up.

Johnny described the neighborhood as "perfection." His summers were spent swimming in the neighborhood pool or playing pickup games of baseball in the open field that sat adjacent to it. "There were acres and acres of trails and woods just outside the neighborhood to ride bikes, motorcycles and get into all sorts of mischief,"[225] Johnny said.

Dirt biking in the woods can be a lot of fun for 12 and 13-year-olds, but it can also be pretty exhausting, particularly on a hot Georgia summer day. After rides, Johnny and his friends would often—and without invitation—take a dip in the backyard pool of a large home nearby. The owner of that home, Dr. Haygood, had no qualms about calling the cops on the trespassers. At the first sign of the police, the kids would scatter into the safety of the woods as quickly as possible.

Despite these impromptu pool runs, the gang never got into any real trouble as children. But in their later years, some of their adventures would result in more serious consequences. When Johnny and his friends were old enough to drive, they would congregate in the parking lot of a local shopping center. On one occasion, some of Johnny's friends were pinched for underage drinking and smoking pot. Johnny was able to "get out of harm's way just before the serious stuff happened," but by his own admission, he was "certainly no angel back in those days. Though to my mom I was! Poor decisions on my part would occasionally cost me a night out or the keys to the yellow Ford Maverick, nicknamed the 'Banana,' that I shared with my sisters, but for the most part I flew just under the radar."[226]

Each of the Pike children holds a special place in their heart for the neighborhood of their youth. Johnny's sister

225   Ibid.
226   Johnny Pike written comments to the author on February 7, 2022.

Cathy even named her son after the street where they lived—Cason. Even though they sold the old house shortly after Denyse's passing in August of 2015, the siblings will still go out of their way to drive by it all these years later. According to Johnny, the "Kingswood alumni" still gather from time to time to relive those wonderful memories.

School Days

By this point in his life, Johnny had traded in baseball and other sports for music and girls. He would sometimes still play ball in a neighborhood pickup game, but with music and girls on the brain, there was no time for high school sports—there was barely enough time for schoolwork! There was simply too much fun to be had elsewhere. "These were the 70s, after all,"[227] Johnny said with a smile.

Although he was an adequate student, Johnny never entertained any serious intentions about college. "Honestly, [it] was more about staying on track to graduate and working during the summers to make a little money, standard stuff," he said. "High school was a great time for me looking back on it. I got along with all the different groups in school; jocks, stoners, brainiacs, band guys, and everyone in between, including teachers and staff."[228]

The Pike Girls Made Life Very Easy For Johnny

At one time or another, most of Johnny's friends had a crush on one of his sisters, making his house "the place to be" in middle

227   Ibid..
228   Ibid.

school and high school. The girl count increased when during her senior year, Julie's best friend Lizzy moved in with the Pike family after a tragic set of events befell her family. Lizzy's mom had died in a car accident, and a week later, her dad succumbed to his grief and took his own life. Lizzy had no siblings and was now alone, a situation Denyse simply wouldn't stand for. She welcomed Lizzy into her home without hesitation. With his mom and four teenage girls now living in the house, "getting into a bathroom...was a near impossibility...[and the smell of] cigarette smoke and White Rain hairspray filled the air,"[229] Johnny said.

Johnny credits his sisters for most of his popularity in high school. "No doubt having attractive older sisters, who just happened to have boyfriends that all liked me and looked out for me, put me in a good place as far as the whole high school experience,"[230] Johnny said. He was also a pretty cool kid in his own right. "I really had it made in high school and wouldn't trade one minute of it,"[231] he said.

Despite his popularity, Johnny had few serious girlfriends in high school—that is, until his junior year when he met Brigette. "She was super sweet, very smart and from a great family,"[232] Johnny said. The two began dating, and John and Brigette stayed together until after graduation when she went off to college. He's still not entirely sure if that was the sole cause of their breakup, but at some point following her departure, Johnny remembered getting a legitimate "Dear John" letter from her. Looking back, Johnny admitted that although she may have been out of his league, she did mean a lot to him, and he probably should have tried harder to make it work. Perhaps if he too had gone off to college...

---

229   Ibid.
230   Ibid.
231   Ibid.
232   Ibid. Page 4.

Jamming

It was not at high school, but at the local skating rink that Johnny met Steve Selvia, Tim Kelly, and Hank Blackmon, who would ultimately become his best friends. The three boys were a couple of years older than high school junior Johnny, but their shared love of music trumped any age difference. Tim and Steve played guitar and eventually convinced Hank to take up the bass so the four of them could start a band. "From there we set up a jam room in Hank's mom's basement where friends from far and wide would come over and witness the four of us, two guitars, and a bass going through a single amp, along with me on drums, playing the same song for hours with no vocals,"[233] he said. It may not have sounded very good to those interlopers who came to listen, but it was fun. Despite jamming for hundreds of hours over the years, the guys never did play an actual gig together. But for Johnny, jamming with those older boys was just the beginning.

A Trip, A Job and a Couple of Bands

After high school graduation in June of 1979, Johnny and some friends took a celebratory trip to Daytona Beach, Florida. When he returned, he resumed working for Eve Windham, his mom's close friend, who had provided Johnny with a part time job at her construction and custom marble bath company while he was a senior in high school. The company specialized in creating unique marble bathtubs, sinks, and countertops, and Johnny helped with their fabrications and installations.

Johnny was friends with Eve's children, and one of her two sons was a drummer who owned a beautiful set of

233   Ibid. Page 5.

164

Ludwig drums. "I would get the opportunity to play his set from time to time," Johnny remembered, which was a real treat. "They were WAY nicer than any I'd ever played."[234]

In February of 1980, Johnny's friend Wade Smith, also a musician, mentioned a copier technician position that had opened at his company, Minolta Business Systems, and he convinced Johnny to apply. Johnny had an interview with Vonell Wilson, the service manager responsible for filling the position. Vonell took a real liking to the young applicant, and Johnny accepted a full-time position with the company. He worked alongside Wade as an on-site tech at the Lockheed Martin facility, the same place where his dad had worked, to service and support upwards of 70 Minolta copiers. While at Minolta, Johnny developed a new skill at which he excelled. He learned everything he could about copiers. It was the beginning of a career that would see Johnny managing service and operations for Minolta, and after a merger, for Konica/Minolta, for almost 30 years.

Perfect Stranger

Though now working in a full-time career position, Johnny never lost his passion for music. Jamming with Steve, Tim, and Hank might have never amounted to much, but it certainly lit a fire. Johnny's prospects changed in the early 1980s when he and Wade, his guitar playing Minolta co-worker, started jamming together. Johnny was on drums (a used set of Ludwigs he bought to replace his beloved red-sparkle Stewarts), and Wade played the electric guitar. They added bassist Johnny Averett and guitarist Lee Paschal, who Johnny had met at Star Maker Music—a small music store in Smyrna, Georgia where

234   Ibid.

165

*Promo piece for Perfect Stranger featuring (L-R) Johnny Pike,
Johnny Averett, Wade Smith and Lee Paschal.
(Photo courtesy of Johnny Pike)*

aspiring musicians often hung out- and together, they became
Perfect Stranger. For several years, the band played the local
club circuit, covering songs from the 70s and 80s. "There were
lineup changes here and there, but that band always included
Wade and me," Johnny said.

Scrub the Pup

Perfect Stranger played from 1989 to 1993 before some
of its members started feeling the heat from their wives,
who weren't fond of the late nights and everything else that
comes with band life. Unable to find new players who were
a good fit, the band decided to call it quits. Johnny was disappointed, to say the least. "It was a real bummer," Johnny
said. "The band was really good, and we had SO much fun
playing together."[235]

But something as small as a band break-up wasn't going

235　Ibid.

to stop Johnny and Wade from making music. The two connected with guitarist Mike Gill and his wife Paula, a solid lead vocalist. This new group initially included Johnny Averett, the bass player from Perfect Stranger, but he left the band for personal reasons and they needed a replacement.

The band was sad to see Averett go but was thrilled with his replacement. His name was Scott King, and everybody loved him. Scott was a masterful musician, but more than that, he was a great guy. He worked at a kennel during the day, where one of his jobs was bathing dogs. When the new band required a name, Scott eagerly suggested Scrub the Pup. The name stuck, and Scrub the Pup began rocking the local clubs with their covers of 70s, 80s, and 90s songs. Scott had a talent for thinking up band names. Many years later he would come up with a name for another band he and Johnny would play in together, Foxes and Fossils.

Being Stood Up Leads To A New Family

It was around that same time in the late 1980s that Johnny attended a technology event sponsored by telecommunications giant Microwave Communications, Inc. (MCI) with his best friend Hank Blackmon and Hank's wife Linda, who worked at MCI. "The plan was for me to meet a co-worker of Linda's who thankfully didn't show up," Johnny said. "Linda did, however, introduce me to another one of her co-workers, Suzi Fawcett, and we hit it off immediately."[236] The two began dating, but after just a couple of dates, tragedy struck the Pike family. Cathy's son, Scott Porto (age 4) and Julie's son, Ryan Yarbrough (age 6), were tragically killed in a car accident. Johnny and Suzi

---

236   Johnny Pike in a written response to interview questions asked by the author. October 17, 2021. Page 2.

put their budding relationship on hold. Though heart broken by the loss of his nephews, Johnny couldn't stop thinking about Suzi, and as time passed, they began dating again. On October 13, 1989, the couple was married in a Catholic church with family and friends in attendance. Following the reception, the couple honeymooned for a week in Jamaica.

Johnny and Suzi both owned their respective houses and decided to live in Suzi's house while renting out Johnny's place. Their professional careers continued to flourish over the early years of their marriage, and when they hit the seven-year mark, they decided it was time to start a family. For Johnny, that would mean taking a break from the late-night gigs and band lifestyle. He informed his bandmates that he would be leaving Scrub the Pup. "There was no real pressure (from Suzi) to quit," Johnny explained. "I just felt I needed to start focusing on raising a family instead of playing drums. I had been playing steadily for quite a few years at that point, so I was cool with dropping out for a little while."[237]

When the couple found out Suzi was pregnant, everyone was ecstatic, but no one more so than Denyse. Unfortunately, just before the baby was born, Denyse was diagnosed with Thrombotic Thrombocytopenia Purpura (TTP), a rare blood disorder that just a decade earlier was almost always fatal. "I remember the doctor telling us, 'It's not cancer, but it's not good,'" Johnny said. "It was awful. She quickly went downhill and was hospitalized for three months, most of which was spent in the ICU."[238] Denyse's hospitalization meant that she couldn't be a part of John David (JD) Pike Junior's birth at Piedmont Hospital on February 23, 1998. Johnny and Suzi brought their infant son to the hospital where Denyse was being treated so he could meet his grandmother for the

---

237 Ibid. Page 2.
238 Ibid. Page 3.

first time, albeit from behind a glass partition. Thankfully, Denyse did make a full recovery.

A little more than two years later, Johnny and Suzi became the proud parents of fraternal twins. Michael and Sammy joined the family on May 31, 2000. This time, "Grandmaw" Denyse was right there to welcome her newest grandchildren into the world.

After a brief maternity leave, Suzi returned to work at MCI, and the children attended a nearby daycare center until they were old enough to go to school. When needed, a dear family friend, Fabs (short for Fabiola) Toussaint would help with the kids, giving John and Suzi some much-needed support when they had to travel for work or just needed time for themselves.

Liberty Jones

In late 2001, an Americana band called Liberty Jones asked Johnny to record drum tracks for an original album they planned to record. A talented group of musicians, the band consisted of Mike "Duck" Duckworth on electric guitar, Jeff Eno on acoustic guitar, Steed Kettles on guitar, Tim Maguire on the bass, and Roger Mathis on both keyboards and guitar. "Putting down drum tracks once or twice a week for about a month, with no real talk at that time of playing shows, was perfect for me,"[239] Johnny said. He accepted their offer without hesitation. In addition to their playing ability, Jeff and Roger were also outstanding vocalists. Mike, Jeff, Roger, and Steed wrote songs together providing material for the band.

They finished recording the self-titled *Liberty Jones* album in about a month and would go on to play a handful

---

239   Johnny Pike in a written response to interview questions asked by the author. August 25, 2021. Page 6.

Liberty Jones performing at Mablehouse Amphitheater—August 2010. (Left to right) Mike Duckworth on electric guitar, Jeff Eno playing acoustic guitar and Johnny Pike at home on his drums. (Photo courtesy of John Pike)

of showcases to promote the album sometimes serving as the opening act for other, better known, Americana artists. Johnny participated in all those events.

It felt great to be back with a real band after so much time away. About a year later in 2003, the band produced a follow-up CD called *Atlanta, GA*. Like the first, this album required the band to play showcase events leading to some great industry exposure and a whole lot of enjoyment for Johnny.

In addition to original tunes, Liberty Jones had a strong selection of cover material, which led to bookings at a few local clubs and several private functions and parties. But all good things eventually must end, and Liberty Jones was no exception. Life got a little too hectic for some of the band members, and they decided to give it up.

Sadly, Steed passed away unexpectedly on April 29, 2015,

Liberty Jones band members (top row standing L-R) Roger Mathis, Jeff Eno,
and Mike Duckworth. (Bottom row seated) Tim Maguire and Johnny Pike.
Steed Kettles not pictured.
(Photo courtesy of Johnny Pike.)

at the age of 50. He was one of the primary songwriters and always a great bandmate. The remaining Liberty Jones band members came together at his memorial service to play a short set featuring some of his original songs. Johnny fondly recalls his time with Liberty Jones and the lasting friendships that developed. "They are a great group of guys who I love dearly," he said. "We're all very proud of the music we made together and what we accomplished, and we still occasionally get together to play."[240]

As the years rolled by, Johnny kept in touch with his old bandmate, Scott King, from Scrub the Pup, who had taken a new gig in a band called The Mustangs. Johnny and Suzi had been to see the band perform, and Scott took

240　Ibid.

every opportunity to tell Johnny what a good addition to The Mustangs he would make. But while he may have had an inner desire to play again, the growing needs of Johnny's young family and the intensity of his professional life were simply not conducive to beginning a new venture that would require playing a steady club scene again.

A Painful Separation and New Love

The year 2003 was another difficult one for Johnny. With JD turning five and the twins barely three, Suzi filed for divorce. While walking away from a 13-year marriage was tough for Johnny, his divorce from Suzi was amicable and the two decided to co-parent the boys. They were able to pull that off and remain close friends to this day. In addition to their primary house, where Suzi would remain, the couple owned a lake house about an hour north of town. They had already sold Johnny's original (pre-marriage) house after being landlords for two years, and they now decided to sell the lake house. The proceeds from the sale would allow Johnny to buy a house just five minutes from Suzi's, making the new parenting arrangement as easy as possible. Their agreement allowed the boys to grow up in "two houses, minutes from each other with both parents completely involved every step of the way,"[241] Johnny said.

In 2005, Johnny met Susan Todd. Susan's son Zac played on the same soccer team as Johnny's son JD, and Susan was also recently divorced. Though not looking for a relationship, Johnny certainly took notice of Susan. "One time in particular," Johnny observed, "Susan went and bought pizzas

---

241   Johnny Pike in a written response to interview questions asked by the author. October 17, 2021. Page 3.

This photo was taken on Johnny and Susan's wedding day. They thought it would be a cool pic of their sons, (L-R) Zac, JD, Sammy and Michael (on drums) as a band. Johnny appropriately named the band «The Last Nerve». The lifespan of this band was short, it ended right after this photo!
(Photo courtesy of Johnny Pike)

for the team's after party."[242] The other parents, including Johnny, offered to contribute to the cost, but Susan wouldn't let them. Her generosity really impressed Johnny, and the two became good friends on the soccer field sidelines. For her part, Susan thought Johnny was still married to Suzi, as they frequently were together at the games. She was gladly mistaken. While romance was not yet on the table, Susan and Johnny often organized playdates for their boys. And these were not your run-of-the-mill get together at the local

---

242   Ibid.

*Susan and Johnny Pike enjoying some down
time in Key West, Florida in October 2021.
(Photo courtesy of Johnny Pike.)*

park playdates, but rather ones that took place at Six Flags
over Georgia, Whitewater Water Park, or the local movie
theater.

Johnny and Susan could feel the chemistry growing
between them as they spent more and more time together
with their children. Johnny remembers months passing
before he "finally got the nerve to officially ask her out for
a "'real date' without the kids." While Johnny may have
broached the subject, he never actually set a date. It took
Susan bringing it up again a week later before anything
actually happened. It's something that Susan still teases him

about today. "On that first date we went to Nuevo Laredo, which has become our absolute favorite Mexican restaurant here in Atlanta," Johnny said. "We've been back no less than 100 times since!"[243] After that first memorable date, Johnny knew that Susan was the girl for him; someone he could easily spend the rest of his life with.

Love blossomed at that Mexican restaurant. The two dated for a couple of years before getting married on August 23, 2008. The ceremony, a simple one, took place in the living room of Johnny's house. Susan and Johnny were joined by their boys Zac, JD, Sammy, and Michael. Also in attendance were Johnny's mom, his sisters, brothers-in-law, their children, Susan's parents, and her brother Dave. Following a honeymoon at the fabulous Breakers Resort in Palm Beach, Florida, they returned to the same home in Marietta where Johnny had lived since 2003. "When Susan and Zac joined up with me and my boys, [we] formed our own version of the Brady Bunch," Johnny said. "She's the best thing that ever happened to me."[244] Susan and Johnny remain very close friends with Suzi (Johnny's ex) and her new husband Tom. "We are an incredibly functional, dysfunctional family,"[245] Johnny joked.

The children have since grown and are now doing their own thing. Zac is currently serving in the United States Navy and is deployed in Sicily. JD graduated from the University of Georgia with a business degree and has secured a terrific job, and twin brothers Michael and Sammy are seniors at the

243   Johnny Pike in a written response to interview questions asked by the author. August 25, 2021. Page 5.

244   Johnny Pike in a written response to interview questions asked by the author. August 25, 2021. Page 5 and Johnny Pike in a written response to interview questions asked by the author. October 17, 2021. Page 4.

245   Johnny Pike in a written response to interview questions asked by the author. October 17, 2021. Page 4

*Promotional photo for The Woodies the husband-and-wife duo with
whom Johnny performs. (L-R) Johnny, Lesli Bryson, Steve Bryson
and Tim Maguire (from Liberty Jones)
(Photo courtesy of Johnny Pike.)*

University of Georgia. They are on track to graduate in the
fall of 2022. "Susan and I could not be prouder of these boys
and how this all turned out," Johnny said. "We have a truly
blessed life together, full of happiness."[246] Johnny can't help
adding with rather proud overtones, "We added another boy
to the mix about six years ago. An English bulldog named
Chubbs. One of the boys for sure!"[247]

246   Ibid.
247   Ibid.

Scott King Asks Johnny Pike to Audition for The Mustangs

Nothing is perfect however, and in 2010, after nearly 30 years with Konica/Minolta, Johnny lost his job when the company laid off an entire region of management. That was a very difficult time for him, but with a substantial severance and feeling a little burned out, he decided to take a short break from the nine-to-five to decompress and maybe find a drumming gig. As luck would have it, The Mustangs were in need of a drummer. Scott King called Johnny, who jumped at the chance to audition.

Johnny could hardly contain his excitement. Landing a spot with such a professional and experienced band that paid good money would be a dream come true. "The Mustangs played all types of corporate gigs, concert series shows, private parties, large weddings, all of which were higher profile than anything I had done in the past," he said. "They even had some regional travel type jobs that I could now do while in-between 'day jobs'"[248].

The band, which at that time included Tim Purcell, Scott King, Toby Ruckert, Scott McDavid on keys and vocals, and Judy Brown on vocals, used all the bells and whistles in their shows, including sequenced horns and strings that required strict adherence to a click track. "They were a cut above any band I had ever played in," Johnny said. "I even had to audition, which was something I'd never had to do before. I had certainly never had to play live with a click track. They weren't sure if I could do it and quite frankly, I

248   Ibid. Pages 6 & 7.

wasn't either."[249] Johnny auditioned in Toby's garage, where he was tested with a handful of the more difficult sequenced songs. He passed with flying colors and joined right away.

Today, Johnny performs with several cover bands. In 2018, he began playing with Rockintrain—a dance cover band that plays hits of the 1970s up to current-day rock and pop—and with Badge, a band that plays 60s and 70s tunes. In 2020, he teamed up with the Angela Reign Band, a group that plays both covers and original rock and country music for a few shows each year. The Woody's are another group Johnny will play with whenever they need a full band.

Overall, Johnny Pike considers himself very fortunate. He has had opportunities to play with a host of great musicians and has made many lifelong friends along the way. For years, he continued to play with his best friends Hank, Wade, and Steve, loving every minute of it. But Hank's unfortunate passing in October of 2017 brought an end to the jam sessions they'd been enjoying for the better part of 40 years. "Those were great times,"[250] Johnny said. But for Johnny, the best was yet to come.

---

249   Author interview with Johnny Pike. December 29, 2021.
    A 'click track,' is a rhythmic pattern using a cowbell hit, rimshot or even a conga that plays at the tempo of the song. In "live" music it is piped to the drummer through the headphones. If the drummer adheres to the click track and the band to the drummer all goes well. If not, disaster could ensue.
250   Ibid.

Chapter 6

THE FORMATION OF TIM PURCELL AND THE MUSTANGS

ollowing his dismissal from Mama's Country Showcase in the summer of 1995, Tim decided to accept offers from both Rodney Mills and Mike Huddleston. Rodney proposed to produce an album for Tim and would arrange for a single-day recording session in Nashville headed up by one of the city's finest session leaders, keyboardist Steve Nathan. Nathan would assemble an A-Team of studio musicians to record Tim's songs. At the same time, Mike became Tim's manager and invested about $7,000 of his own money to cover the expenses involved with recording the album.

Tim's job would be to assemble a band to promote the soon-to-be recorded album. The plan was to play showcases and maybe a club or two, performing songs from the new CD as well as some of Tim's other compositions. It took him a while, but he ended up with some great players.

The first of those players was Duncan James, a guitarist and erstwhile singer. "He was from England where his

The Mustangs CD back cover photo featuring (top) Duncan James, Tim Purcell and Lanice Morrison. (bottom) Barry Smith and Tony Cottrill. (Photo from CD cover courtesy of Tim Purcell)

father had once served as the 'Lord Mayor of Liverpool',"[251] said Tim. Duncan was almost a decade older than Tim and had come to America on a personal mission to find and play "real" country music.

"I arrived in Atlanta in 1992 wanting to be a part of the country scene that was heating up at the time," Duncan recalled. "I was drawn to the more traditional side of it, not the pop/country artists. I liked Ricky Scaggs, Randy Travis, Alan Jackson, Dwight Yoakum, Lee Roy Parnell and, of course, the legends like Haggard, Jones, and Cash. It surprised me when I got to Atlanta that the bands weren't playing much 'real' country like they do in say, Texas."[252] Duncan had no interest in the Shania Twain-style music that was so popular at the time, ironically the very stuff Tim had been playing at

---

251   Author interview with Tim Purcell. October 4, 2021.
252   Duncan James email reply to questions from Tim Purcell. January 28, 2022.

1. Pain, Pain Go Away
   (Tim Purcell)
2. Things Have Changed
   (Jim Fallon and Tim Purcell)
3. Liberated Man *
   (Tim Purcell)
4. The Road To Forever +
   (Jim Fallon and Tim Purcell)
5. The Luckiest Man In Town
   (Jim Fallon and Tim Purcell)
6. If I Could Stop The World
   (Tim Purcell and Joel Burkhart)
7. Could It Be Enough
   (Jim Fallon and Tim Purcell)
8. Ain't Foolin' No One But Me
   (Jim Fallon and Tim Purcell)
9. Smile And Say Goodbye
   (Tim Purcell)

All Songs c. and p. 1996 Tim Purcell

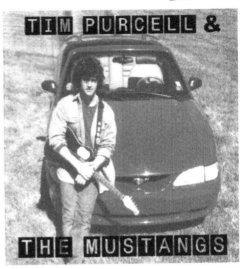

The CD front cover photo for the first recording published by
Tim Purcell & The Mustangs
(Photo courtesy of Tim Purcell)

Mama's. Tim recalled that Duncan was a great guitarist, and a virtuoso at finger picking. "He had a real cool style of playing," Tim said. "Getting him on board got the ball rolling."[253]

Duncan's good friend Lanice Morrison—arguably one of the best bass players and singers in Atlanta—came next. Lanice had a pronounced stutter, but that disappeared when he sang in his rich, baritone voice. Lanice was not only a great musician, but a world-class individual, said Tim. At the time, he was working with several other bands in the area, but when Duncan got him to listen to some of Tim's songs, Lanice, a stay-at-home dad like Tim, agreed to give it a shot. Purcell now had two of the best players in Atlanta lined up.

Next up, a drummer. Tony Cottrill's band had just been fired from the house band position at Cowboys, a mega country dance club in Kennesaw. Tony was looking for a

---

253   Author interview with Tim Purcell. October 4, 2021.

Promotional poster listing The Mustangs
for various performances
(Photos courtesy of Tim Purcell)

new drumming gig, and Tim made him an offer. Tony was on board.

For years, Tim had been ignoring advice that he should get out in front of the band and play guitar, rather than being stuck behind the keyboard. He decided to take that advice to heart when assembling The Mustangs, and started to look for a keyboard player that would free him up to take his place at the front of the band. He turned to Barry Smith, a great player whose affection for the University of Georgia Bulldogs football team was surpassed only by his love for his family and Jesus Christ. Barry got a little slice of heaven in January, 2022, when his beloved Bulldogs became NCAA football champs.

By this time, Tim's former college housemate John Huie was a top agent with CAA in Nashville and was able to set up meetings for Tim with top record labels and publishers in the city. Tim began shopping his songs up and down Music Row, and the response seemed to be the same everywhere.

"We really like this, what else do you have?"[254] Label executives and publishers also had a cryptic piece of advice offered in the form of a question; "Do you want to be a singer or a songwriter?"[255] Not understanding why he couldn't do both, Tim kept plugging away. "I think they just wanted to know where my real passion was," Tim said. "Artists tour and songwriters, for the most part, live in Nashville and they do a lot of collaboration with each other. It's tough to do both."[256]

Huie was happy that Tim was finally making a real go of it, but he was skeptical of Tim's affiliation with his manager, Mike Huddleston. Huie thought Huddleston had good business sense, but feared Huddleston wasn't equipped to navigate his way around the music industry. As it turned out, Huie was right, and not just about Mike.

Huie had long been telling Tim that if he wanted to make it in the music business, he needed to be in Nashville. Nashville was where connections and opportunities presented themselves, which Tim finally understood on his last visit to Music City. Just before making that trip, he participated in a songwriter showcase at The Buckboard in Smyrna and made a big impression on a representative from Sony Records who was in attendance. In a late-night phone call following the showcase, the Sony rep said he wanted to see Tim in Nashville "as soon as he could get there"[257]. It was great timing as Tim had previously scheduled a writing session at Acuff-Rose Publishing in Nashville early the next week. That trip, on the surface, looked like it was going to be a game changer—turned out, it was.

When Tim met with the Sony executive, he treated Tim

---

254   Author interview with Tim Purcell. November 29, 2021.
255   Ibid.
256   Ibid.
257   Ibid.

like a king, promising access to the Nashville studio whenever Tim wanted. After that meeting, the songwriting session at Acuff-Rose went exceedingly well, resulting in a song that actually got demoed. Buoyed by the success of the trip thus far, the 40-year-old musician decided to attend a songwriters open-mic at one of the local bars. Tim was the third of eight to play, and when his turn rolled around he played his allotted three songs, including the one he'd written that day, to polite applause. Tim thought he did pretty well, but the artist who followed him—a young, good-looking singer/songwriter—was simply amazing.

"He played three songs; one made you think, one made you laugh, and one made you cry," Tim said. "He was a great guitar player, a great writer and a great singer."[258] Tim remained at the pub for the rest of the night just so he could meet the guy and tell him how good he thought he was. As Tim approached the artist turned and told Tim he was glad he had stuck around. "He introduced himself to me and told me, 'I thought your songs were great.' I thought you were great,'"[259] Tim said. Tim demurred with a bit of self-deprecation, but the man saw right through that and asked him what he was doing the next day. When Tim told him that he was driving back to Atlanta that night, the singer's exuberance waned. "Oh, you live in Atlanta," he said. "Well, take my card and give me a call when you come back."[260]

"That's exactly what Huie meant," Tim thought as he drove back home later that night. "You have to be there to take advantage of any opportunity that might come along."[261] Tim contemplated his career the rest of the way home,

---

258   Ibid.
259   Ibid.
260   Ibid.
261   Ibid.

evaluating his life and deciding exactly what he wanted—and what he didn't. As a 40-year-old with a young family that now included three daughters, he realized that he really didn't want to tour the country on a bus to promote songs that he had yet to write. For Tim, this was an epiphany. He had a great life and didn't want to spend months at a time away from his family. He still had his band and could still write songs while staying close to home. Tim made a life-defining decision that night—he decided to focus on just having fun and making good music, leaving stardom to someone else.

The following day, he informed a very disappointed Mike Huddleston of his decision. Mike responded by giving Tim a large invoice for the work he had done. The two wrangled over the amount of the invoice and finally agreed to a figure that neither liked but both accepted. The two haven't spoken since.

Free from the burden of chasing fame, Tim could relax and enjoy the music he and The Mustangs were making at clubs and events in the Atlanta area. He could just focus on having fun with a great group of guys. One such fun time happened on the second day of an extended gig in Athens, Georgia at a large country dance club. Late on Saturday afternoon Tim, Duncan, Barry, and Lanice decided to get an early dinner before heading over to the club. The restaurant was somewhat crowded, and the hostess informed the group that it would be a few minutes wait for a table and asked for their names. According to Tim, Lanice responded with his signature pronounced stutter, saying, "L-L-L-Lanice—like Janice, with an L." The others gave a hearty chuckle at Lanice's joke. "Barry, right on cue, stepped forward, saying, 'I'm Barry. That's like Larry with a B.'" Of course, Tim couldn't stop himself from joining the fun. "I walked up and said, 'And I'm Tim, that's like Jim with a T.' Duncan followed, saying in his deep voice with his British accent, 'My name's

Duncan …'" Unfortunately, Duncan realized too late that he didn't have a rhyming name at the ready. Luckily, Tim came to his rescue: "It's like Punkin, with a D."[262]

Around 1997, Lanice's wife was transferred to Nashville, and he left the band to go with her. While in Nashville, he took a one-time gig filling in on bass for a church praise band. It was relatively easy music for Lanice to play and as usual, he did a great job. When the service ended, a congregant with white hair and a beard approached Lanice and told him he would be going on tour in a couple of months. The man's usual bass player wouldn't be available for four dates, and he wanted to know if Lanice would be able to fill in. Turns out, the man was Michael McDonald of Doobie Brothers fame. Lanice jumped at the chance. McDonald was so impressed with Lanice's playing that by the end of those four gigs, he offered Lanice the permanent position and let the other bass player go. Lanice played with him for the next few years. Tim and all of The Mustangs had the opportunity to see their former band mate perform with McDonald at Chastain Park Amphitheater in Atlanta where they opened for Steely Dan. What a thrill!

Having to replace Lanice wasn't easy. Tim called his old friend Tommy Strain, a legendary guitar player who knew every good musician in Atlanta, hoping he might recommend someone who could fill Lanice's shoes. Without hesitation, Tommy suggested Richard Meeder. Tim did not know Richard but knew his brother Scott, the absolute number one drummer in Atlanta. Turns out talent runs deep in the Meeder family. Richard played a fretless bass and he had all the chops. He agreed to join the band.

Tony Cottrill had also decided to move on from The Mustangs, to relocate in Nashville and pursue a career in the

262   Ibid.

recording industry. George Sandler became the band's new drummer. Just before Lanice left for Nashville, Tim met Judy Brown at a neighborhood pool party. Judy's sister-in-law and Tim's friend, Jane Brown, told him that Judy could really sing and asked Tim if he might let her sit in with the band. As a favor to Jane, Tim invited Judy to sing in his studio and was pleased to find that she did have a quality lead voice and after a bit of practice, was able to sing fine harmony as well.

Tim invited Judy to sit in with the band at a gig in Newnan, Georgia. With the departure of Lanice, who had sung lead on several songs, Tim was now the only lead singer in the band and felt that he could use another person to ease the vocal burden. He began to toy with the idea of hiring Judy to sing full-time with The Mustangs. The first few times she sat in, the club passed a hat around to get some money to pay her. That was nice, but you can only do that a couple of times. A decision needed to be made as to whether to bring Judy in as a member. Tim was all for it, but some of the other band members weren't so enthusiastic, thinking that a female presence in the band was just asking for trouble—typical band superstition.

But Tim was less concerned with gender than equity. He explained to Judy that other members had to buy equipment, maintain it, set it up, break it down, and play all night, while Judy would only sing seven or so songs. Consequently, he offered to compensate her at one half share of the proceeds from the two-night gig, an offer she readily accepted. Her attitude changed on payday, however, when Tim handed her $110 for the two nights at the club in Newnan. She quickly protested that $110 for two nights just wasn't worth it.

Tim spoke to the other band members and they all agreed to increase Judy's share, but with a condition. At this point, the band did not have its own stage lights, so Tim killed two birds with one stone and made Judy's pay raise contingent on her purchasing and being in charge of lighting. She agreed, and Tim thought all was good. Before long however, she was asking that the band's name be amended to Tim Purcell and The Mustangs Featuring Judy Browne. Tim, who no longer cared about pushing his own brand, decided to drop all personal references in the band's name and from that point on they were known simply as The Mustangs.

Though the band had experienced some significant turn-over in those first two years, the transformation was not yet complete. In late 1998, Duncan James, who was disappointed at having never discovered the true country music he had been searching for, left the band and returned to England. "I eventually got disillusioned as Nashville kept heading to where it is now," Duncan said. "It's just not country anymore. It's all pop."[263] Tim, meanwhile, got wind that Toby Ruckert was no longer playing with The Buckboard Bandits. He wasted no time in reaching out to Toby and asking him to join the band. Once Toby heard Tim's music, he was on board.

"I received a call from someone by the name of Tim Purcell," Toby remembered. "He said, 'Hey, our guitar player is getting ready to leave and I heard that you're leaving the Buckboard. Would you be interested in maybe working with us?'" The question was followed by an invitation to dinner at the Purcell home in Smyrna. "We had a very nice sit down," Toby said. "We chatted about it and it seemed plausible. I said I'd give it a try."[264] His first gig with The Mustangs was on New Year's Eve, 1998, at a VFW in Buchanan, a small town west of Atlanta.

Toby's role in the band grew from there. One of his responsibilities was to chart songs for the band. That skill

---

263   Duncan James in an email response to questions posed by Tim Purcell. January 28, 2022.

264   Ibid.

was particularly useful when it came to the Price Oil Celebrity Golf Tournament and concert in Destin, Florida where The Mustangs served as the "host" band from 2004 to 2008. "There were usually 12-14 famous musicians who were paid to perform at the Saturday night dinner/concert," Toby explained. "As the host band, we were required to learn three songs for each of the artists so we could back them up. We would rehearse three or four times using the charts that I wrote and together we would work out the background vocals. We put some real effort into it and the artists could tell. They loved us."[265]

Toby had mastered the art of charting during his time at The Buckboard. When the Buckboard Bandits keyboard player and band leader, Keith Thomas, left the band to open a demo studio, Toby went to work for Keith and began charting songs for the fledgling artists that recorded there. Toby uses the Nashville number system, which assigns a number (representing the order in the scale) rather than a name for each chord in a song. Using this system in a live performance, a band can easily accommodate an artist's request for a last-minute key change. Moreover, if just one band member knows a song he can mouth the numbers or even hold up fingers to the other players on stage. This meant theoretically, that a band could play songs they've never even heard. It really is a marvelous tool!

One night in 2000, The Mustangs former bass player Lanice and his buddy, Mike Bruce, came out to see the band perform at Whispers Pub. Before Lanice's stint with The Mustangs, Mike and he played together for years in a very popular band called Hillbilly Romeos. That night, Tim invited Lanice to sit in and sing a song. Lanice asked if Mike could join in on drums. Tim agreed, not knowing that Mike was very drunk

265   Author interview with Toby Ruckert. February 11, 2022.

at the time. As Lanice, Mike, and The Mustangs performed, Mike lost his balance and fell. He didn't simply fall off the drum stool, but off the entire riser as well. He wasn't hurt, but that ended his time on stage for that night. Funnily enough, Tim had no recollection of this a few years later when The Mustangs hired Mike to replace George Sandler. Mike reminded him about it and they had a laugh. "In the time Mike played with The Mustangs, I can't recall him even taking a drink, much less being drunk," Tim recalled.[266]

In 2001, The Mustangs were playing at the Cadillac Ranch, a club in Cumming, Georgia, when what appeared to be a totally benign event caused another major shakeup in the band. "[We had] hired a big crew to film the evening's performance to be a part of a promotional video," Tim remembered. "The crew came in with cranes and remote gadgets that swung around and swirled with large cameras attached. It was a major production. I oversaw the audio recording and single-tracked all the instruments and vocals so I could go back and mix the music to make it as good as possible for the video. At the end of our set we always did a little dance number where we'd play *Brick House*, and stuff like that, in a medley. I asked the crowd to really respond, more than normal, for the video. I also asked some girls who had been standing up front to come up on stage and dance. Ten girls rushed up and started dancing. At one point, the camera was focused on Richard Meeder playing bass when some sexy-looking babe saunters over to him and starts [suggestively] dancing near him, all getting up in his face and rubbing her body on him. Shortly after, Richard's wife, a very conservative Christian woman, saw the video and told Richard she didn't want him to play clubs anymore."[267]

266   Ibid.
267   Author interview with Tim Purcell. October 4, 2021.

Richard asked Tim if he would allow him to remain with the band for corporate functions and only replace him for the club work; Tim said no. He didn't think it was fair to ask another bassist to play the clubs, which was harder work and paid less money, and let Richard play the easier, higher paying corporate gigs and concerts. Meeder was out.

Once again, Tim turned to his old friend Tommy Strain for help—and once again, he came through. "Oh wow! Have I got the guy for you,"[268] he told Tim. "The guy" was Scott King. Tommy had played in Bareback with Scott and thought him to be an outstanding player and singer. He gave Tim Scott's number.

Several days passed and Tim—having called Scott on three separate occasions without a response—turned to Tommy again asking for another name, as Scott clearly had no interest in talking to him. Tommy offered to call Scott on Tim's behalf, and ask Scott to call Tim back as a personal favor. "Tim's a great guy and the gig (audition) is only one weekend," Tommy told Scott. "Please call him."[269] Scott did so and agreed to join Tim and The Mustangs on stage at the Blue Rodeo in Jasper, Georgia on Friday, February 12, 2001.

The band "got to the first chorus of the first song and it sounded like angels singing. I knew right then I wanted to stay," Scott said emphatically. "The Mustangs had four weekends in a row booked at that club and after the first weekend was over I went up to Tim and I said, 'What's it going to take to do another weekend or two with you up here so I don't have to take my equipment home?' Tim thought for a minute and said, 'Well, you can join the band, or you can pack your gear up.' I joined the band right then."[270]

---

268   Ibid.
269   Author interview with Scott King. October 26, 2021.
270   Ibid.

Tim recalls it a bit differently. "After the first set, Scott asked, "What do I have to do to be in this band? You have the best vocals I've ever heard,'"[271] Tim said. Tim also knew immediately that he wanted Scott to join the band, but he didn't want to make joining The Mustangs seem too easy. "Let's see how the rest of the night goes. Then let's go home and sleep on it," Tim said. "I called Richard the next morning and told him not to bother coming in that night. So Saturday night, after the first set, I invited Scott to join the group."[272] Regardless which version of the story you believe, the result was the same. Scott King was now a Mustang. Both Tim and Scott agree that a hard-core, life-long friendship was formed then and there.

By 2004, The Mustangs consisted of Tim, Judy Browne, Toby Ruckert on guitar, Scott McDavid on keyboards (Barry Smith left the band to devote himself full time to his church), Scott King on bass, and George Sandler on drums. Tim, officially giving up any lingering designs on stardom, now focused his attention on booking the band for corporate events, outdoor festivals, and occasional club work. The higher the pay, the better.

One of the clubs the band played was The Rusty Rooster. "The place was huge," Scott recalled. "It was a converted grocery store that had a mechanical bull and all the bells and whistles of country nightclubs at the time."[273] The Mustangs weren't the house band, but the owner liked them and they performed there often. One particular night, Tim, who coached all of his daughters' softball teams, had to go to The Rusty Rooster directly from a game. He had packed his equipment and a change of clothes in the van before he

---

271   Author interview with Tim Purcell. October 4, 2021.
272   Ibid.
273   Author interview with Scott King. December 17, 2021.

left home, knowing he would be cutting it close, planning to change into his stage clothes at the club. But when he arrived at the club and went to the dressing room to change, he found that he had accidentally packed a pair of his wife's jeans instead of his own. "So while the other Mustangs wore their country finest stage clothes, Tim had to perform in his cowboy shirt, boots, and his grey-green Sansabelt nylon coaching shorts, just because he didn't take the time to look at the jeans in his hands before he left the house,"[274] Scott said. Scott and the others never let Tim forget that one.

The Rusty Rooster had a VIP section where the band members were encouraged to mingle between sets and have a drink with the patrons. A very attractive (VIP) woman who often came to the club always insisted upon having a drink with the band members at the end of the night. Because she was one of the club's wealthier clients, often giving big tips and not to mention really pretty, the band always accommodated her. They quickly learned that she was the ex-wife of Rick Camp, a legendary retired relief pitcher for the Atlanta Braves.

Camp was a pretty good pitcher on some really bad teams. Like many pitchers, he wasn't much of a hitter—something his .074 lifetime batting average proves. Yet, his hitting is perhaps the thing for which he is best remembered.

The game on July 4, 1985, started late due to a two-hour rain delay. That meant the spectacular fireworks display the Braves put on each year following the holiday game would be pushed back late to in the evening. When the game finally commenced, it turned into a very long one, and the crowd (or what was left of it at 2:30 a.m.) was still awaiting the fireworks when Camp strode to the plate with two outs in the 18th inning. The Braves trailed the New York Mets 11-10. With a count of two strikes, Camp hit a long drive over the

274   Ibid.

left field fence, his one and only major league home run, tying the game at 11 and forcing the crowd to wait even longer for the fireworks display. The Mets eventually won the game in the 19th inning with a score of 16-13 in what has been described as one of the craziest games ever, and the greatly diminished crowd finally got to enjoy the fireworks sometime around 4 a.m.

The loss was charged to Camp, but he got to keep the bat with which he hit the tying home run, a keepsake he treasured and kept on his trophy shelf. While having drinks with Camp's ex, someone asked her if Rick still had the bat he used to hit that unlikely home run. "He did" she replied, "until he pissed me off and I threw it in a lake!" Imagine, one of the most famous bats in Braves history winding up at the bottom of some lake!

Scott remembered another funny incident that took place during his time with The Mustangs. "When we had to travel, Tim and I would often ride together in the van," he said.

"One day we had to leave early for a gig, and I had to leave my house at 4:30 in the morning to get to Tim's. I showered the night before and that morning I dressed in a hurry in the dark and ran out the door. At Tim's, as we prepared to leave, I told him I had to go to the bathroom before we left. I noticed that, in my haste to leave my house, I had put my boxer shorts on backwards. I was fixing them when Tim knocked at the door and said, 'Are you almost ready, man,' to which I replied, 'Yeah, I'm just putting my shoes on.' Tim said, 'You take your shoes off to pee?' I answered, 'Yeah, doesn't everybody?' He probably thought I was pretty strange, but when I told him the whole story, we both had a good laugh."[275]

The keyboard position in the band had seen more turn-over than the others. When Barry Smith left the band in

275   Author interview with Scott King. December 17, 2021.

Johnny performing as the drummer for The Mustangs during
the Smyrna Birthday Party, an annual event at which The
Mustangs performed for nine years in a row.
(Photo courtesy of Johnny Pike)

2003 to pursue a full-time opportunity in the music ministry at his church, Scott McDavid replaced him. McDavid was an exceptional player, producer, and engineer who had written movie scores and jingles, and who taught Tim a lot about the recording process. When McDavid left the band in 2015, they hired Keith Thomas, but he lasted only about four months. Ultimately, the band hired Greg Scoheir, who played keyboards with The Mustangs from 2016 until 2018.

In 2002, drummer George Sandler left the band and was replaced by Mike Bruce. Mike was an outstanding person, an author, and so funny he certainly could have been a stand-up comedian—he's also the friend of Lanice who fell off the stage back in 2000 while sitting in at Whispers Pub. Mike left The Mustangs in 2009 when Billy Bob Thornton, who in addition to being a famous actor is also a singer/songwriter who plays a blend of Americana, blue grass, and country, offered Mike a spot in his band. Kerry Denton stepped in to take Mike's place.

"Kerry is an example of a professional musician in a part time band," Tim said. "I say part time because The Mustangs basically only performed on weekends and not necessarily every weekend. Kerry provided for his family with the money he made playing music and doing studio work."[276] It wasn't uncommon for Kerry to notify The Mustangs that they needed to get a sub for him because he had been offered a job that paid more money. This was not a good situation and it was almost a relief when Kerry called Tim to tell him he was leaving the band. He had been offered a job with another Atlanta group that worked more frequently. Tim needed to find a replacement for Kerry, and Scott King suggested his good friend Johnny Pike.

Johnny was very excited when he got that call. He had just lost his 30-year job with Konica Minolta and decided to take some time off before looking for another job. He was looking to start back up with a band and getting a spot with one as professional and experienced as The Mustangs was a phenomenal opportunity for him.

Johnny had never been required to audition for a spot in a band, but this time he was. He was confident of his ability but still a bit nervous about having to play with a sequencer (click track) as many of The Mustangs songs utilized sequenced horns or strings. He accepted the challenge head on and pulled it off with flying colors, making a great impression on everyone in Toby's garage that day. Scott never had a doubt!

Those first few months playing with The Mustangs caused Johnny some anxiety, and that led to his having some crazy dreams,[277] all centered around him forgetting to pack some of the necessary equipment in his car. In prior bands, he would just set up his drum kit, maybe a few mics, and be

276   Author interview with Tim Purcell. October 20, 2021.
277   Author interview with Johnny Pike. December 29, 2021.

Lowcountry boil party 'typical food dump' from the Edisto
Island home party of September 5, 2015
(Photo courtesy of Mary Thomas)

ready to go. With The Mustangs, he had to set up a small mixing board with headphones for the click track in addition to his drums and mics. He would dream about making it to gigs late, forgetting his mixing board or headphones (he never did), and other foolish things.

With other bands, Johnny always felt confident. But this band was so much more professional than anything he was used to, and because of that he worried about everything. It wasn't unusual for him to pull over on the interstate just to make sure he had packed all the equipment he needed. He was a bundle of nerves, but after he played with the band for a few months and got used to the guys, all that anxiety went away.

One of Johnny's favorite gigs with The Mustangs was an annual private party called the "Lowcountry Boil" hosted on Labor Day weekend by Mike and Mary Thomas at their home.

The Mustangs (L-R—Toby, Tim, Amy Wallace, Scott and Johnny (in the back) performing at the Smyrna home of Mike and Mary Thomas during the 2012 lowcountry boil party. (Photo courtesy of Mary Thomas)

The name comes from the coastal region of South Carolina and Georgia, often referred to as the lowcountry. The "boils" would begin around 2:00 p.m. and featured hourly food dumps of shrimp, crab, lobster, corn, sausage, and potatoes, all boiled together in a big pot over an open flame, until 6:00 p.m.. Guests would bring side dishes to eat along with the main spread. "Those parties were just amazing,"[278] Johnny said.

Before meeting Mary, Mike lived in Georgia's lowcountry, where he first began having boil parties. The tradition continued after their marriage and is now in its 20th year. The parties started out small, hosted at the couple's home in Woodstock, Georgia. It was when they moved to Smyrna that they added live music to the event.

---

278   Ibid.

Mary Thomas's daughter Allison Forbes would sometimes sing a song or two with The Mustangs at the lowcountry boil parties. This one is at the Smyrna home of Mike and Mary Thomas in 2012 (Photo courtesy of Mary Thomas)

The Mustangs first performed at the party in 2009. Mike and Mary knew Tim and Terri Purcell and Larry and Ellen Adams (Maggie's parents) from church. In fact, Mary's daughter Allison Forbes was baptized on the same day as Maggie. Mary's son Drew Forbes, while a freshman in high school, dated Toby's daughter, Kelsey.

Those connections, however, had nothing to do with why The Mustangs began performing at the Lowcountry Boil. "The way that came about is actually quite funny," Mike said. "We have two very good friends, Randy Hutson and Kim Schwartz, who had been dating for a while. They first met at a country dance club where The Mustangs were playing. Randy had gone to the club to see his friend Scott King's band play."[279]

---

279   Author interview with Mike and Mary Thomas. January 28, 2022.

Tim's daughter Rachel with The Mustangs at the
September 3, 2016 lowcountry boil at the Edisto
Island home of Mike and Mary Thomas.
(Photo courtesy of Mary Thomas)

Because of their individual relationships with band members, the two couples (Kim and Randy and Mary and Mike) found themselves together at the City of Smyrna's Annual Birthday Party where The Mustangs were performing. That's when Randy told Mike that "he was planning to ask Kim to marry him and he was going to do it on Labor Day."[280] Mike had the idea of asking The Mustangs to play at his annual Low County boil, since they were playing when Randy and Kim first met. "It will be a full circle of where you met and how you got engaged," Mike said.

It would have made for a very romantic story. However, Mike was unaware of two things; first, how expensive the

---

280   Ibid.

*Relaxing during a break at the lowcountry boil party on Edisto
Island, Tim and Scott featured here with Tim's friend Charlie
Strange and sound man Doug Godbold–September 3, 2016.
(Photo courtesy of Mary Thomas)*

band was (he thought it would cost a couple of hundred dollars but it was more like $2,500); second, that Randy was on pain medication, which he had combined with beer on the evening he told Mike of his proposal plan. That intoxicating combination caused Randy to have no recollection of his and Mike's conversation. Mike followed through with his part of the plan, explaining it to Mary who agreed it was a terrific idea but, knowing what The Mustangs charged for a performance, wondered if paying that much money would be worth it.[281] Despite the sticker shock, the Thomases went ahead and hired the band. "Randy and Kim were at the party, but Randy did not ask Kim to marry him that day,"

---

281   Ibid.

Mike said. "In fact [he] had not even purchased a ring at that point. He had no idea that anything special was afoot as he had no recollection of his conversation with me that night at the Smyrna Birthday Party." The story does have a happy ending, however. The couple got engaged on New Year's Eve of that same year, and the Hutsons continue to attend the Lowcountry Boil just about every year.

Following the party in 2012, Mike and Mary moved from Smyrna to Edisto Island in South Carolina. The move did not stop them from asking The Mustangs to perform at their party. They even rented a house for the band members to use for the weekend they performed.

"That party was so much fun that we couldn't go back to not having a band,"[282] Mary said. With the exception of 2013, when Allison Forbes' band, Lost Tribe, performed, The Mustangs played at the Lowcountry Boil every year from 2009 to 2018. Over those years, Allison—now the lead singer in a Charleston band called Rooks and Raven—would always join in for a song or two, and in 2010, Foxes and Fossils even performed a set at the party.

Mike recalled the great times that they had with the band members at night after the party had ended. "We would start a bonfire by the pool, and Tim, Toby, and Johnny Pike played acoustic guitars while Scott played his ukulele," Mike said. "They led us in song as we sat around the fire." Mary added, "It always amazed me that after playing in the hot sun from two to six they would sit around the pool and jam. It was a lot of fun."[283]

Following the 2011 untimely passing of Mary's nephew, Bryan Allison, a musical tribute was added to the party. The second set, from that time forward, would always begin

---

282   Ibid.
283   Author interview with Mike and Mary Thomas. January 28, 2022.

with a rendition of *Amazing Grace* in remembrance of all the family and friends who had passed during the previous twelve months. "In 2022, that remembrance will include Scott King,"[284] Mary added.

In addition to the low country boil parties, Johnny also recalls with a special fondness the "green room" memories with his band mates. The funniest stuff always seemed to happen when the band was backstage waiting for the gig to begin. "A lot of the gigs required us to be there quite early for sound checks, etc., and there was a lot of down time between setting up, doing sound checks, and performing," Johnny said. "We had so much fun in the green room listening to stories, especially Toby's stories, which were always entertaining."[285]

The Beginning of the End for The Mustangs

The Mustangs had a great run during the first 13 years of their existence. Corporate functions, city festivals, clubs, weddings, private parties, and events like the Price Oil Celebrity Golf Tournament kept them busy year round.

One of the more famous performers at the Price Oil event one year was Branford Marsalis, the brother of trumpeter Wynton Marsalis. A renowned composer, bandleader, and saxophonist, Branford is well known for his jazz band—the Branford Marsalis Quartet—and for his work with the classical group Buckshot LeFonque. His fame rose even higher when he led the Tonight Show Band from 1992 to 1995. After his performance with The Mustangs at the Price Oil event, he took a real liking to the band and would contact the members when his tours came through Atlanta, giving them passes to his shows.

---

284   Ibid.
285   Author interview with Jonny Pike, December 29, 2021.

The Mustangs also had a tie-in with WKHX, a local country radio station in Atlanta. The band would perform on site whenever the station did live remote promotional broadcasts—things like grand openings of businesses, or special sales events at car dealerships. In the middle of a set at one such event on a summer Saturday morning, a bored Judy Brown decided to place a phone call to Branford. She held the phone to the microphone so the other band members could hear. They heard Judy say, "Yeah, we're playing this promotional thing at a car dealership and there is absolutely no one here. Yeah, I can hold on." Branford, who was recording in the studio that morning, handed the phone off and another voice said, "Hello, is this Judy? I've heard so much about you guys. This is Harry Connick Jr., How's it going?"[286] The starstruck band members spoke to him for a few minutes before resuming their performance. Scott added that Branford Marsalis was both a wonderful man and an amazing talent. "I'm sorry we lost touch with him," he said.

The Mustangs were on a roll, but as Tim had seen so often in his career, success is a fleeting thing. History was about to repeat itself. The downturn in their run of success began in November 2008, when top executives from Ford, Chrysler, and GM left their offices in Detroit, boarded their private jets, and flew to Washington DC to seek a financial bailout from Congress for their near bankrupt automobile manufacturing companies.

Perhaps requesting this extraordinary corporate welfare program wouldn't have garnered as much negative press if those top corporate executives, who were all raking in salaries and bonuses well north of seven figures, had not disembarked in Washington from luxurious private jets to request

---

286   Author interviews with Tim Purcell on December 31, 2021 and Scott King on December 17, 2021.

the handout. Headlines chastising these executives and their companies spread across the country. The outrageous salaries and perks of the company's CEOs were featured in every major newspaper and on virtually every radio and television news program.

California Congressman Brad Sherman pressed the issue at the hearings, asking the three CEOs to "raise their hand if they flew here on a commercial plane."[287] Not a single hand went up. The congressman wasn't done yet. "Second, I'm going to ask you to raise your hand if you are planning to sell your jet and fly back commercial."[288] Again, no one raised their hand. Thomas Schatz, president of Citizens Against Government Waste, added, "They're coming to Washington to beg the taxpayers to help them. It's unseemly to be running around on a $20,000 flight versus a $500 round trip [ticket]."[289]

Before the dust settled, all large corporations were feeling the heat as the very concept of capitalism came under fire. Every major company in the United States—and their CEOs—had suddenly become the target of the public's ridicule and disdain. Almost overnight, major corporations—including those for which The Mustangs performed—cancelled their events. Those companies didn't want anything to do with flashy galas or anything that resembled excess.

The Mustangs lost all their high-paying corporate gigs. For the first time in recent memory, they weren't working on New Year's Eve. The band's revenue stream dwindled and they found themselves at a crossroads. Though continuing to play club jobs, the gigs were few and far between. Some

287   Levs, Josh; Anderson, Emily; Nicolaidis, Virginia; and Bash, Dana. Big Three Auto CEOs Flew Private Jets to Ask for Taxpayer Money. CNN, November 19, 2008. Page 1. http://www.cnn.com/2008/us/11/19/autos. ceo.jets/.

288   Ibid.

289   Ibid.

gigs they played were only one night a week and the money simply wasn't there. The trend continued, and in 2012, Judy Browne had had enough. She left The Mustangs to form a duo with an excellent guitar player, Marvin Taylor. She believed it would be a better financial opportunity for her.

Her departure was not good news for the band, and they thought her leaving might mean the end of The Mustangs. Scott suggested that Tim try to recruit someone from his church choir, but he could think of no one who was in any way qualified. Then he remembered Amy Wallace.

Some years earlier, when Tim was serving on the staff-parish committee, his church decided to add a contemporary service to its worship options. Contemporary worship services rely heavily on praise bands, and subsequently, the praise band leader. Charisma, commitment, and stage presence—as well as the ability to sing—all go into the making of a good praise leader. There were many applicants and Tim was on the review committee. Some were better than others, but only one stood out to him—Amy. It was on the strength of Tim's recommendation, and her obvious talent, that she was hired for the position. Tim decided to ask her if she would be interested in joining The Mustangs.

He was asking a woman who, in her entire life, had never sung anything but gospel and contemporary Christian music, to join a country-rock band. She nervously agreed to audition at Tim's home studio. He remembers she sang *Midnight Train to Georgia*, and her voice just blew him away. All the band members took an immediate liking to Amy, and how could they not? She was cooperative, always prepared, and always on time. Her husband even helped move equipment. She was fantastic and couldn't have been a better fit.

Scott was particularly fond of Amy. She was a fine arts teacher at North Marietta Christian Academy and he suggested that he and Tim attend her school's special talent show, a revue featuring the best of her high school singers, as a show of support for her. That's when Tim and Scott first heard Chase Truran. The poised and gifted young lady was so impressive, that after the show Tim asked Amy where she would be attending college the following year. To his amazement, Amy told Tim that Chase was only a high school freshman.

About a year after Judy left the band, Scott McDavid also moved on. He was a full-time musician and with the demise of The Mustangs' corporate gigs, there just wasn't enough money for him to pay rent in Atlanta. He relocated back to Birmingham, Alabama and moved in with his brother. He continued to commute for a while, but when the gigs began to dwindle, he moved on to California to look for a job writing scores for movies and television productions.

The Mustangs last performed together at the Marietta City Square Concert Series on Saturday, September 24. "It was the last show of the city's 2018 concert season, and it drew a huge crowd," Johnny said. "What made the event so memorable was the extraordinary number of friends and family who were there to hear the band."[290]

---

290   Author interview with Johnny Pike. December 29, 2021.

Part II
FOXES AND FOSSILS
The Post-Mustang Era

Chapter 7

SAMMIE "THAT'S SOME GREAT SAMBOURINE" PURCELL

amantha "Sammie" Purcell is the youngest child of
Tim and Terri Purcell. She was born on December 2,
1994, and has two older sisters, Maggie and Rachel. Her
mother, Terri, served as a lawyer for Coca-Cola Enterprises,
Inc. and The Coca-Cola Company, while Tim worked as
a stay-at-home dad. He had retired from his job at Lowe's
back in 1986 and had since been living out his dream as a
full-time musician. "My dad was smart like mom," Sammie
said. "But he was definitely the goofier of the two."[291]

Sammie's parents were relatively easy going, except when
it came to academics. "They were pretty tough when it came
to school,"[292] she said. But despite their tough disposition
towards schoolwork, her parents were mostly lenient with

---

291   Written discussion between the authors. October 29, 2021.
292   Ibid.

One year old Sammie and her dad enjoying a 'drink' together while watching an Atlanta Braves baseball game. Dad was putting away a beer while Sammie fiddled with an unopened plastic bottle of Coca-Cola. (C 1995) (Photo courtesy of Sammie Purcell)

their youngest child. "They probably coddled me a bit,"[293] Sammie admitted.

Growing up, Sammie had two close friends in her neighborhood. The young girls lived right across the street, so the three of them were able to play outside in each others' yards moving freely from house to house. But when Sammie was still rather young, her friends moved away leaving no playmates in the neighborhood Sammie's age. "I really didn't have any kids to play with close to home,"[294] she said.

She kept herself busy by making friends at school and playing around the house. "We had a basement where dad

293   Ibid.
294   Ibid.

had his studio and all of his music stuff," she said. "The rest of the house was all situated on the first floor. It was pretty open…[between] the living room, dining room [and] kitchen."[295] When Sammie was three years old, Tim and Terri "knocked down the back wall of the house to create a master suite for themselves, adding a hallway, a bathroom and a bedroom which meant that my sisters didn't have to share a room anymore," she said. "That made the house a good bit larger."[296]

Playing around the house also meant spending more time with her sisters, particularly Maggie, who was closest to her age. "I mostly served as a really annoying little sister," Sammie recalled. "I don't think I was very close to Maggie or Rachel when I was younger. Again, I just annoyed Maggie and we would yell and hit and gripe at each other a lot."[297]

Sammie hasn't seen the video in a long time, but she does remember watching one of those sisterly arguments unfold on an old home camcorder tape. Sammie has no recollection of the incident, but after watching the recording, she couldn't deny that it captured the essence of her and Maggie's relationship. "In the video I was a toddler—maybe one and a half—and Maggie is holding a garden hose," Sammie said. "She just points it at me on full blast knocking me down." After a moment's thought, Sammie added, "I probably did something to deserve it."[298]

Sammie has very fond memories of going on bike rides with her dad. The two would ride on a trail back behind their house that was partially paved, partially unpaved. In typical, eloquent kid fashion, Sammie would call the paved

---

295   Ibid.
296   Ibid.
297   Ibid.
298   Ibid.

Sammie (right) and her friend Savannah (left) cooling off at the Smyrna neighborhood pool. (Photo courtesy of Tim Purcell)

stretch "smooth road" and the other stretch "bumpy road." On these trips, Tim would carefully strap his daughter into a seat on the back of his bike, and the two would ride the trail all the way down to Nickajack Creek, hang out for a bit, and head home.

She also recalls numerous summer trips to the neighborhood pool as a child. It was there that Sammie met Savannah; an encounter that sparked a lifelong friendship. One hot summer day at the pool Savannah was annoying her dad, James. In an effort to distract her, he told her to go give that little blonde girl a popsicle. "I was that little blonde girl," Sammie said. "We have been really good friends ever since… we became inseparable."[299]

---

299   Ibid.

Sammie, age 9, playing softball for Rhyne Park Allstars
(Photo courtesy of Sammie Purcell)

Sammie also loved sports as a child, and started playing softball at the ripe old age of four. She continued to play all the way through high school, where she received many accolades for her defensive play.

Neither she nor her parents devoutly attend church anymore, but growing up, Sammie and family would go almost every Sunday. She joined a children's choir at Smyrna First United Methodist Church when she was just four years old, and eight years later, in seventh grade became a member of God's Light youth choir. Sammie spent six years in God's Light, five of them alongside Maggie Adams.

As a member of God's Light, Sammie and the other members were responsible for raising funds each year to subsidize a choir tour. "Every June, just after school let out for summer, we would get on a bus and travel across the country, singing at different churches along the way to our destination,"[300] Sammie explained. On those tours with God's Light, the destinations included Niagara Falls, the Grand Canyon, Pike's Peak, and New York City. Each summer, the tour concluded with the group's arrival back in Smyrna, where they would have a big pot-luck dinner and perform one last concert for family and friends. In her senior year Sammie became co-president of the choir. In that role she took a leadership position at weekly choir meetings and at the monthly fundraising luncheons.

The High School Years

While at Campbell High School, Sammie grew to love literature, and was particularly fond of her English teachers, Mr. Max Jones and Mrs. Susan Smith. One of her fondest memories of school was when Mrs. Smith acted out the poem, *Sir Gawain and the Green Knight.* "She used a different voice for every single character," Sammie said. Mrs. Smith, it seems, had a bit of a flair for the dramatic. For one assignment, Sammie and her classmates had to memorize the prologue to Geoffrey Chaucer's *The Canterbury Tales*, something they were all less than excited about. Mrs. Smith told the students it was imperative that they learn the words, because one day they might be at a party, and someone might ask them if they know the prologue. And then, when they start reciting it, someone across the room might just start reciting it back—and that, Mrs. Smith said, could be how they find their soulmates. Sammie has yet to try this tactic.

While at Campbell High, Sammie matriculated in the International Baccalaureate Program (IB). Founded in 1968,

300   Ibid.

IB is a nonprofit foundation headquartered in Geneva, Switzerland, that provides a curriculum with globalized educational standards. It is offered in countries throughout the world including many US public schools as a magnet program for qualified students. Maggie Adams and Toby's daughter Kelsey were also in IB at Campbell; something that would never have happened if not for the solidarity of Campbell parents.

Years before Sammie entered the program, when the county school board was preparing to offer IB in Cobb County, parents from Walton High School challenged the idea that lowly Campbell would play host to the program arguing that the more highly rated Walton would be a wiser choice since it was located in a "better" part of the county. Sammie was still a small child in diapers when Tim received a call from a concerned Campbell parent, informing him that this group of parents from Walton was attempting to force the school board to move the program to their kids' school. In response, the Campbell "phone tree" sprang into action, rallying concerned Campbell parents to attend the school board's "called" meeting.

Tim received the head's up just before the meeting was scheduled to begin and with no time to spare, hustled Sammie into his van and hurried off. "Along the way, Sammie messed her diaper in dramatic fashion," Tim said. When the two arrived at the school, Tim prepared to change her in the parking lot. But there was one problem—in his rush he had forgotten to pack Sammie's diaper bag. Just as panic set in, another parent that Tim knew well, equipped with her own baby's well stocked diaper bag, offered to change Sammie, urging Tim to go on into the meeting and promising to deliver Sammie as soon as she was clean. The mom who volunteered to help did a great job, cleaning Sammie up

Samantha Purcell, 16-month-old daughter of Tim Purcell of Smyrna, pitches in on the protest Friday with the sign 'You Are Choosing Our Future' taped to her stroller.

A clipping from the local newspaper showing young Sammie entering the IB meeting.
(Photo courtesy of Tim Purcell)

and replacing her soiled clothes. She even taped a sign to Sammie's stroller promoting Campbell's case. As she pushed Sammie into the meeting hall, a newspaper reporter snapped a photograph of "the baby with a cause," which appeared in the local paper.

Sammie doesn't recall this—she was just a baby, after all—but she certainly appreciated IB. "It was a pretty rigorous program," she said. "[We] were basically working up to a bunch of tests senior year. We had to take oral exams and write long, extended essays on topics of our choosing. It was probably harder than college, honestly."[301]

Sammie was an outstanding student who made all As and Bs in high school, but she didn't concern herself solely with academics. In addition to singing in God's Light, she played softball on the high school team (also on a year-round travel team), and performed in high school musicals.

---

301   Authors discussion. February 8, 2022.

Family, Friends and Mischief

Sammie was a good kid—but even good kids get into mischief. She recalled one moment of mischief that happened on a family vacation. She and her cousin Barrie were ten and nine respectively at the time, and their parents had allowed them to go kayaking on a lagoon that abutted the beach. The lagoon looked rather small and was at most four feet deep. Both girls were excellent swimmers and would be wearing life jackets so their parents didn't set any specific parameters or rules for the girls' adventure. Turns out, the lagoon stretched out much farther than anyone knew—all the way to a lake a couple towns away. As the girls paddled around in the lagoon, their parents relaxed under beach umbrellas looking out at the beautiful Gulf of Mexico.

When they turned to check on the girls after what seemed like only a few minutes, Sammie and Barrie were nowhere to be found. A frantic search ensued. Sammie's uncle Steve, Barrie's dad, waded far out into the waist-deep lagoon shouting for Barrie. Aunt Elaine, her mom, knocked on the doors of strangers renting lagoon side homes with high decks that looked out over the water, hoping that vantage point would help her locate the girls. All of this was to no avail. True panic was setting in. Cool-headed Terri ended up finding the wayward mariners, some twenty minutes later, paddling about in the what the girls still considered "the lagoon." None of the parents were aware when the girls took to the water, that a canal connected that little lagoon with a series of lakes that run along the coast. Terri figured it out and while Steve, Elaine and Tim were searching the beachside lagoon, got into her car and drove down to the next lake where she found them. "My parents were actually okay about it," Sammie said. "We didn't really break any rules, and nobody knew how far the lagoon went. But my cousin's parents were really mad, and I remember just being so upset by the fact that she got in trouble. It really wasn't anyone's fault! Just a bad misunderstanding."[302]

Sammie has fond memories of many vacations taken along Florida's "Red-Neck Riviera" while growing up. In high school, she was allowed to take friends with her on spring break trips with the family. "We (she and her friends) would usually try to go to the beach with each other on spring break and my parents were most times the supervising adults," Sammie said. "When we were old enough to drive, we would be allowed to borrow the car, and drive down to Seaside, which was close to where we were staying, and get ice cream and just hang out. It was nice to have some time to ourselves without any pressures from school."[303]

Sammie had a good core group of friends in high school. Most of them had been friends since middle school, but the ones who joined the group in high school just slid right in. Together, they would go to football and basketball games and afterward head to the Waffle House or a local burger joint—anywhere so the night didn't have to end. They hung out together all the time, frequently having sleepovers on weekends. "We would get movies from Blockbuster, get Jet's Pizza or Taco Bell, play Just Dance on the Wii, and stay up way too late,"[304] she said.

---

302   Ibid.
303   Ibid.
304   Ibid.

Sammie (left front) dons a black wig during her middle school performance of Aladdin. (Photo courtesy of Tim Purcell)

Singing And Acting

Tim was a major influence in shaping Sammie's interest in singing, something he said was an obvious talent of hers even when she was just a toddler. Because of her dad, she was exposed to and grew to love music early in life and, thanks to her sisters' participation in middle school and high school productions, began developing an interest in musical theater as well. In middle school, Sammie performed in the plays *Aladdin*, *Bugsy Malone*, and *Seussical: The Musical*, a show based on the Dr. Seuss classic, *Horton Hears A Who*.

Neither Sammie's musical pursuits nor her interest in acting abated after she graduated from middle school. She continued to enjoy both singing and acting at Campbell,

*Sammie (3rd from left) and some friends
trick or treating on Halloween
(Photo courtesy of Tim Purcell)*

where she participated in musicals and plays throughout her four years of high school. She performed with Maggie Adams in *The Wedding Singer* when she was a freshman and Maggie was a sophomore. Sammie was the understudy for the role of Holly, while Maggie was the understudy for the part of Julia.

In her second year, Sammie took on a dual role playing the parts of both Olive and Rona in *The 25th Annual Putnam Country Spelling Bee.* For that show, the school's drama department had an A Cast and a B Cast, the actors alternating roles every other performance. In junior year, Sammie played the part of Doralee in the school's version of *Nine to Five,* and in her senior year she was the lead in *Xanadu,* a satire based on the critically panned 1980s movie.

Of course, by then, Sammie was also a "professional" singer with Foxes and Fossils. It was in her sophomore year

16-year-old Sammie (L) having a good time with big sister Maggie
singing Karaoke at Lonnie's in Nashville, Tennessee.
(Photo courtesy of Tim Purcell)

at Campbell High School that her dad called on her to come sing a song with him. She had never heard Simon and Garfunkel's *America* (it was, after all, written and performed by the duo more than a quarter century before her birth), but that didn't stop her from picking up on the harmony after just a few listens. Harmony so beautiful, it launched a band.

In addition to her academic studies, musical performances both in and out of school, and athletic pursuits, Sammie also found time to work. She had the occasional baby-sitting job and also worked full time at a golf course as a cashier in the clubhouse and as a cart girl out on the course, taking snack and drink orders for golfers.

As mentioned earlier, Sammie was a softball enthusiast for many years leading up to high school. As a member of Campbell's varsity team from freshman to senior year, she

*Sequence Showing Sammie snagging a ground
ball at third base and making the throw to first
(Photo array courtesy of Tim Purcell)*

was the team's starting third baseman and was awarded Defensive Player of the Year multiple times. "I had a habit of just dropping to my knees to stop the ball," she recalled. "In softball, the corner (third base) is sort of forced to play as close to the batter as possible to cover bunts/slaps. My knees were constantly bruised up!"[305]

Sammie's high school career concluded with her graduation in May 2013. With her acceptance to Vanderbilt University, Sammie's future looked very promising. With great anticipation she looked forward to college and to performing with the Foxes and Fossils throughout the summers.

The College Years

"Leaving for school was a little weird," Sammie said. "Luckily, Maggie had done it before me, so I got to see her

---

305   Written comments provided by Sammie Purcell. February 23, 2022.

sort of leave first. It was actually a lot easier than one might think. Nashville is really close (three and a half hours) to Atlanta, so it was easy to come back for weekends if we had a show and most of the shows were in the summer, anyway."[306]

At Vanderbilt, Sammie majored in Communication Studies and Spanish and continued to score As and Bs. She also participated in a musical revue troupe called Original Cast. "It was probably the defining thing I did in college," she said. "Each semester, the student director and producer of the show would pick a setlist of songs from different musicals and then apply them to an original storyline or theme. I produced a show my sophomore year and directed a show my junior year. Auditioning for parts in a revue was a little different than for a normal show. We would basically audition (suggest) the songs that we wanted to sing, for the most part, and then go from there."[307]

Sammie was reluctant to evaluate her performances with the group, but quick to discuss the pitfalls that befell her and other cast members as they rehearsed and performed. "There was one year that basically our entire group had mono [mononucleosis] at one point or another," she remembered. "I just happened to catch it during the week of the show, and completely lost my voice. My big songs that year were *I Miss the Mountains* from *Next to Normal* and *Another Hundred People* from *Company*. Neither of those songs are easy. I really could barely get a note out, especially above a certain pitch, and it was probably the worst experience of my life. The cast was super supportive though. We were literally sitting backstage switching vocal parts around so I could kind of slide by and focus on my solo parts."[308]

---

306   Ibid.
307   Ibid.
308   Ibid.

The Vanderbilt cast who performed in musical reviews—a collection of songs centered around a theme. This cast photo is from March 2, 2017. (Photos courtesy of Terri Purcell)

Sammie and her dad pose for a photo during her senior year of high school. (photo courtesy of Tim Purcell)

Graduation from Vanderbilt—2017 (Photo courtesy of Tim Purcell)

Sammie's First Full-Time Job

After graduating from Vanderbilt in May of 2017, Sammie remained in Nashville and accepted a position with a company called ThirdHome. The home exchange company promotes itself as a way for people to house-swap at destinations all around the world. Members exchange their vacation homes rent-free with other members in the club. Initially Sammie worked in member services, but later settled into a sales and marketing position where she was responsible for writing property descriptions for new homes that came into the club. But by August 2019, Sammie realized that she didn't really want a career in sales and, unfortunately, the company didn't offer much room for growth any other way.

Back To School

Sammie had always been a talented writer, so enrolling in a Masters' program for Journalism at Boston University made sense as a next step. She took her first classes at BU in the fall of 2019, and initially thought she might want to go into investigative journalism. That interest was reinforced, but also challenged, when Boston Globe reporter Michael Rezendes—whose work on the Boston Globe's Spotlight team helped break the Boston Catholic Church Diocese sex abuse scandal (the movie *Spotlight* is based on his work)—spoke to her class. "I'm finding that I might not have the stomach for it," she said of investigative reporting. "It takes a very special person because you cover some tough subjects."[309]

Sammie was able to finish her degree, but not before the COVID-19 pandemic disrupted in-class learning. In March of 2020, she returned home to complete the spring semester via distanced learning. That "break" provided an opportunity to record more Foxes and Fossils music in her dad's home studio. Sammie returned to campus at the start of the fall semester in 2020, but still had to attend classes virtually.

The pandemic also had a negative impact on Sammie's graduation ceremony. Commencement 2020 was a virtual experience, though in 2021 the University offered an in-person ceremony for the first time since the pandemic started. Sammie returned to Boston for graduation weekend but chose to skip the formal ceremony and just hang out with her close friends/classmates for maybe the last time. She ended up receiving her diploma, quite unceremoniously, through the mail.

---

309   Ibid.

Writing

After graduation, Sammie went to work as a staff writer for Reporter Newspapers in Atlanta, a position she started on February 1, 2021. She covers news stories in the neighborhood of Buckhead as well as the cities of Dunwoody, Sandy Springs, and Brookhaven. This includes a wide range of subjects, from crime, to city council meetings, and the arts. She loves writing the occasional movie review.

As if a position as a journalist doesn't keep her busy enough, Sammie has developed a newsletter that comes out every Friday. It is a free publication in which she reviews movies, television shows, or anything else that is of interest to her. She has entertained thoughts of making the newsletter available by subscription, but hasn't yet decided how she wants to handle that. She continues to enjoy sports and plays on an intramural softball team in the Atlanta Sports and Social league.

Dogs and Other Things

Sammie currently rents an apartment in the Atlanta area, one she shares with her beloved beagle Willie Nelson. Though she is a fan of Willie Nelson the country star, she did not choose that name for her dog. Rather, Willie was named by the Nashville Humane Society when they "rescued" him from a laboratory where he was a subject in experiments testing CDB dog treats. Willie Nelson never had the opportunity to try any of the drug laced treats, though, as he was in the control group that was used to test the flavors of the treats. While at the laboratory, Willie Nelson had a tattoo placed in his right ear identifying him as GZF8. "I think they kept him on a concrete block. He wouldn't even pee on grass when I first got him," she said. "He's a little strange! He was a nightmare for about a year, but has calmed down for the most part. I love him dearly."[310]

Sammie obtained Willie Nelson through a joint adoption event sponsored by the Country Music Awards (CMAs) and MuttNation Foundation, a charitable organization started by dog-lover and country music superstar Miranda Lambert, which explains the dog's "country" name. The two agencies partnered to rescue dogs and find them suitable foster homes. "My friend from work fostered Willie for a couple of weeks before the auction because they didn't have room for every dog at the Humane Society, and that's how I met him,"[311] Sammie said.

Willie Nelson is not Sammie's first dog. When she was around eight years old, her parents brought home Annie, a terrier mix that was the Purcells' first family dog. Everyone loved Annie, and was heartbroken when she passed away. "My mother didn't want to get another dog," Sammie remembered. But that sentiment didn't last too long, and Larrie (a girl dog—hence the "ie") joined the family when Sammie was about 15. "Larrie is about the strangest dog in the world," Sammie said. "She's reluctant to play, doesn't like the dog park, and will go two days without touching her food. But she and Willie love each other and do well together."[312]

---

310   Ibid.
311   Ibid.
312   Ibid.

Chapter 8

MAGGIE
"MEAN MARGARET"
ADAMS

The Early Years

aggie's paternal grandfather, Robert (Bob) Adams, was 27 years old and attending artillery school in Fort Sill, Oklahoma when his wife Lucile gave birth to their only child, Larry, on February 8, 1957.

By the time Larry was born, Bob had already served in the military for six years. He would go on to devote 22 years of his life in service to his country as an Army officer, including a tour in Vietnam. Bob's father and brothers also served in the army—all West Point graduates—so it came as no surprise when Larry followed in his family's footsteps.

Lucile and Bob lived both overseas and in multiple states during his career. Following Bob's retirement from the military in 1973, he accepted a position as personnel manager at George Washington University in Washington D.C. Meanwhile, Lucile worked at Zayre's, a discount department chain

*Maggie's paternal grandparents, Robert (Bob) Adams (L) and
Lucile (Overton) Adams (R) on their wedding day in July 1955.
(Photo courtesy of Larry and Ellen Adams)*

that had a store in the D.C. area utilizing her sewing skills
and serving as a manager in the fabrics department. Later
on, while still in D.C., she accepted a position with the State
Department, assisting foreign service personnel who were
either beginning or ending their duty abroad.

Ellen Watson was born in Morristown, New Jersey, on
August 21, 1960. Larry first met Ellen at the end of 1980,
when she was an undergraduate and he a graduate student at
the College of William and Mary in Williamsburg, Virginia.
"Ellen told a mutual friend that she was interested in me, and
that friend told me," Larry said. "I did eventually ask her out,
but it took a while."[313]

Ellen remembers it differently. "I was getting an under-
grad degree at William and Mary," Ellen said. "Larry was
getting a graduate degree in Business Management at the

---

313   Author interview with Larry Adams. January 6, 2022.

Maggie's maternal grandparents, (R) Harry Watson and (L)
Margaret Fulton Watson, on their wedding day in June 1946.
(Photo courtesy of Larry and Ellen Adams)

same school. I worked part time in the public documents
section of the school library and I controlled access to all the
government documents. Larry came in to request a document and I said something really dumb. I don't recall what
I said, but I know I used a dumb word. We didn't even
exchange names."[314] Despite what she might have said, Larry
took note. "I really didn't need government document help I
just went over to the desk to talk to her,"[315] he said. While he
didn't get her name, he would forever remember those eyes.

Frustrated with the lack of undergraduate dating material,
Ellen and some friends decided to check out the grad students, who they thought would be more mature."We found
out about a party that was at the graduate student center and
that is where we (Larry and I) first met for real," she said. "I
liked him because he didn't have a big ego. He had just come

314   Ibid.
315   Ibid.

out of a relationship and wasn't ready for anything long term or serious. In fact, he even had a list of people he wanted to date before getting serious with anyone."[316]

Not long after she met Larry at the party, Ellen's roommate's grandparents came and took the girls to dinner at the Surry House. On the ferry ride to the restaurant, Ellen saw Larry once more. "This time he was with a girl, and we spied on them," she said. "My roommate's grandparents thought it was hilarious."[317] Larry never noticed Ellen and didn't even know she was on the same boat.

Ellen would encounter Larry a third time at a spring sorority dance. "I'd had a bit too much to drink and told a friend that I wanted Larry to ask me out," she said. "He did, and we ended up dating for the couple of months while we lived in the same city."[318]

Larry graduated in June of 1981 and immediately went into the Army, putting dating Ellen on hold. He moved to Oklahoma where he attended artillery school at Fort Sill, the same post where his father served. His first deployment from artillery school was in Turkey, after which he ended up being stationed at Fort Campbell, Kentucky.

Though unable to date in person, he and Ellen carried on a long-distance relationship over those years. Larry's end of the relationship was exclusive, but Ellen continued to have dates for school dances and the like during her last year of college—an arrangement to which Larry consented. "Fortunately, nothing came of those dates," Larry said. "I proposed to her on my mid-tour leave in the summer of 1982."[319] The two were married on December 18, 1983, and the ceremony was followed by a four-night honeymoon cruise to the Bahamas.

316   Ibid.
317   Author interview with Larry and Ellen Adams, March 29, 2022.
318   Ibid.
319   Author interview with Larry Adams, January 6, 2022.

Larry and Ellen (Watson)
Adams on their wedding day,
December 18, 1983.
(Photo courtesy of Larry and
Ellen Adams)

Larry still had several months remaining in the service, so following the honeymoon he returned to Fort Campbell accompanied by his new bride. The couple took up residence in Clarksville, Tennessee, a border city just two miles from the base. Ellen took a job as a headquarters secretary, a position that required both experience and clearance. Fortunately, Ellen had gained both from a prior position at the Pentagon, a job she held for about a year after college.

After Larry's military service ended in June of 1984, the couple moved to Atlanta. They chose Atlanta because Ellen's sister Carolyn lived there, and because the city had a thriving job market. Larry quickly found work as an underwriter with Allstate Insurance Company. In 1985, the couple purchased a home in Marietta, Georgia. For the next 37 years Larry held many different positions with Allstate before retiring in August of 2021 as a senior compliance analyst/consultant.

Ellen began her new life in Atlanta as a bank secretary, but soon after accepted a position with Sales Technologies, a software company that sold programs meant to improve a company's sales force performance. At some point the company shifted gears and began tailoring their product specifically for pharmaceutical sales and changed the name to Synavant.

Music had always been a big part of both Larry and Ellen's lives. Shortly after moving to Atlanta, the two joined the chancel choir at the First United Methodist Church of Marietta, where they sang for the next several years—Larry, with his strong tenor voice and Ellen with her rich alto.

In January of 1988, Larry and Ellen moved into a new home in the city of Mableton. It was a bit of a trek, but they still continued to sing in the choir at the Methodist Church in Marietta, now about 30 minutes away. Their new home was situated at the entrance to a cul-de-sac and had a big yard. There was only one gnawing problem: it had no basement, just a crawl space under the house.

The Adams Family

On April 5, 1990, the couple had their first child, David Christopher, born at Piedmont Hospital in Atlanta. Three years later, Ellen gave birth to Margaret Christine on September 25, 1993 at Northside Hospital. Like David before her, Maggie brought so much joy to the family. Larry described his daughter as an easy-going baby. "She would just roll with it, you know," he said. "She'd be happy in a jumpy chair for a long while."[320]

Years passed, and though they loved their beautiful house and its big yard, Larry and Ellen wanted a house with a basement where their now teenage children could have their

320   Ibid.

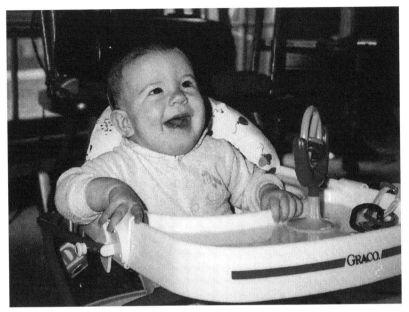

This photo of Maggie was taken on February 5, 1994,
when she was just four and a half months old.
(Photo courtesy of Larry and Ellen Adams)

own space when they had friends over. With that goal in mind, the couple found a house in the same neighborhood and moved into it in 2005. The new home featured four bedrooms and two bathrooms on the second floor, with a family room, den, dining room, and living room on the first. More importantly, it had a fully finished basement with yet another bedroom. The open floor plan of this home, along with its higher ceilings, made it feel much bigger than their previous home. This home was perfect for their growing family.

Unfortunately, after 15 years with Synavant, Ellen was laid off. With time on her hands, she decided to enroll at Georgia State University for a Masters degree in Library and Media Technology. With her advanced degree in hand, Ellen accepted a position as a media specialist in the Cobb County School System in 2004. She later attended the University of

David and Maggie enjoyed taking this Christmas photo circa 1999.
(Photo taken from Larry Adams Facebook page)

West Georgia in Carrolton where she obtained a specialist degree in instructional technology.

Smyrna First United Methodist Church

Having two young children, the couple found it impractical to continue singing in the choir at a church a half an hour away. "We just couldn't get there on time,"[321] Larry said. So, the family began attending services at the First United Methodist Church of Smyrna.

---

321   Ibid.

When they walked into the new church, they were pleasantly surprised to see that Lynn Dee Martin, who had been the assistant choir director and organist at their former church in Marietta, had become the new choir director in Smyrna. When Maggie was about 12, she began taking voice lessons from Lynn Dee and continued to do so for several years.

Larry and Ellen joined multiple choirs at the Smyrna church. They both sang weekly in the Chancel Choir, performing traditional hymns and anthems, often at two services on Sundays. Larry also enjoyed singing (alongside Tim) in the Chamber Choir, which offered a selection of more difficult classical and modern choral music. Larry is also a member of New Praise, a group that performs more contemporary music. He also sings with a men's gospel group called The Jonquil City Boys. Ellen eventually left the Chancel Choir and joined the church's praise team, which is the band that provides music for the contemporary service. This group is led by Amy Wallace, who was also a member of Tim's band The Mustangs (See Chapter 6—Tim Purcell and The Mustangs).

In addition to singing in multiple church choirs, Larry joined the Society for the Preservation and Encouragement of Barbershop Quartet Singing in America, performing with The Marietta Big Chicken Barbershop Chorus. Thankfully, the society in recent years has simplified their name to the Barbershop Harmony Society. Larry was active for about seven years, during which his group won multiple division contests and even sang in international competitions in places such as Calgary, Miami, and Philadelphia. While he was singing with The Marietta Big Chicken Barbershop Chorus, he and three friends formed their own barbershop quartet known as Bad Habits.[322] He eventually gave up singing with that quartet in 1997, as it cost too much money (competition entry fees) and took too much time away from his family. "Like most hobbies, it can become all consuming,"[323] Larry said.

Dogs, Art and Music

For as long as she can remember, Maggie has loved dogs. In fact, her world revolved around them. "I remember, at the age of five, wanting to be a dog, wanting to marry a dog,"[324] she said with a laugh. Her first dog was a schnauzer named Jessie, who she played with in her large, fenced-in backyard. Jessie died when Maggie was about nine years old, prompting her family to bring home Roxy, a black-colored mix. "She was a great dog," Maggie recalled. "The whole family loved her. She died in 2015."[325]

Maggie was so obsessed with dogs that even the walls of her bedroom were painted with a sponge pattern of dog paws and bones. She fondly remembers receiving a big book she refers to as "A Bible of Dog Breeds" when she was just seven years old.

As a young child, Maggie also liked to draw and color,

---

322   The Big Chicken is a Marietta landmark standing 53 feet tall. The structure was originally built in the 1960's to promote S.R. "Tubby Davis's new eatery, *Johnny Reb's Chick, Chuck and Shake restaurant,* the five-story-tall chicken was designed by Hubert Puckett, an architecture student at nearby Georgia Tech and features a moving beak and rotating eyes. The Big Chicken now graces the front of the Kentucky Fried Chicken that replaced Johnny Reb's. Pilots use the Big Chicken as a landmark for navigation and radio stations mention it when describing traffic.

323   Author interview with Larry Adams. January 6, 2022.

324   Ibid.

325   Author interview with Maggie Adams. January 5, 2022.

Maggie with her beloved dog, Jessie, (L) circa 1998-1999 and with her second dog, Roxy, (R) on Christmas day 2008. (Photos courtesy of Larry and Ellen Adams)

an interest she may have acquired from her dad's side of the family. "My grandma on my dad's side was quite artistic," she recalled. "I actually have one of her paintings. It is of a beach sunset scene that she painted from a photograph. It's really gorgeous. My dad was also quite artistic when he was growing up."[326] It should come as no surprise that much of Maggie's own artwork depicted dogs of some sort. "I traced dogs from my dog book and then later drew them from memory,"[327] Maggie said.

She also loved music, a trait that much of her family shared. Lucile Tilghman Overton, Larry's maternal grandmother, may have originated the singing gene so prevalent in the Adams family. "My grandmother had a radio show on which she performed a few times a week," Larry said. "The kids probably got it from her."[328]

Larry and Ellen recall Maggie and David singing in the car on family trips. They would sometimes harmonize together, especially when a song that Maggie liked would

326   Ibid.
327   Ibid.
328   Author interview with Larry Adams. January 6, 2022.

come on the radio—that is, if they weren't wearing their own private headsets. "I would sing around the house," Maggie recalled. "So much that my brother would get annoyed with me because I never remembered the words, so I'd just sing gibberish to whatever melodies I had stuck in my head."[329]

David has a good voice as well and is also a good guitar player. He took piano lessons for about six years in his youth, then picked up an old guitar of Larry's when he was in the eighth grade. In high school, David was in a couple of heavy metal bands, a style of music Maggie referred to as "Screamo."

School--Pre-K Through Junior High

Maggie started Pre-K at Covenant Christian School in Smyrna in 1998, just prior to her fifth birthday. She remained at Covenant Christian through first grade, and in 2001 performed her very first solo as part of the Christmas pageant choir. "I remember being dressed as some farm animal, a donkey or something," Maggie said. "I performed at an early age, and I guess I wasn't afraid of doing it."[330] That lack of fear surprised Maggie's family, as she was a pretty shy kid. "My mom called me 'her little shadow' when I was under ten years old,"[331] Maggie said. "But then you get [older and] a little too cool, you don't even want to be seen with your parents."[332]

In September of 2001, Maggie enrolled in Eastside Christian School in Marietta, where she attended grades two through eight. In seventh grade, she tried out for a part in *The Music Man*. She auditioned for the lead role of Marian

---

329   Author interview with Maggie Adams. January 5, 2022.
330   Ibid.
331   Ibid.
332   Ibid.

Maggie "rocked it" in the lead of Ida in her eighth-grade production of the musical 'Honk Junior'. She is only fourteen and a half in this March 2008 photo. (Photo courtesy of Larry and Ellen Adams)

Paroo, River City's spinster music teacher and town librarian. Unfortunately, lead parts were generally reserved for the older eighth grade students, and a disappointed Maggie did not get the part.

But the following year, when Maggie was finally in the eighth grade, she did land a leading role. That year's musical was called *Honk! Jr.* It was based on Hans Christian Anderson's *The Ugly Duckling,* first published in 1843. "I was the ugly duckling's mother," Maggie said. "While being a mother duck was not the coolest part to have, you know what? I rocked it. Acting, dancing, the whole thing. It was a lot of fun."[333] Ellen noted that though Maggie wanted a part other than the mother duck, the part of Ida fit her perfectly. "When you saw the whole play, you realized, 'Of course she's Ida,'" Ellen said. "It wouldn't have made sense for her to be anything else.'"[334]

---

333 Ibid.
334 Author interview with Larry and Ellen Adams. March 3, 2022.

Family Vacations And A Trip To The ER

Maggie and her family took many vacations while she was growing up. "Mom's side of the family is really big and a lot of them live in San Diego," she said. "We went there every other year. My San Diego cousins were closer in age to me than my Georgia cousins, so I always enjoyed going there. While in San Diego, we went to the world-famous Zoo and Wild Animal Park, which to me, as an animal lover, was amazing."[335]

While Maggie was growing up, her extended family would occasionally vacation in Hilton Head, a beach resort in South Carolina. "Some of my fondest memories are in Hilton Head," she said. "My cousins from Georgia and San Diego would all come. We had a great time."[336]

In addition to all the fun, vacations were a time when Maggie tended to have accidents. "I got hurt on a few vacations," she recalled. "Everyone expected it."[337] While she can remember most all of those mishaps, one incident really stands out in her mind. It happened when she was only five years old. "We were at Folly Beach, outside of Charleston, SC, and a family friend had invited us to their Charleston home on the water that day to go boating," Ellen said. "Larry wasn't there, as he was attending a work-related meeting in another town."[338] While Maggie was playing on their dock, she cut her knee trying to get into the water. Maggie picked up the story from there. "When I was walking back to the house to get a bandage for my knee, I stepped on a rough wooden plank on the dock and got a one-inch splinter in my tiny little foot,"[339] she said.

The thick, sharp splinter was so embedded in Maggie's

335   Author interview with Maggie Adams. January 5, 2022.
336   Ibid.
337   Ibid.
338   Interview with Larry and Ellen Adams. March 3, 2022.
339   Interview with Maggie Adams. January 5, 2022.

Maggie (front center) playing in the semifinal soccer game for Eastside Christian School on their way to a league championship.
(Photo courtesy of Larry and Ellen Adams)

foot that not even her uncle—who is a pediatric pathologist—was able to remove it safely. Maggie was in a great deal of pain. Ellen and her brother-in-law had to take her to the local emergency room where the splinter was removed. The resulting laceration was so large that it required stitches. "I'm not sure my wife has ever forgiven me for missing that traumatic event,"[340] Larry joked. Maggie noted that after that incident, "everyone called me Princess Maggie, which I think [caused] a complex that probably stuck around."[341]

Swimming and Soccer

Maggie always enjoyed swimming and joined the local Smyrna team at a young age. She loved being one of the Smyrna Sharks, as the team was called. She and her brother David participated in the program throughout their childhood

340   Author interview with Larry Adams. January 6, 2022.
341   Interview with Maggie Adams. January 5, 2022.

years, and their parents supported their athletic endeavors. "Ellen, for several years, served as the president of the Smyrna Swim Team, actively recruiting new members and doubling its size by the time she was done,"[342] Larry said.

Maggie followed in her brother's footsteps, playing soccer in the Smyrna recreational league and also at Eastside Christian School. Her team at Eastside Christian even won a championship one of those years, primarily due to the ability of one of Maggie's teammates, Emily Sonnett, who in 2020 played on the U.S. Olympic team. Maggie opted to not participate in high school soccer, choosing instead to swim competitively. She enjoyed the social aspect of sports as much as she did the competition. She just loved being a part of a team.

Church Performances

Maggie and David both participated in God's Light Choir at Smyrna First United Methodist from grades seven through twelve. Every summer, the choir goes on a ten-day tour financed primarily through church fundraisers. Over the years, they've performed in many wonderful places all over the country. Maggie said that going on those trips was her primary reason for joining that choir, as it was for many of the kids.

One of the choir's major fundraisers is called *Love Makes the World Go 'Round*, an annual variety show with songs and skits that takes place on Valentine's Day weekend. Ellen was in charge of that program during the time that David and Maggie were in God's Light, and the siblings performed in the show every year. Maggie was one of Ellen's go-to acts. "I knew I could count on her to pull off a solo,"[343] Ellen recalls. Today,

---

342   Author interview with Larry Adams. January 6, 2022.
343   Author interview with Larry and Ellen Adams. March 3, 2022.

Maggie and David singing a duet (Be Still and Know) during David's last God's Light Choir tour in the summer of 2008. (Photo taken by Dan Henninger and courtesy of Larry & Ellen Adams)

Ellen looks back fondly on those years, even though they were a source of major stress at the time. Every *Love Makes the World Go 'Round* show is theme based—one year it's Disney, one year it's country, another year is Broadway, another is movies, and so on. Ellen warmly remembers the Disney year. "Maggie sang the song *Part of Your World* from *The Little Mermaid*," Ellen said. "It's one of my favorite performances. She was so cute in it and just knocked it out of the park."[344]

As mentioned before, Maggie was more focused on the trip than the fundraisers. "Two busses filled with kids traveling to places to which they might otherwise never go,"[345] Maggie said. On her first choir tour in 2007, she went to the Grand Canyon, where God's Light performed a couple of songs right beside the huge natural wonder. Other tours traveled to South Dakota, Washington DC, and New Orleans, Louisiana. On their trip to Niagara Falls the group also visits New York City. Early one morning on Maggie's trip to NYC with the choir, they all went to Rockefeller Plaza and joined the 'outside audience' for *The Today Show*. That was

---

344   Ibid.
345   Interview with Maggie Adams. January 5, 2022.

the year when Roberta—Terry Heinlein's wife- was selected from the crowd for a complete make-over and actually made an appearance on the show!

On the tour, God's Light sang at numerous churches. Maggie recalled one year when the choir made a stop at a predominantly Black church. "It was much more soulful than the churches we were used to," Maggie said. "We got a lot of feedback and shouts of praise from the crowd. It's a much better response than the polite clapping we were used to. I sang a solo and got some of that feedback. It was one of the coolest experiences."[346]

High School

Maggie and David both attended Campbell High School in Smyrna. Maggie was a very good student, and was in the same magnet program as Sammie. "I was in the International Baccalaureate Program (IB) in high school," She said. "It's an international program with the same curriculum in every country. It is a pretty prestigious program in high schools, and I graduated with the IB diploma."

While a good student, Maggie admits that her grades basically correlated to how much she cared in any particular class. "My brother had to get all As to get into the Air Force Academy, which he knew he wanted from a young age," Maggie said. "It was very important to him. My social life was more important to me. I had a lot of different interests, and I wasn't going to focus only on academics to try and get straight As. I really didn't need to or want to. I always tried to do my best, but I had a tendency to procrastinate."[347]

Maggie really enjoyed IB Art class, where in their last

346   Author interview with Maggie Adams. January 5, 2022.
347   Ibid.

The God's Light Choir taken on one of their tour stops in Jasper, GA on August 18, 2012. Maggie is standing third from the left.
(Photo taken from Larry Adams Facebook page)

David (center), Maggie (behind David to the left) and Sammie (behind David to the right) on the Jumbotron when God's Light Youth choir sang the National Anthem at the Atlanta Braves baseball game in June 2008.
(Photo courtesy of Larry and Ellen Adams)

two years students get to pick a particular area of interest to explore artistically. "Mine was how war was influenced by music and vice versa," she said. "My family was a big military family and my brother had just entered the Air Force Academy."[348] As a result, Maggie produced a lot of art with darker themes. The course was under the direction of Mr. Ross, and Maggie got a score of six out of seven on her final IB Art exam. "That's something I was really proud of,"[349] Maggie said. Maggie's favorite courses of study were English and Spanish. She received a seven on her IB Spanish exam, and could speak it fluently in high school. She still raves about her Spanish teacher, Melyn Roberson, and her English teacher, Max Jones.

While still in high school, Maggie had the opportunity to sing at Carnegie Hall as part of The American High School Honors Performance Series. For that program, high schoolers from the US and Canada learn the parts to several songs over the summer and then come together for one week to practice and perform. Maggie took the world-famous stage on Saturday, June 26, 2010 at 8 p.m. She was beyond excited. "I now know that anyone can sing at Carnegie Hall if they pay for it, but at the time I didn't know that," Maggie joked. "It was a great experience."[350]

The trip was not without its problems, however. "I did get in a little trouble on that trip," Maggie admitted. "I was caught being in another person's room beyond the curfew. I was such a social butterfly that I wanted to hang out with my friends longer. They [the program officials] called my parents but they brushed it off knowing that I wouldn't do anything I wasn't supposed to."

348   Ibid.
349   Ibid.
350   Ibid.

Ellen (L) and Larry (R) celebrating Maggie's seventeenth
birthday in Panama City in September 2010.
(Photo courtesy of Ellen and Larry Adams)

Maggie had always been a social butterfly—sometimes getting her into a bit of trouble. "I did get into trouble with my
parents for attending a few of the wilder parties in high school,"
she said. "But overall, I think I was a healthy balance of chal-
lenging and good for my parents. I was more of a challenge
than my brother I think, but I turned out okay. I never let my
'butterflying' get in the way of things that were important,
like school and general well-being, but I wasn't perfect."[351]

To reinforce the point, Maggie offered another example. "There was one time when I was so looking forward to
going to a concert by the pop-punk band Say Anything," she
said. "But, I got in trouble for attending a party that I wasn't

---

351   Ibid.

supposed to, and my parents took away my concert tickets. I was really sad about it."[352]

Larry confirmed Maggie's status as a social butterfly. "She made friends easily and had a lot of them," he said. "Her high school friends are spread all over, but she still gets together with them every now and then."[353]

With all these things going on, Maggie still didn't lose sight of her interest in music or in bands. "I was obsessed with a band called My Chemical Romance," she said. "They were like my NSYNC. I had posters in my room which are still there. My room is frozen in time from when I was 16. I cleaned out some stuff, but the posters are still on the walls. I was just boy crazy, and the lead singer was really cute."[354]

Maggie wasn't as active in the musical theater scene as Sammie was, but she did participate in *The Wedding Singer* alongside Sammie in her sophomore year. She also participated in Campbell Idol a couple of times, the school's version of the popular reality show *American Idol.* In Maggie's senior year she lost to Sammie, who was a junior. Sammie may have had a slight advantage, however. Both Larry and Ellen noted that the performers had to provide their own accompaniment. "Sammie had Tim provide a great accompaniment while Maggie had to download something off YouTube,"[355] they both recalled. Regardless of the accompaniment, Ellen quickly added, "Maggie's choice of song wasn't that great, and she wasn't too comfortable on stage. Overall, it wasn't her best performance."[356]

---

352   Ibid.
353   Author interview with Larry & Ellen Adams. March 29, 2022.
354   Author interview with Maggie Adams. January 5, 2022.
355   Interview with Larry & Ellen Adams. March 29, 2022.
356   Ibid.

Joining Foxes and Fossils

Maggie always wanted to be part of a band, but never really thought about starting one of her own. But then, an opportunity arose in January of 2010, while she was still just a junior in high school. The memory of how Tim asked her to join his new band is foggy, but she does remember being excited about it. "I thought, 'This sounds fun. Cool. Of course I'll do it,'"[357] she said.

Larry, who knew Tim from singing with him in the SFUMC Chamber Choir, said that Tim had always complimented Maggie whenever she had a solo. Still, he was surprised when Tim called him. "He said he was trying to formulate a plan for a new band," Larry explained. "He initially wanted to find three girls."[358] Tim already had Sammie on board and wanted to ask Larry if he wouldn't mind if Maggie joined too. Larry thought it would be a great opportunity for Maggie, and Ellen agreed. "Holy Moly, this child was born under a lucky star," Ellen remembers thinking. "For something like that to just fall into your lap is just mind-blowing to me. I thought it was a great opportunity for her though she may have been too young to really understand that."[359]

In early February of 2010, they began to rehearse a few songs together in Tim's studio. A few weeks later, Tim, the girls, Tim's friend Darwin Conort, and fellow Mustang Scott King, appeared at a pizzeria called Bella's for what would be the first of many Foxes and Fossils performances.

Maggie joined the band for live performances from 2010-2012 before going off to Belmont University in Nashville,

---

357   Interview with Maggie Adams. January 5, 2022, and written comments provided to the author. May 13, 2022.

358   Interview with Larry & Ellen Adams. March 29, 2022.

359   Interview with Larry & Ellen Adams. March 29, 2022.

Tennessee. She would commute back to Georgia during the summer months of her first two years of college to join the band for live shows, but by the end of the summer of 2014 she found it increasingly hard to get away. That basically ended her tenure as the band's elder Fox.

Trying Out For The Voice

In the fall of 2011, Maggie and Sammie tried out for a spot on the popular television show, *The Voice*, which was holding auditions in Atlanta. "When Sammie and I got the opportunity to try out for *The Voice*, I was filled with hope, nerves, and excitement," she said. "We auditioned separately, but looking back, we might have had a better chance doing it together. It was still early in the show's lifespan and I don't think we knew we were allowed to audition as a duo."[360]

A friend of Maggie's dad had a connection to someone on the show and was able to get Maggie and Sammie a pass allowing them to skip the first audition. "That's the one (the first audition) where you have to wait in line for hours and sleep over,"[361] Larry said. The girls, at the second level, had a scheduled appointment for their audition.

"I walked into a large room with a long table of judges." Maggie recalled. "I don't remember who they were, but they were not the ones on the TV show."[362] There were test cameras filming her performance to see what she looked like on camera. Maggie chose to sing *Thinking of You* by Katy Perry. "I don't remember if I sang the whole song or got stopped

---

360   Written comments provided to the author by Maggie Adams. May 13, 2022.

361   Interview with Larry & Ellen Adams. March 29, 2022.

362   Written comments provided to the author by Maggie Adams. May 13, 2022.

part of the way through," she said. She also doesn't recall the judges' reactions. Tim and Larry accompanied the girls on the trip, but were not allowed to go in the audition room. However, they could hear the girls singing from outside the room.

The judges were very positive and said great things about the girls, but neither of them was selected. Maggie does not regret the experience. "I was glad I did it, regardless of the outcome," she said. "I have always had a terrible time with song choice when it comes to auditions. I don't think my choice here helped me."[363]

Searching For The Right College

Maggie had always intended to attend the University of Georgia, until she discovered Belmont University in Nashville. After doing some research, she decided that if she really wanted a career in music, Belmont—and Nashville—was the place to be. After touring the campus with her parents, she decided Belmont was the right fit. She enrolled in the fall of 2012.

"I found out about Belmont University from my dad," Maggie remembered. "I wanted to go to UGA and I was accepted there. Instead, I went to Belmont, initially majoring in commercial voice, but switching halfway through to entertainment industry studies. I also minored in classical voice."[364] Maggie changed her major after deciding that she didn't want to spend her life doing the constant self-promotion that's required of a singer. "It's difficult to make it as a singer," Larry said. "I think she made a wise decision."[365]

363   Ibid.
364   Ibid.
365   Interview with Larry & Ellen Adams. March 29, 2022.

One requirement of commercial voice majors at Belmont is to perform in choruses, said Larry and Ellen who attended two of Maggie's performances. "There's a big show at Christmas they do every year," Ellen said. "It actually is aired on public television and parents are invited to attend the taping."[366] "There were so many different musical groups at Belmont and each group sang a couple of songs. Maggie was in this ginormous women's chorus," Larry said. "They were great!"[367] Even after changing her major, Maggie continued to perform in shows.

When Maggie enrolled at the university, she had already made the decision to immerse herself fully in the college experience. Like most college students she was excited to explore her new-found freedom. For Maggie, that meant remaining in Nashville during the summer months. "It's the city that I love, surrounded by music and people that inspire me," she explained. "Moving back home felt like stifling my newfound independence. I had opportunities to intern, work, and grow in new ways in Nashville that I would not have back home."[368] Of course, remaining in Nashville for the summers required a seven-hour round-trip commute every time Foxes and Fossils had a gig. During the summer of 2013, Maggie made that commute a total of six times.

By the summer of 2014, the time and expense of joining the band for summer gigs began to take its toll. Mindful of the burden on Maggie, Tim only booked three shows that year. It just wasn't right to ask her to drive eight hours for $50. It seemed like F and F was at an end. That winter, however, Tim and Scott figured out a way to save the band and

366 Ibid.
367 Ibid.
368 Written comments provided to the author by Maggie Adams. May 13, 2022.

in the process open up a new world of possibilities and insure a bright future for Foxes and Fossils.

For her part, Maggie never envisioned Foxes and Fossils as a long-term commitment. "I was excited about tapping into new realms of possibilities with music," she said. "I felt like my time with Foxes and Fossils had come to a natural and amicable end. I enjoyed it when I was involved, but the travel back and forth from Atlanta to Nashville was not worth it when I felt at the time like I could explore other avenues of music-making in Nashville."[369]

Larry, while supporting Maggie's decision, really missed hearing her sing. "That's why I was so happy when she and Tim revived Foxes and Fossils in the studio, because it gives her that place to sing,"[370] he said.

Olivia Management

Maggie managed to graduate from Belmont a semester early thanks to credits she was awarded for courses she completed in IB during high school. She received her degree in December 2016. The following month she began work as a paid intern at The Nashville Entrepreneur Center, and then nine months later landed her first real full-time position with Olivia Management, an artist management and consulting company based in Nashville. The company, owned by Belmont grad Erin Anderson, hired Maggie as its first full-time employee. Maggie was an assistant, and her duties ranged from booking flights for artists' tours, to ordering merchandise, to resolving a myriad of problems that came out of nowhere—often with little direction and very little lead time. "That's the nature of

369   Ibid.
370   Interview with Larry & Ellen Adams. March 29, 2022.

Maggie and Lucile Adams, her paternal grandmother, celebrated Maggie's graduation from Belmont University in December 2016. (Photo courtesy of Larry & Ellen Adams)

artist management," Maggie said. "And part of the reason why it was exciting."[371] Maggie gravitated toward the marketing side of the job, which called for more creativity. Her responsibilities in this area included managing social media, creating marketing campaigns for tours, albums, crowdfunding, and more. "I even got to try my hand at signing and managing my own artists, which gave me a lot more respect for artist managers," she said. "It's an all-consuming job."[372]

Maggie had the opportunity to manage tours for several acts, including The Secret Sisters when they played at two Austin festivals—SXSW and Willie Nelson's festival, Luck Reunion—in 2017. In 2018, the Secret Sisters' album, *You Don't Own Me Anymore*, was nominated for a Grammy as Best Folk Album of the Year, and Maggie accompanied Erin to the awards ceremony.

Maggie looks back with fondness at her time at Olivia

---

371   Written comments provided to the author by Maggie Adams. May 13, 2022.

372   Ibid.

Management. "I'm so glad I did that, it was a great experience overall. It led me to realize that what I enjoyed most was marketing," she noted. "I started to focus mostly on tour marketing, and that is when I began to think it might be fun to expand my horizons in that area."[373]

From that point, Maggie kept her eyes open for other positions in Nashville that would better utilize her marketing skills. She discovered that Basement East, a well-known venue in Nashville, was hiring a marketing manager. She applied for the position and was hired. "Erin (Olivia Management) was a wonderful role model and mentor," Maggie said, "I learned so much from her about the music industry; hard work, dedication, boundaries, and the subtle nuances of artist management."[374]

Basement East

Dave Brown and Mike Grimes opened Basement East in 2015, following the success of their other club, The Basement. On March 3, 2020, a massive tornado hit the Basement East and nearly destroyed the entire building. The venue re-opened in the spring of 2021.

Maggie joined the Basement East team as the marketing manager just a few months later in June 2021. According to Maggie, Basement East is synonymous with community. "There's something about it that draws you in, and makes you feel like family," she said. "Artists of all genres play there, and I knew that if I worked there, I'd have the chance to work with and see all kinds of artists. I've always loved seeing live music, and Basement East felt like the perfect place for me to lean into that."[375]

---

373   Ibid.
374   Ibid.
375   Ibid.

The photo (top) was taken of the Adams family in Nashville in 2017 (L-R) David, Larry, Ellen and Maggie. The two photos below were taken on a family trip to Israel in 2018. On the right, Maggie and her dad are posing under a Roman Aqueduct. On the left, Maggie is enjoying a ride on a camel.
(Photos courtesy of Larry & Ellen Adams)

Maggie's Road To Forever

It is often said that to a dad, no boy is ever good enough for his daughter. There may have been some truth to that sentiment with regard to Maggie's high school and college boyfriends. "There was one we loved and some not so much,"[376] Larry admitted.

Then Maggie met Luke Preston. They knew each other from Belmont and had mutual friends, but never really ended

376 Author interview with Larry & Ellen Adams. March 29, 2022.

up in the same place at the same time. "We began to run in closer circles after we graduated in December of 2015, and we would see each other more regularly through mutual friends while at music festivals and concerts,"[377] she said. They saw each other at the Pilgrimage Festival in Franklin, TN while they were both celebrating their birthdays (Maggie's is September 25 and Luke's is September 26), and then again at Bonnaroo in June of 2016. At Bonnaroo, Maggie started to take notice of how funny and handsome she thought Luke was. Then the two bumped into each other again in August of 2016 at Live on the Green in Nashville. "That was when the spark started," Maggie said. "We bonded over mutual musical heroes at a bar afterwards."[378]

Maggie and Luke began dating in early 2017 and have been together ever since. Larry and Ellen really liked Luke and were very welcoming of him in their home. In 2020 when he couldn't go home for Christmas due to the COVID-19 pandemic, Ellen hung a Christmas stocking for him and treated him like one of her kids. She didn't want him to feel that he was anything less.

After a few years of dating, Ellen sensed that Maggie and Luke might be headed toward engagement, but Maggie was never one to let on. "I once asked her,'" Ellen said, "'Is he your forever guy?' She said, 'Oh, probably, I don't know.'"[379]

It was Luke who would offer a more telling response to that question when he approached Larry and Ellen to ask their permission to marry Maggie. "I jumped up and down for about 30 seconds," Ellen said. "Luke treats Maggie well and is so respectful of her."[380] Larry went down to the base-

377   Written comments provided to the author by Maggie Adams. May 13, 2022.
378   Ibid.
379   Ibid.
380   Author interview with Larry & Ellen Adams. March 22, 2022.

ment and grabbed two diamond rings that belonged to his mom. "I said, 'Luke, here are two diamond rings,'" he said. "If you want, you can pick one to give Maggie, if not, that is okay too."[381] Luke was blown away by the offer. He was prepared to purchase one, but thought this was so much cooler. He picked the two-carat ring and had it cleaned and sized.

Over the years, Luke got much more comfortable with Maggie's family. "He was awkward around us at first," Ellen said. "He would give me a side hug, but one day, I told him I wanted a full-on hug. Now he does that."[382] Sometimes, Luke will even stay with Ellen and Larry while Maggie goes to Tim's house for a recording session.

Luke carefully planned every detail of the proposal. He first determined which dates his and Maggie's family were available to join them in Nashville. He arranged with a friend who owned Pearl Diver, Maggie's favorite bar, to close the facility from 5-7 p.m. to set the scene. He also invited Maggie's closest friends to join in. Finally, he planned his ruse to get Maggie to the bar. He told her that her friends, Sarah and Alic, were in Nashville for a private event. Luke and Maggie planned to meet them at Pearl Diver around 5. He recruited another one of her friends to take her for a manicure, so that her hand would be ready for the pictures of the engagement ring. To avoid tipping her off, that friend made up a story about receiving a gift certificate to a nail salon, and that she had enough credit on it to treat a friend as well. "I felt honored to be the chosen friend to receive a free manicure,"[383] recalls Maggie. The stage was set.

Luke and Maggie entered the alcove of the pub, where,

381   Ibid.
382   Ibid.
383   Written comments provided to the author by Maggie Adams. May 13, 2022.

Luke proposed to Maggie at the Pearl Diver on December 5, 2021.
She said YES! The magic moment was captured by one of Luke's
friends and fellow songwriters, Jon Sherwood.
(Photo taken from the Foxes and Fossils fan page)

getting down on one knee, Luke asked Maggie to spend forever with him. A three-piece string band—featuring Lydia
Luce, one of the artists that Maggie worked with at Olivia
Management—played *In My Life,* Luke and Maggie's favorite
Beatles song. Maggie enthusiastically said yes. The couple
then turned the corner into the pub where Maggie, for the
first time, saw her family, friends and future in-laws. Someone asked Luke what she said, to which Maggie yelled, "I
said YES!" She was over the moon.

Maggie posted a video to Instagram in which she described
the evening. "I was so happy my family and friends could be
there," she said in a video. "The whole bar was decorated
for Christmas. It was so beautiful, and so overwhelming, so
perfect."[384]

---

384   Ibid.

When the couple arrived home, they found that their apartment had lost power. Naturally, the rest of the evening was spent by candlelight, providing a most romantic ending to a perfect night.

The Couple's First Dog

Any relationship involving Maggie would be incomplete without a dog. "My fiancé and I got our first dog, Emmylou, in July of 2020 during the pandemic," she said. "She is a German shepherd, golden retriever, lab, pointer and pit bull mix. She is a smart, energetic dog, to say the least. We didn't know what we were getting ourselves into. She is a very good girl, very alert. A lot of the German Shepherd shows, and she barks a lot at other dogs out the window."[385]

---

385   Ibid.

Chapter 9

CHASE
"THE FREAK"
TRURAN

A Rich Family History Of Musical Talent

Scott Truran was born to Allen George Truran and Lois May (Kiligas) Truran in Pittsfield, Massachusetts on March 2, 1961. He had two older half-sisters named Wendy and Lauren. Both were Lois' children from a previous marriage to Adolf Von Ulrich, which ended in 1953.

Both of Scott's parents were entertainers. Allen (Al) was the band leader for Al Truran & His Orchestra, a 17-piece unit that played throughout New England. Lois was a Broadway and Off-Broadway star who performed under the stage name Karyl Stewart. Her many musical performances included the Broadway shows *Call Me Mister* and *Song of Norway*. She also sang with the big bands of Art Mooney, Henry Jerome, and Hal McIntyre.

Even the greats have to start at the bottom, and according to Scott, his mom was no different. "Before she made it on

Lois May Kiligas Truran,
Chase's paternal grandmother
(Photo courtesy of Scott &
Karon Truran)

Broadway, when she was in her early teens, she performed at a radio station in Pittsfield, Massachusetts and was paid in doughnuts," he said with a laugh. "It was like, 'Can I get money?' 'No, we pay in doughnuts.'"[386]

Mel Torme And Lois's First Big Entrance

At the beginning of her Broadway career, Lois met Mel Torme, one of her musical idols, in an unusual way. It was the late 1940s and she had just arrived in New York. Before she could perform, she needed to pick up her Broadway credentials from The Actor's Equity Association, the union that represents Broadway performers.

---

386   Author Interview with Scott and Karon Truran. March 17, 2022.

Lois and Al Truran
(Photo courtesy of Scott and Karon Truran)

When she arrived at the union building, she pushed the heavy shining door with significant force, accidentally knocking the person who stood on the other side to the ground. Much to her horror, the man that she had pushed over was Mel Torme. He had a large scratch on the side of his face, and Lois apologized profusely as his attendants helped him stand up. She told him she was a huge fan, and Torme—ever gracious—told her it was alright, and even took the blame for not paying attention to where he was going. The two got to talking, and Lois explained that she was just starting out on Broadway. Torme responded by offering her tickets to his show.

A few years later, while at home in Massachusetts, Lois met big band leader Al Truran. Al needed a vocalist and asked Lois if she'd consider singing for his band. Lois, however, was devoted to Broadway and had no desire to leave the stage for a band gig. But Al was persistent, and finally Lois agreed to give it a try. She couldn't know it at the time, but joining Al's band would start a relationship that would lead to the couple's marriage in 1955.

A few years later, Al took Lois to New York to celebrate their anniversary. They were eating at a very nice restaurant when Mel Torme and his entourage walked in and took a table not too far away. Al told Lois how much he loved Mel Torme and how cool it would be to meet him. Lois replied by telling Al the story about knocking Torme to the ground, and then had an idea. She wrote a note: "The girl who knocked you on your keister in the Union Building is sitting in the next booth, and would love to have her husband meet you."[387] She asked a waiter to deliver the note to Torme. When Torme read the note, he waved Lois over to his table, giving Al the opportunity to meet one of his favorite singers.

Al Truran & His Orchestra

Lois might have been the Broadway star, but Al had quite a range of musical talent as well. He played saxophone, acoustic bass, and keyboards in his band. Scott recalled one of the many funny stories his dad told him about those days on the road. "After traveling about six hours in a bus with 17 guys, the acoustic bass player (not Al on this occasion) realized that he had forgotten his instrument," Scott said. "'How the hell can you forget a standup bass?' Al asked him. 'It's as big as the bus!' So, dad had to contact the local high school and borrow a bass."[388]

Scott recounted a story about another gig that almost ended in disaster. "His (Al's) drummer got so drunk in the

387 Ibid.
388 Ibid.

*Promotional posters for Al Truran and His Orchestra led by
Scott's father, Allen (left) and Karyl Stewart and Her Orchestra
led by Scott's mother, Lois, under her stage name (right)
(Photos courtesy of Scott and Karon Truran)*

first set that he was playing all over the place, and at the break
he ended up passing out in the bushes," Scott said. "Luckily,
the drummer from Elliott Lawrence's big band happened to
be in attendance and offered to fill in. He ended up playing the remainder of the show. After the show, the wife of
the inebriated drummer went up to my dad and asked for
his check. My dad said, 'I'm not giving him a check. He's
throwing up in the bushes. He's not getting a check!'"[389]

Moving South to Florida

The Truran family moved to Sarasota, Florida in 1968
when Scott was just seven. After suffering through several

---

389   Ibid.

New England winters, Al had decided to move south. "You don't have to shovel rain,"[390] Scott recalled his dad saying with a smile.

In Florida, Al and Lois became realtors. They still dabbled in music, with Lois performing in plays at the local theater and Al continuing to diddle around with the saxophone, bass, and keyboards. But the days of touring were over.

Scott Truran The Drummer

That same year, young Scott decided that he wanted to play drums. "My first drum teacher was Maurice Purtill, Glenn Miller's original drummer," Scott said. "He would come to my house every Friday to give me lessons and would tell story after story."[391] Scott turned out to be somewhat of a prodigy. Through his parents' connections, he met legends like Count Basie, Duke Ellington, and so many others. In his youth, Scott played gigs with the likes of Eartha Kitt and Canadian jazz trumpeter and band leader Maynard Ferguson.[392]

By the time he was 12 years old, Scott had become a member of the musician's union and was quickly called up to play his first club gig. When the owner of the club saw Al carrying Scott's drums inside, he naturally assumed Al was the drummer they had hired. Imagine their surprise when Al said, "No, it's my kid." It was a jazz gig—right in young Scott's wheelhouse. After a fantastic performance that night, the band hired Scott as their regular drummer.

In 1979, Scott received a prestigious jazz award, presented to him by Louis Armstrong's widow, and in 1980 he got

390   Ibid.
391   Ibid.
392   Ibid.

*Scott Truran at age 18 playing drums at the Sarasota Jazz Festival in Sarasota,
Florida. On the right is a photo of Scott that same year receiving a jazz award
from Lucille Armstrong.
(Photo courtesy of Chase Truran)*

a recording contract with American Sound Records out of
Nashville. He was also a songwriter. That same year, Bill-
board magazine's "Deejay's Picks" had Scott's novelty blues
song, *You're so Ugly Baby*, at number seven, right behind
Diana Ross' hit song *I'm Coming Out.*

An Inauspicious Encounter with Karon

Alva Davis enlisted in the U.S. Air Force at the age of
17. At the age of 19, he married telephone operator Betty
Tucker. Four years later while Alva was stationed in Tampa,
Florida, Betty gave birth to their first daughter, Kellie, on
March 22, 1961. Less than a year later, after they were trans-
ferred to a small radar base in Aiken, South Carolina, middle

daughter Karon (pronounced KAY-ron) was born on March 19, 1962.

The couple was again transferred, this time to Anchorage, Alaska, where on February 1, 1965 their youngest child, Lonna, was born. Two more transfers were in the couple's future. Alva and his family moved to Biloxi, Mississippi, where he was stationed for about five years, and finally to Eglin Air Force Base in Florida. He retired from the military in 1975 and moved his family south to Naples, Florida, where Karon and her two sisters sang in their high school chorus.

Much like Scott, Karon hails from a musical family. Her paternal grandfather, three uncles, and one aunt all played the guitar—her grandfather, who was left-handed, had to flip his guitar over and play it upside down. Most of her father's nine brothers and sisters grew up singing in church in Mobile, Alabama. Karon's mother Betty and her Aunt Lyda would act in plays and sing duets in school and church.

Karon first met Scott toward the end of October 1986 when he was performing with his band, Midnite Flite, at a club called The Witch's Brew in Naples. Karon was there with her sister Lonna and their dad "Mr. Smooth came out with a wireless mic, singing to the audience around the tables,"[393] Karon remembered. Scott was singing *One in a Million,* by Larry Graham.

"That's when I noticed Karon," Scott said. "I walked out to the table at the break, and I said, 'Sir, I don't know which of these young ladies you're with, but I hope it was okay that I came out and sang to them.' Her father replied sternly, 'I'm with BOTH of them—they're my daughters.' I thought,'Well, this has gotten off to a great start.'" [394] Despite the initial awkwardness, "We hit it off right away. I remember

393   Ibid.
394   Ibid.

The photo on the left is of Karon's dad, Alva Davis. On the right is Karon's mom, Betty (Tucker) Davis. Below is the couple on their wedding day— August 29, 1957.

The extended families (left) Scott's sisters Lauren Truran and Wendy Truran posing with Scott. (Right) Karon's sisters, Lonna Cooper (left of photo), Kellie Priller (middle) and Karon (right) (Photo courtesy of Scott and Karon Truran)

thinking he was so straight laced," Karon said. "He would be perfect if he were just a little funny!"[395]

Ironically, Scott WAS funny. In fact, he had performed as a stand-up comedian doing musical comedy impression in shows on Royal Caribbean Cruises. Scott said that the night he and Karon met, he was trying to put on a different, more serious persona. Luckily, Karon saw right through it. From that day on, she asked everyone and anyone to go to The Witch's Brew with her so she could see Scott again.

Karon attended the University of South Florida where she received her associate of Arts degree. While at the School of Nursing, she took a summer job with a physical therapist and loved it so much that she changed her major from nursing to physical therapy. She was working on a bachelors degree in

---

395   Ibid.

Promotional photo of Scott's band,
Midnite Flite, circa late 1980s. (Photo
courtesy of Scott and Karon Truran)

Health Sciences at the University of Florida. After meeting
Scott, she changed her plans. "I thought, 'we have a great
relationship, so we probably need to stay together'," Karon
said. "So I withdrew from school and went on the road with
him in December 1986. My dad wasn't too pleased with me
at that point, but I think he's happy with my choice now."[396]
Scott's recurring gig with Royal Caribbean Cruises posed
one potential problem for Karon—she couldn't accompany
him on the ship unless she was a member of the band. "Do
you think you could learn the bass parts to the songs?"[397]
Scott asked her. She said she'd try, and after a few sessions
with the band's keyboard player, she had learned an entire
set. "I would play the bass parts, and sing a couple of songs,"
she said. "We had another female vocalist at that time, but
the following year she quit the band and I started singing all

396   Ibid.
397   Ibid.

*Scott and Karon (left photo) performed together from 1986
to 1995 aboard the Royal Caribbean Cruise Ships. They are
pictured here with their band circa 1990s. The photo on the right
is Karon circa 1995 at 33 years old.
(Photo courtesy Scott and Karon Truran)*

the female leads. All my hard work paid off as we were able
to travel together for many years doing what we loved."[398]

The band alternated between the cruise gigs and land
gigs, just to get a break from the water and the tight accommodations aboard the ship. "We had a blast on the cruises,"
Scott said. "We played only 13 hours a week."[399] Karon said
the rest of their time was spent scuba diving, playing golf,
eating at the ship's buffets, or gambling in the casino. "We
had a great life!"[400] she said.

---

398   Ibid.
399   Ibid.
400   Ibid.

*Scott and Karon on their wedding day in June of 1997
(Photos courtesy of Scott and Karon Truran)*

Life Off the Road

But nothing lasts forever. In 1995, Scott and Karon decided it was time to settle down and have a family. They got off the road and moved to Woodstock, Georgia, where they opened a restaurant called The Countryside Café with another couple with whom they were friends. The café featured creative American cuisine. The husband of the couple was an outstanding chef and his wife helped out in the kitchen. "They said to us, 'We'll be the kitchen people and you can be the front of the house people,'"[401] Scott said. The Trurans remained with the restaurant until 1996, when they finally decided to leave their crazy schedule behind. "We were used to working 13 hours a week on the ships, and in the restaurant business we were working 13 hours a day,"[402] Karon said.

---

401   Ibid.
402   Ibid.

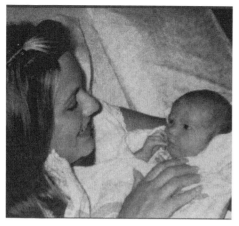

(L) Karon and Chase on the day of Chase's birth in August 1999
(Photo courtesy of Scott and Karon Truran)

On June 14, 1997, Scott and Karon were married at Kennesaw Mountain Vineyard in Kennesaw, Georgia. The couple took a one-week honeymoon in Blue Ridge, Georgia at a mountain cabin retreat, and purchased their first home in Woodstock later that year. Their first child, Chase Truran, was born on August 12, 1999. Two years later, their family was completed with the birth of another daughter, Kennedy Truran, a special needs child born with DYRK1A (deletion) Syndrome, on August 17, 2001.

Raising Chase

According to Karon, Chase was always very smart for her age. When Karon went into pre-term labor with Kennedy, Chase was just about a year and a half. "[She] stood in the hallway of the hospital with her dad when a nurse wandered by and said to her, 'Oh, how are you today,'" Karon recalled. "Chase looked at her without responding, prompting the nurse to ask Scott if she could talk yet, to which Chase responded, 'Actually, I'm absolutely phenomenal!'"[403]

Scott and Karon would continue to catch glimpses of Chase's talents. One such sign came as she was approaching her second birthday. In those early days, they would often read books to Chase, an activity the family treasured. They soon realized that Chase didn't just enjoy books, but could memorize the exact wording on every single page, even in the case of fairly complex children's books like *The Monster Who Ate My Peas*. "If I skipped over even one page of the book, Chase would scrunch up her face, and say, 'That's NOT right!'"[404] Karon added with a chuckle.

Chase's remarkable memory was on display when it came to music as well. When she heard a song on the radio, she would seem to instantly learn the entire arrangement, melody, and lyrics, even though she had heard them only once or twice. In the car with Karon, Chase would always ask to hear the instrumental *Frankenstein* by The Edgar Winter Band. Upon hearing the song, she would mimic the drum interlude with her body motions. She would start and stop with incredible precision. "She seemed to know the entire arrangement of the song at only 18 months old," Karon said. "Chase simply had an innate sense of rhythm and arrangement."[405]

While Chase doesn't recall jamming out to *Frankenstein* in her car seat, her clearest early childhood memory of singing is from when she was maybe five years old. "I was in the bathtub, and I started singing *Tomorrow* from the musical *Annie*," she said. "I really belted out the last note, and my mother came running into the bathroom."[406] "I couldn't believe what

---

403   Ibid.
404   Ibid.
405   Ibid.
406   Author interview with Chase Truran. March 30, 2022.

A family photo of Karon, Scott and one year old Chase circa 2000
(left) and a photo of two-year-old Chase with her sister Kennedy
(right side of photo at left) in Spring 2002
(Photos courtesy of Scott and Karon Truran)

I heard," said Karon. "I asked, 'Chase, was that you?' She held the last note and had this great vibrato."[407]

"That's when I realized I must have done something special," Chase said, "[My mother] was making such a big thing of it. I remember smiling from ear to ear and experiencing a sense of wonder in that moment."[408]

Karon knew that she somehow had to channel Chase's talent. "There was a community theater called Clubhouse Kids where the children performed original musicals,"[409] Chase said. She signed Chase up immediately. In her first play, Chase performed two solos, one of which she got because she was the only child who could memorize the melody and lyrics. At only six years old, she was one of the youngest kids,

407   Author interview with Scott & Karon Truran. March 17, 2022.
408   Author interview with Chase Truran. March 30, 2022.
409   Ibid.

(Left) Chase posing with her preschool class—she's the sassy one with her hand on her hip. Photo to the right is Chase at her preschool graduation ceremony in May 2004 (Photos courtesy of Scott and Karon Truran)

but she was so tall that nearly everyone thought she was eight or nine. Chase has clear memories of this experience. "Clubhouse Kids performed all original songs in their productions," she said. "One of my first solos was a song called *Don't Try and Pin Your Feathers On Me*. I played a neighborhood girl who the boys used to call a chick, and she didn't like that. That's what the song was about. I really enjoyed doing theater as a kid. I remember that being a big highlight."[410]

Those Early School Days

Chase started pre-school in August of 2002 at the Antioch Christian Church in Canton, Georgia, and in 2004 started in kindergarten at Holly Springs Elementary School. She remained there through second grade, and in 2007 transferred

---

410   Ibid.

Chase was always the actress with a flare toward the dramatic. She is pictured in the photo on the left at age six or seven. The 2006 photo on the right shows six-year-old Chase singing at a church function. Her dad, Scott, can be seen in the background playing the drums. Karon is also in the band, but not pictured in the frame. (Photo courtesy of Scott and Karon Truran)

to Avery Elementary School, where she remained from grades three through five.

Chase said that she always followed the rules in those early years of school, and would cry if a teacher got upset with her for any reason. "I really cared about what my teachers thought of me, so I would do my best to really keep it in line," she said. "I would probably cry if a teacher just made a mean face at me."[411] Consequently, Chase never really got in trouble. Well, except for maybe one time in kindergarten.

"It's a really weird story," Chase said. "I sometimes had trouble with multi-step directions. I remember it very clearly because it has scarred me to this day. We were learning about shapes, and we had these little shape cutouts. [The teacher] gave us a tortilla and told us to cut a star, a circle, and a square from the tortilla. Then, the teacher said, 'I'll come and grill the tortilla and we'll make quesadillas.' I did what I was told, it looked great, and she said, 'Oh, and by the way, you can eat

411   Ibid.

282

the leftovers.' When she said leftovers, I thought she meant [I could eat] the whole tortilla and just leave the three little shapes. So, I did just that. As I was going up to the grill, I was looking around at my classmates, and they had eaten the cut-out shapes and still had the tortilla on their plate. I was like, 'Oh no, oh no, I've screwed up! I've really done it this time. When I got up there, [the teacher] looked at me and said, 'Chase, I've had enough of your nonsense.' That was so upsetting. I cried."[412]

This teacher had a diagram of a jungle in the classroom, and each student had a monkey placed somewhere in the jungle. The monkeys were moved to red, yellow, or green, based on the students' behavior on any particular day. "Well, my monkey got moved to yellow, which was a big deal because that was the step before red,"[413] Chase said. The teacher even sent Chase home with a note to give to her parents. Though Chase cried when she presented the note to them, Karon and Scott just fluffed it off, saying, "It's fine. It's just a tortilla, honey. It's alright." "Now that I think about it," Chase continued, "I did get in trouble a few times for rolling my eyes. I didn't know that was sassy, I was just so dramatic all the time and I didn't even realize what my face was doing."[414] She figured out pretty quickly that that was not something she was supposed to do.

Chase had a very kind heart in elementary school. "My classmates used to call me Mama Chase," she said with a laugh. "I'm not sure why. I think I just tended to take in kids that I thought needed a friend. My parents used to jokingly call my friend group 'the island of misfit toys,' but from my perspective, they were the cream of the crop."[415]

---

412   Ibid.
413   Ibid.
414   Ibid.
415   Ibid.

Chase recalled several very caring teachers throughout her school years but remembered one with particular fondness. David Boggs took a particular interest in her, and asked her to join the chorus. "It was like a choir group," she said. "But we also participated in a couple of parades in the community."[416]

Chase stayed busy in those elementary school years. In addition to participating in the school chorus, she took dance and was still a member of the Clubhouse Kids theater groups outside of school. Additionally, she sang with the praise and worship band on Wednesdays and Sundays at Branches of Christ Church in Acworth, Georgia.

Chase always had a funny, sassy edge. Scott recalled an incident that took place when she was about six years old while the two were in Target store together. Scott instructed Chase to stay close to him. "There are not always good people around," he told her. "Chase stopped, looked back at me and said, 'Who are these people you speak of? I've never seen these people,'"[417] Scott said. He tried again, and told her that there are some bad people in the world so she needed to stay close to him. "She stopped, turned to face me and said, 'Dad, if I believed in fate, I wouldn't be playing with loaded dice,' and just kept walking," Scott said. "I laughed so hard and had no idea where she got that line but was impressed that she used it appropriately. We later found out that it was a line she picked up from the DreamWorks movie *The Road to El Dorado* that she had seen two years earlier."[418]

Chase performed in school talent shows every year in elementary school. It was in third grade that she got to perform her first school solo. "I sang the song *Tomorrow* from the musical *Annie*,"[419] she noted.

416   Ibid.
417   Author interview with Scott Truran, March 17, 2022.
418   Ibid.
419   Author interview with Chase Truran, March 30, 2022.

North Cobb Christian School and Korean Music

In August of 2010, Chase enrolled in North Cobb Christian School (NCCS), a private institution where she would remain until she graduated high school. In 2013 during the summer before high school, Chase once again displayed her individuality. Chase and Scott remember those days with a chuckle.

That summer, Chase decided to try and learn the Korean words to a very popular song called *Gangnam Style* by South Korean singer Psy. "I was always into foreign languages," Chase said. "I also learned the words to some French and Chinese songs."[420] Thinking she was neglecting her summer reading for something he found superfluous, her dad told her he thought she was being ridiculous. "You're never going to use this stuff," Scott said. "It doesn't matter." "It does matter," Chase protested. "It's something I really want to do."[421] Scott insisted that she would never use it, but left her to her own designs.

In the final weekend of summer, Chase and a few friends went to a local IHOP to grab a bite to eat after seeing a play. For some reason, Chase thought it would be funny to exit the vehicle with a twirling motion. Rather than appearing "super cool" however, "I twisted my ankle and fell to the ground,"[422] she said. "My ankle swelled up to the size of a softball as I was inside IHOP eating pancakes,"[423] she laughed. The following day, Chase went to the ER where she learned that she had torn the ligaments in her ankle. Unable to walk, she was stuck, either on crutches or in a wheelchair and would remain so all the way up until school began, kicking off with the NCCS annual retreat.

In August 2013, Chase and her classmates boarded a bus

420   Author interview with Chase Truarn, May 23, 2022.
421   Author interview with Chase Truran, May 23, 2022, and with Scott Truran, March 30, 2022.
422   Author interview with Chase Truran, May 23, 2022.
423   Ibid.

for a three-day excursion to a camp in northern Georgia. The campground was comprised of mostly gravel, which made it nearly impossible for Chase to maneuver in a wheelchair and very difficult to get around on her crutches. So, while most of the students were enjoying outdoor activities, Chase was sitting alone in her cabin when a group of girls—international students from South Korea—walked in. Chase made her way over to them, introduced herself, and engaged them in conversation. The girls shared their Korean snacks with Chase, and eventually the conversation turned to music. Once the girls learned that Chase could sing, they pressed her to perform. Never one to turn down an opportunity, Chase crutched her way to the front of the room and sang *Gangnam Style* in Korean to the enthusiastic claps of her audience. They all had a great time, and she made some good friends that day. The experience even prompted her to join the International Club at school, and she later became its vice president.

Chase was nominated to Homecoming Court in 2013, thanks in part to all the support she received from her many friends in the International Club. Scott now admits that, in retrospect, he may have been wrong about *Gangnam Style*.

Swimming

Chase participated in athletics in middle school, playing volleyball and joining the swim team in seventh grade in 2011. Competitive swimming was not something Chase had ever attempted before, but on a whim, she decided to try out. She was so excited and determined to join the team that she went and purchased all the equipment necessary for the tryout before she attended the general interest meeting. "I

Chase on the NCCS Homecoming Court in fall of 2013
(Photos courtesy of Scott and Karon Truran)

got the swim caps, the goggles, the swimsuits, everything," she noted. "We were in the meeting and some of the other parents approached my parents saying, 'Are you sure Chase can do this? You have to be really athletic to swim. I don't know if she can keep up with the other kids,' etc.'"[424] All this was said within earshot of Chase. It was incredibly rude and did nothing to bolster her self-esteem. She took it in stride however, using those remarks as motivation.

Initially, Chase was absolutely terrible. "I don't think anybody else has been that bad at swimming in the history of humankind," she said. "It was so bad. My parents said I looked like a piano falling into the pool when I was diving for the first time. My hands [flailed] all over the place."[425]

---

424   Ibid.
425   Ibid.

But by the end of the season, Chase was recognized as the most improved swimmer and was actually scouted by local coaches who said she had great potential for college swim teams and beyond. "Looking back, I guess that story is a testament to the fact that I can do anything I put my mind to if I really want to do it,"[426] she said proudly. She may have had a promising future in swimming, but she gave it all up in high school, choosing instead to devote herself completely to the arts.

High School Musicals

In her freshman year of high school, Chase had a major role in *The Sound of Music*, playing Mother Abbess. Chase's rendition of *Climb Ev'ry Mountain* "blew the doors out," Scott said. "People were running everywhere asking, 'Who IS that?' The director was running up and down the aisles saying, 'She's 14, She's 14!' She killed that song. She hit everything."[427]

Chase recalled that performance as well, and remembers Matthew Hendrix, the school's arts director, with fondness. "At rehearsals [for *The Sound of Music*], he would always say, 'this is the part where Chase steals the show' when it was time for my solo," she said. "It would make me go totally red, but I was so encouraged."[428] As the person in charge of the entire arts program, Hendrix had a huge influence on Chase. "Oh my gosh, he had such a way with the kids," she said. "He was a very special teacher because he really cared about the students and treated us like we knew what we were talking

426   Ibid.
427   Author interview with Scott Truran, March 17, 2022.
428   Author interview with Chase Truran, March 30, 2022.

In her freshman year of high school, Chase (left) scored a major role, playing Mother Superior Abbess in The Sound of Music. In her junior year, Chase (right) played the role of Ismene in Antigone Now, a one act play. (Photos courtesy of Chase Truran, captured by Pam Doughty)

about, as if we were peers. He was someone that you always felt you could really talk to. He was an excellent director and a truly encouraging person who always believed in me and urged me to take on those big roles. During rehearsal the cast would sometimes break off and have these deep, philosophical roundtable discussions, lead by Mr. Hendrix, about ethics or morality- things you don't typically associate with rehearsing a play. Those conversations were a really important part of my life. I think I learned more about life during those theater rehearsals than in other classes meant to teach those things."[429]

---

429   Ibid.

Chase (Left) performing the role of Mayzie La Bird in Seussical the Musical in her senior year of high school. Chase (right) in the role of Fiona in Shrek the Musical in her junior year of high school. (Photos courtesy of Chase Truran, captured by Pam Doughty)

The Academy Singers

Amy Wallace was another of Chase's teachers who had a profound influence in her life. Chase participated in the school choir from grades six through eight. After eighth grade, students were allowed to audition for an elite high school group called The Academy Singers. "That was a big deal for me," Chase recounted in an interview. "Being in The Academy Singers was the dream of my life when I was in middle school."[430] After Chase had auditioned, Amy called her to tell her she got in. "I was in the living room when the call came saying that I was in," Chase said. "It was a really big moment. My mom was sitting there with me, and I stood up on the ottoman because I was just freaking out waiting

---

430   Ibid.

*Chase performing with the Academy Singers in the Valentine Cabaret
of 2015. Here she is pictured singing "At Last" by Etta James, or
perhaps "Ribbons in the Sky" by Stevie Wonder.
(Photo courtesy of Chase Truran, captured by Pam Doughty)*

to hear my fate. 'Welcome to the group,' Amy said. I was like, 'Oh my gosh!' I was so excited, and I was jumping all over the couches. My mom and I were both jumping up and down. It was a great moment that I remember vividly."[431]

The Academy Singers consisted of 10 or so students. Chase participated in the group from grades nine through twelve and credits it with providing her a real opportunity to sing some serious music. "We did a lot of really advanced choral music," she said. "I also got to do solos, duets, and other ensemble pieces ranging from classical and musical theatre to full-on contemporary. Plus, we did shows at the school. That's actually where Foxes and Fossils (Scott and Tim) found me."[432] Amy was the lead vocalist for The Mustangs. Scott and Tim attended the Academy Singers'

431   Ibid.
432   Ibid.

Valentine Cabaret in February of 2014 to show their support for her. "They saw me do a solo that night," Chase said. "I might have been singing *Ribbon in The Sky* by Stevie Wonder."[433] Tim immediately recognized Chase's immense vocal talent and after the show asked Amy what college she would be attending the following year. "College?" Amy replied. "She's just a freshman."[434] Tim and Scott were gobsmacked.

That chance encounter would have a profound impact on the course of Chase's life. Once again it all began with a call from Amy Wallace. "In May of 2015, I was with my mom in the car when we got a call from Amy who said Foxes and Fossils were trying to keep their band afloat because one of the girls was going to college," Chase said. "She told me 'They're looking for someone who could step in. Would you be interested?' I was 15. It was a real gig. Of course I was interested!"[435]

When Tim asked Chase's parents if she could audition for Foxes and Fossils, Scott and Karon thought it was a great opportunity for her. "We were ecstatic because it was a place for her to grow," Scott said. "Tim called me on the phone to ask if I would be okay with this because they sometimes traveled for jobs. He also invited me to attend their rehearsals to make me feel more comfortable."[436]

After just a couple of practice sessions with the band, Chase participated in her first two professional gigs with Foxes and Fossils, both hosted by the international accounting firm Ernst and Young.

---

433   Ibid.
434   Ibid.
435   Ibid.
436   Ibid.

This 2017 photo shows Chase posing prior to her Senior Prom (left). The photo on the right shows Chase (right) and her sister Kennedy (left) sharing a precious moment after Chase's high school graduation in the Spring of 2017. (Photos courtesy of Scott and Karon Truran)

A Busy High School Career

Chase's work with Foxes and Fossils and The Academy Singers didn't stop her from participating in her high school Worship Team, which she did from sixth to twelfth grade. "We had Chapel at the school gym once a week for about an hour," she said. "There was some prayer and maybe a sermon from either a guest speaker or a teacher. They would alternate the person who would sing each week."[437] Chase performed many solos during those years. The group mostly sang popular Christian music or hymns, such as *In Christ Alone* or others that you might hear in a non-denominational Christian church service. She also continued to sing on Sundays with her church's praise band up until her high school graduation.

---

437   Ibid.

Throughout her four years with The Academy Singers, Chase had many wonderful experiences. At Christmastime, the group would dress in Victorian costumes and sing carols throughout the town of Acworth, Georgia. They also made appearances at churches, assisted living homes, and several community functions throughout the year. They even had an opportunity to sing at the Governor's Mansion. The Academy Singers traveled with the arts department each year to Disney World and Seaworld. Chase visited Belmont University on the groups' annual trip to Nashville, where they learned about the music business. Maggie Adams of Foxes and Fossils fame actually spoke to the group about her time at Belmont and her career in music promotion on one such trip. It was Chase's first time meeting Maggie.

Chase recalled a prank she coordinated during the 2017 Academy Singers Spring Showcase her senior year. She and her good friend, Austin, were the only seniors that year. They hatched a plan to surprise everybody, including director Amy Wallace, by sneaking off stage toward the end of the opening song, *Another Day Of Sun* from the movie *La La Land*. At the end of the song, they would roll back onstage on scooters. The theater department already had one scooter, painted with golden sparkles, that had been a prop in a previous production. Chase had a second scooter in her garage at home. She drew her mother into the conspiracy by having her help paint it to match the one at school. "We ended up flying in during the climax of the song and everyone nearly fell off their chairs laughing,"[438] Chase said.

Chase also participated in Spring Term while at North Cobb Christian School. Spring Term was a program the school offered in which students could travel internationally. "One year, we all went on a trip to Ireland and sang in

438   Author interview with Chase Truran, May 23, 2022.

Chase singing "Another Day of Sun" from the movie La La Land after entering the stage on a scooter. It was part of a 2017 prank orchestrated by Chase and her friend Austin, both high school seniors.
(Photo courtesy of Chase Truran)

Irish castles and churches and did community service work," Chase said. "My mom went along. It was a total blast."[439]

Chase also joined the Tri-M Music Honors Society. This was an arts community service organization in which students were allowed to participate if they maintained a good enough GPA. This group would support the arts community by helping to set up and break down for different events in the community.

Chase excelled academically. During her junior and senior years, she had dual enrollment in high school and at Shorter College, where she completed courses in math, literature, English and French. She also took Advanced Placement (AP) classes at high school. She was inducted into the National Honor Society and graduated with a GPA of 4.3.

Despite her outstanding academic achievements, Chase

---

439   Author interview with Chase Truran, March 30, 2022.

Chase and her friend, Austin, a fellow graduate, closed out their high school careers with a performance of "The Prayer" by Celine Dion and Andrea Bocelli (Photo courtesy of Chase Truran)

was not the school's valedictorian. She was not even the salutatorian, an honor she missed by just a couple of tenths of a point. Her class rank was not a major source of concern as she had already been accepted to college and would begin that new adventure in August of 2017 at Belmont University.

Performing With POTS

The summer after Chase's freshman year of college, she spoke with her cousin, who owned the Dry County Brewery in Kennesaw, Georgia, about the possibility of performing there during the brewery's first anniversary celebration. The outdoor festivity would include a couple of bands and some food trucks. Many people attended, including Chase's family and Jorge, someone who Chase had been seeing for a few weeks. This would be Jorge's first opportunity to meet Chase's family and also the first time that Jorge would see Chase perform live. "The pressure was on,"[440] she said.

Unfortunately for Chase, the temperature that day was about 104 degrees by the time she took the stage. Chase had just about reached the end of her first 60-minute set and was singing *Rumour Has It* by Adele when she started feeling faint. "My vision just started to go, and I was looking out at the audience and singing, but I was kind of fading," she said. "I was in the middle of a song and didn't know what to do."[441] From the audience, Karon could see what was happening and rushed onto the stage to put a stool underneath her daughter, hoping that by sitting she could finish the song. It was to no avail. Chase collapsed into Karon's arms. Thinking it might be heat related, Chase was carried to the Brewery's industrial freezer where she sat for about twenty minutes and cooled down. "I was so mortified," Chase recalled. "It was really embarrassing."[442]

After her time in the freezer with a worried Jorge and Karon, a somewhat recovered Chase returned to the stage for her second set. It went flawlessly, and toward the end of the set, she said to the audience, "I'm going to do *Rumour Has It* again since I didn't finish it the first time and I really like the song." She started singing it again—and once again, passed out. "Now we just say the song is cursed, and I haven't sung it to this day,"[443] she laughed.

Unbeknownst to Chase at the time, her fainting spells had a cause. She was later diagnosed with Postural Orthostatic Tachycardia Syndrome (POTS). The condition "affects

440   Author interview with Chase Truran, May 23, 2022.
441   Ibid.
442   Ibid.
443   Ibid.

blood flow and its symptoms include lightheadedness, fainting, and an uncomfortable, rapid increase in heart rate."[444] The symptoms are exacerbated by heat, dehydration and standing for long periods of time, meaning that Chase's performance on that hot summer day created a perfect storm to set in motion the symptoms of POTS.

College

Chase began her college career in August of 2017 at Belmont as a commercial voice major.[445]* "I was sucky at everything else," she said of her decision to choose voice. "I flunked out of piano class twice. It was the only class I ever failed in my life."[446] Despite her self-deprecation regarding musical instruments, Chase can play a little guitar and ukulele, although "neither of them very well," she said. "Although I've played guitar in my own shows and ukulele in gigs with Foxes and Fossils," she added. "Scott and I [even] played the ukulele together in one or two songs on stage, most memorably *Follow Your Arrow* by Kacey Musgraves. Speaking of instruments, I do also have a mandolin, and it's very special to me because it was Scott King's first ever mandolin from when he was 15 years old. He gifted it to me on my 16th birthday at the Crafty Hog gig. Oh, and I would be remiss not to mention the tin whistles I played on a few songs on the Ireland trip!"[447]

Music school really wasn't at all what Chase expected, and

---

444   Cleveland Clinic, Your Health Questions, Answered. Postural Orthostatic Tachycardia Syndrome (POTS), https://my.clevelandclinic.org/health/diseases/16560-postural-orthostatic-tachycardia-syndrome-pots.

445   *Commercial Voice is considered to be modern music, pretty much anything that is not classical.

446   Author interview with Chase Truran, May 30, 2022.

447   Ibid.

*Chase during the Belmont years
(Photo courtesy of Scott and
Karon Truran)*

before long she decided to change paths. "The way the program works is you creep into commercial voice studies, but you start in classical for the first two years," Chase said. "I completed my entire classical study while I was there, and then I took a couple of commercial classes that were lower level—music theory and that sort of thing. Then I just sort of realized that the kids there and the environment weren't for me. It was very cut-throat because everyone was trying to be somebody and prove they were better than you. I wasn't challenged enough vocally, and [the students] seemed fake. I didn't like it."[448]

Despite some disappointing experiences, Chase's time at Belmont wasn't totally bad. "There was one teacher at Belmont, Dr. Kelly Garner, who really stood out to me," she said. Chase took Garner's course, a seminar on Commercial Music. In their second year, commercial voice majors were allowed to audition before a variety of teachers in the voice program. Those teachers would then select the student with whom they would like to work. "Dr. Garner was the voice teacher I auditioned for," Chase said. "She was really important for

---

448   Author interview with Chase Truran, March 30, 2022.

me. After I auditioned for her, I became part of her group called Voxology."[449] Voxology was an all-girl R&B and gospel choir in which Chase was able to sing many solos and perform in a variety of churches. Dr. Garner also invited Chase to be included in a private R&B and gospel group she led off campus called Vox12, that performed in the Nashville community and actually did some recording. Twice a week, Dr. Garner also served as Chase's private commercial voice teacher.

Chase thought that Dr. Garner was wonderful because she seemed to understand the dynamics between the students. "It's sad that we bonded over that, but she encouraged me daily and gave me hope that my experiences at the school weren't representative of the music industry as a whole and that I would likely have much more success out in the real world with music and relationships,"[450] Chase said. Dr. Garner was also very honest with Chase. "She was the teacher I went to for a private vocal lesson the summer before I auditioned at Belmont. She had me sing both of the audition pieces I had prepared, and after I was finished, she told me, 'No, you're good. You don't need a vocal lesson,' and she gave me my money back," Chase said. "That gave me a lot of confidence, and when I went to audition, I got in. All in all, she was a bright spot in my Belmont experience."[451] Chase noted that Dr. Garner really loved the girls in Voxology and encouraged them. "She was cool and very grounded, not at all pretentious, and was an incredible voice teacher and vocalist,"[452] Chase said.

Regarding the competitive nature of the music industry, Chase is not a fan. "It can be that way, but I prefer to

449   Ibid.
450   Ibid.
451   Ibid.
452   Ibid.

work with people who are humble—people who celebrate one another's strengths—people who have a desire for more than just getting themselves to the top," she said. "I guess in general I don't think it's right to only want the good things for yourself. I believe that all musicians have room at the table. We all bring something unique and special, and I would say to any musician, bring what only you can bring. I believe that there's an audience, a community, and a spotlight for every creative person with passion, heart, and talent, and if we can support and uplift one another, there's a much brighter future out there for the industry."[453]

The Man in Her Life

Chase didn't really want to use a dating app to find her soulmate, but in July of 2018 she did experiment with one. Just before starting her second year at Belmont, Chase decided to put up her profile on an online dating app. "It is not something I ordinarily would do because I think it's creepy, but I decided to give it a try," she said. "One week later, when I was home, I [went] on the app and there was a message from a Jorge Castro. He said, 'Hey, I think I know what school you go to,' because I had included in my bio that I went to a music school. I said, 'Okay, which one.' He said, 'Belmont,' and he told me that he had a feeling it might be because he went there too, so I immediately felt more comfortable talking with him since we were both in college and were going to the same school. He actually lives in Atlanta about an hour and a half from me, as well, which is funny."[454]

About a month later when school began, the two met in

453   Ibid.
454   Ibid.

*Chase and Jorge visiting an apple orchard together
in the fall of 2020.
(Photo courtesy of Chase Truran)*

person on campus. It was August 31, 2018, a date engrained in Chase's mind. "We went out for a night on the town," she said. "We had dinner and chatted, and we went around Nashville together seeing the sites."[455] They really liked each other and continued dating throughout the school year. "The funniest thing is that we actually have a picture of us together before we knew each other,"[456] Chase said. It was taken when the solar eclipse was visible in Nashville in August of 2017. "There's a picture of some kids on the lawn [watching the eclipse], and you can pick us out sitting just a couple of feet apart in the photo, which we both think is pretty cool,"[457] she said.

Chase and Jorge decided to transfer from Belmont together since he was also not feeling challenged enough in his audio engineering program. They both entered the University of

455   Ibid.
456   Ibid.
457   Ibid.

*Chase (bottom row on the left) with her Old Gold A
Capella group at the University of Iowa—circa 2019
(Photo courtesy of Chase Truran)*

Iowa (UI) as third-year students in August of 2019. Though
no longer majoring in a music-related course of study, Chase
managed to join a singing group at UI called Old Gold A
Cappella. "I lived off campus and was looking for something
musical to get involved with on campus just to meet people
and potentially make some friends," she said. "I saw a listing
for auditions and decided to go. There were probably about
15 people in the group, and, when I was asked to join, I
was so excited to come onboard. My best memory from college was when we did a joint fall concert the first year that
I went to Iowa."[458] The concert was a friendly way to feel
all of the other a cappella groups out and see which groups
would make their mark on campus. "[Each ensemble] sang
three songs, and I had a big solo in one of ours," Chase said.
"It was *Godspeed* by Frank Ocean. I finished with a big note,
and everyone started freaking out, clapping. It was crazy and

---

458   Ibid.

was such a huge moment for me and my group. After the show, some of the other a cappella groups came up to give hugs and introduce themselves. Somewhere in the conversation, someone invited our group to a big party they were throwing that night to get all the a cappella groups together and celebrate the performances. When I arrived at the party and walked into the room, a member of another group said, 'Our champion has arrived!' It was the coolest thing because before then, I didn't know anyone from the other groups at all, and we ended up having a great time that night. I never dreamed that I could do anything like that in Iowa. The whole experience made me feel humbled and surprised that I could make so many friends just by doing a solo."[459]

The Sting of Loss

In 2020, Chase experienced a huge loss. Her Grandma Lois passed away on May 14 at the age of 93. Chase was close to both her paternal grandparents, who attended every one of her events when she was younger. But she was especially close to her Grandma Lois. Lois, a former Broadway and big band singer, who had also studied opera provided her granddaughter with endless tips on how to improve when Chase took opera as part of her college curriculum. "She would always give me pointers telling me to 'use your diaphragm, get more air,'" Chase remembered. "She would give me the hardest time about it, but she was right." With the COVID-19 pandemic in full swing, the family wasn't able to have a proper service for their matriarch, which was very difficult.

---

459   Ibid.

Jorge and Chase's first (left) and last (right) day at the University of Iowa in 2019 and 2021, respectively. (Photos courtesy of Scott and Karon Truran)

Graduation from the University of Iowa

Because of the ongoing pandemic, both Chase and Jorge graduated from the University of Iowa in a virtual ceremony on Saturday May 15, 2021.

They, along with their parents and Jorge's siblings, watched the graduation from the comfort of Chase's apartment in Iowa as it was live-streamed. "As our names were called, we threw our [mortarboards] into the air," Chase said. "We had breakfast and tried to make it nice. We're both first generation college graduates from our families, so it was a proud moment, and it was pretty cool."[460]

A few days later, the university held a celebration in the football stadium with students and families sitting socially distanced in the bleachers. Shortly thereafter, Chase and Jorge returned home to Atlanta. "We had a big joint graduation party in Jorge's backyard," she said. "He has a very big, fenced-in, grassy yard. Both of our families and many friends

---

460   Author interview with Chase Truran, May 23, 2022.

*Chase in her cap and gown following graduation from the
University of Iowa—May 15, 2021
(Photo courtesy of Karon Truran, captured by Jorge Castro)*

came to celebrate with us. We had a mariachi band, and I
sang some songs. There was incredible food, a mechanical
bull and dancing all night. I have so many pictures from that
[party]. It was a blast and made every college experience—
good and bad—totally worth it."[461]

Post College

Following college graduation, Chase moved back home
with her parents. She and Jorge spent months building out
a recording studio in the attic and former media room of
her parent's home, where, according to Scott, she records
every single day. Jorge drives almost three hours roundtrip
to get to the studio to work with her five days a week. He
does all of the audio engineering and co-produces the songs
with Chase. He also takes care of some of the management
responsibilities that go along with her budding career. He
is, according to Chase, an outstanding and creative track-
ing and mixing engineer and has a rich understanding of
acoustics. "I trust him with anything on that side of music

461   Author interview with Chase Truran, March 30, 2022.

and beyond," Chase said. "He's very, very good."[462] Jorge and Chase are not yet engaged, though Chase believes that it is just a matter of time. "We are waiting for our financial situation to improve, but love and relationship-wise, we are there,"[463] she happily noted.

Promoting Chase

Scott's parents always encouraged him to pursue his dreams in music and to have fun. As a result, he and Karon have had a wonderful life in music together. They toured the world performing on Royal Caribbean Cruise Lines, and had an absolute blast making good money, not having a care in the world. "My parents were all for it," Scott said. "We just had a great life doing music. [That's why] with Chase, we totally encourage her to follow her dream. I told her 'it would be a shame for everybody on the planet if you don't pursue it because you've got something special that people want to hear.'"[464] Scott also credits Tim for being so supportive of Chase and bringing her into his band when she was just 15 years old.

"Tim always says, 'We'll have been Chase's first band when she makes it,'" Scott noted. "He has been very sweet that way, as have Scott King, Johnny, Toby, Darwin, Sammie and Maggie."[465]

"They are all very kind," Karon added. "Tim has so much confidence in Chase. Sometimes he'll tell her to come to the studio to record but doesn't send her any music. When they

462   Author interview with Chase Truran, May 23, 2022.
463   Author interview with Chase Truran, May 23, 2020.
464   Author interview with Scott and Karon Truran, March 17, 2022.
465   Author interview with Scott Truran, March 30, 2022.

(Top) 2020 photos of Chase and Jorge's attic recording studio
(Photo courtesy of Chase Truran, captured by Jorge Castro)
(Bottom) Chase singing a duet of "It Had To Be You" with her dad, Scott, on
drums at Christmas In Concert, a live, virtual event hosted by Chase in 2020.
(Photo taken from Chase's Fan Page courtesy of Brad Burns)

get there, she hears the music for the first time and he tells the guys, 'Watch this!' and she goes in there and it's one and done. It's almost like a trick that he shows everybody."[466]

What's Next For Chase?

Chase is enjoying her time with Foxes and Fossils but is also preparing for a career as a solo artist. Scott King's death put many things in perspective for the band. Neither Foxes and Fossils nor its members are immortal, and time is not their friend. As time passes, the fossils are aging, and the other foxes are growing into their own time-consuming and demanding careers. Chase is pursuing her own career as a solo artist. At the time of this writing, a new single is in production with an expected release in June 2022. There are also a couple of other things that she and Jorge have been planning. Ultimately, Chase would love to share her music around the world, and she is excited about the possibility of those new adventures. "I would love to play in London," she said. "I'm really interested in the music scene there. What I've heard is that the culture of house shows there is a lot different. They (the clubs) attract a more diverse audience as opposed to our mostly younger groups of people attracted to house shows in this country. It's just a music culture that I'm excited about in general."[467]

Despite her plans for a solo career, Chase expects to continue to be part of Foxes and Fossils for as long as they exist and will make whatever accommodations are necessary to make that happen. "I can take some of my recording equipment on the road with me and if I needed to do anything for

---

466   Author interview with Karon Truran, March 30, 2022.
467   Author interview with Chase Truran, May 23, 2022.

(Left) Chase during the recording of "Goodbye Yellow Brick Road" for Foxes and Fossils at Tim Purcell's basement studio (Photo courtesy of Scott and Karon Truran) (Right) Chase at the 2020 Josie Music Awards at which she was nominated in three categories. (Photo courtesy of Chase Truran)

the band, I could do it easily [on the road]," she said. "I can make it work. I'm definitely not planning on leaving Foxes and Fossils anytime soon."[468]

As things are now, Chase believes she can easily handle both her work with the band and a solo venture. She is also excited about the possibility of returning to live shows with Foxes and Fossils. "I love to perform live," she said. "The thought of it brings a little anxiety now because it's been so long, but that will take care of itself once I get back on stage."[469]

---

468   Ibid.
469   Ibid.

Chapter 10

THE FORMATION OF FOXES AND FOSSILS

January to March 2010

With The Mustangs' decline in job opportunities, and the coming of that fateful day in January 2010 when Tim asked Sammie to sing harmony on *America,* the story of Tim's musical exploits had come full circle. His idea of success had morphed from a record deal to the ideals of a father who only wanted to make beautiful music with his daughter.

After listening to the *America* recording, he wondered, what would it take to produce music like this live. The sound he and Sammie made together was, in his mind, magical. He asked her what she thought about doing a few performances together, or maybe even starting a band. When she responded affirmatively, he started focusing on making that happen.

Tim's innate ability to recognize and assemble musical talent sets him apart from most. "The main component of Foxes and Fossils is Tim," said Terry Heinlein, Tim's friend and the band's videographer. "He is a master at multitasking.

He works on different songs in various stages, often doing the audio and the video at different times."[470]

Imagine simultaneously working on five songs with lead vocals, multiple backup singers, drums, percussion, hand-claps, bass, two or more guitars, and keyboards—all with separate audio and separate video files. Thinking about all that is enough to make one's head spin. And coordinating all of that with the busy schedules of eight different band members at one time living in five different states … amazing!

Tim tends to downplay his own musical talent, which is quite impressive, constantly giving accolades to those around him. The simple truth, however, is that despite the enormous talent of the Foxes and Fossils band members, the band would not exist without Tim.

While he and Sammie sounded great together, he instinctively knew that the addition of another female vocalist would take that sound to an angelic level. He spoke to Sammie about her choir mate, Maggie Adams, and wondered if she would be interested in joining. The two girls weren't super close, but Sammie agreed that she would be a perfect addition. Tim decided to gauge Maggie's interest. He had been watching Maggie sing and perform in church youth choirs since she was a little girl. "I've always been thrilled and impressed with her tonality and her stage presence; the whole thing,"[471] he said.

Maggie recalled that Tim approached her one morning as she and some friends were eating breakfast at Chick-Fil-A to see if she would be interested in joining the group. "I said okay," she remembered. "I was pretty excited."[472] The addi-

---

470   Written comments provided to the author by Terry Heinlein. February 11, 2022.

471   Tim Purcell in a pre-performance interview at Bella's Pizza, March 21, 2010.

472   Written comments provided to the author by Maggie Adams. May 13, 2022.

tion of Maggie shored up the vocal section of the band. It was now time for Tim to assemble the musicians. Tim's first choice was obvious. He turned to his old Hapeville High School buddy Darwin Conort, the person with whom Tim had played in his very first band, American Apple. The two had a long history of making music together, and Darwin was the perfect guitarist and singer to join the group.

The addition of Scott King, the bassist for The Mustangs, completed the new band. Scott had some misgivings when Tim initially asked him to join. "When first approached by Tim to play, I thought it might be a waste of time playing with some high school girls," he said. "But after giving it more consideration, I figured, it's just for one night. Tim didn't fill me in at the time that he planned to book other jobs."[473] In any case, the economy had changed and so there weren't as many live venues for bands out there. "Playing for the two bands wasn't really a conflict at all," said Scott. "So, the way I saw it, I still got to play music with some of my favorite people."[474]

Scott really enjoyed playing with The Mustangs, so much so that he once told Tim, "I want to die a Mustang." He viewed playing with the new band like the other side of the same coin. "I was playing with the same guys, the vocal level was where I liked it, a real high standard in vocals," Scott said. "I didn't really think anything about it other than it was a side job. We got to play some different material and play some different venues, and it was a cool thing for the girls to get to do. Plus, it only took a few days out of my summer to do it, so I was all for it."[475]

Tim did not initially ask Toby Ruckert, The Mustangs' lead guitarist, to be in the band, but he did ask him for help in

---

473   Author interview with Scott King. December 17, 2021.
474   Ibid.
475   Author Interview with Scott King. December 17, 2021.

a different, equally significant role. "When they first formed, Darwin was playing the guitar," Toby said. "Tim and Darwin have a long history together. Tim was very open with me about it. He said 'I'm putting this band together with my daughter Sammie and Scott's going to play bass with us. A friend of Sammie's, Maggie, is also going to sing, and Darwin's going to play guitar, but we need a good sound man. Are you interested?' I said, 'Sure, it sounds like fun.'

The Mustangs weren't working much at the time, so it was an opportunity to make a little extra money. I enjoy running sound, it's fun."[476] So, Toby took on the role of sound man for the band's very first gig at Bella's.

With the band assembled, Tim turned his attention to rehearsals. Sammie noted that they practiced as much as possible, pretty much every day unless she or Maggie had a lot of homework. Maggie agreed that practices were fairly frequent, but in an interview held just prior to the start of the band's first performance in 2010, she said they were also quite fun. "It's kind of like friends chillin' out and singing together," the then 16-year-old said. "It's not really like strict practices."[477]

She found the experience to be very different from singing in youth choirs, the only groups she had sung in before. She also got a kick out of how funny the musicians were, making special note of the way Tim mistyped the title of the song *American Honey,* turning it into *American Homey.*

Tim wouldn't say if his spelling errors were intentional antics meant to be humorous or if they were legitimate typos. He did, however, verify the frequency of rehearsals, noting that all five members practiced together only one time, but he and the girls got together more frequently. He also said

476   Author interview with Toby Ruckert. February 11, 2022.
477   Maggie Adams in a pre-performance interview at Bella's Pizza, March 14, 2010.

that Darwin came to his house separately three or four times to work on his material. Together, the band members developed a 20-song setlist. "It was a lot of work for me, but I think it [was] worth it,"[478] Tim said.

While the band members were concentrating on tightening their sound and practicing their vocal arrangements, Tim had the added burden of finding a place to play. He set his sights on a small Smyrna pizza establishment on Atlanta Road by the name of Bella's Pizzeria. After speaking to the owner, they set a date for the band's debut—they would perform two sets at Bella's on the evening of Sunday March 14.[479]

All that remained was to select a name. Tim initially thought Ear Candy would work, but soon changed his mind. He later thought that Beauty and the Beasties would be a more appropriate way to describe three older men and two young girls playing in a band together. But at the last minute, Scott King—ever great at coming up with clever band names—came up with Foxes and Fossils. When Tim mentioned that name to the Bella's crowd just prior to the start of the show, it was met with applause. The band members liked the name too, so it stuck.

---

478   Author interview with Tim Purcell. May 23, 2022.

479   Author Interview with Christopher Ketchum, May 2, 2022. It has long been accepted that the date of the Bella's performance, the recordings from which resulted in the Foxes and Fossils Live at Bella's DVD, was March 21, 2010. That is the date that appears on the DVD. However, Chris Ketchum, David Weaver, John Hazeldene and Doug Godbold have uncovered significant and indisputable evidence that the show was actually held on March 14, 2010. Among the plethora of evidence Ketchum produced to support this date are these facts: 1. A Darwin Conort Facebook post of March 13, 2010, notifying Jill Ewing that he was playing at Bella's with Tim and his daughter this Sunday, March 14; 2. A March 13, 2010, Facebook post from Donna Beaubien, in which Tim and Darwin were tagged, that included photographs of the Bella's performance; 3. Larry Adams Facebook post from March 8, 2010, inviting friends to see Maggie and Sammie sing at Bella's at 7:00 PM this Sunday (March 14, 2010).

Foxes and Fossils' First Performance
Bella's Pizza—March 14, 2010

The big night finally arrived. The girls had spent the past few weeks promoting the show, hoping to have a full house. "We created a Facebook group event about a month before the show and invited all our friends on Facebook,"[480] 16-year-old Maggie said in an interview before the show. "We had also been asking everyone at school,"[481] Sammie added. "And reminding them all week long!"[482] Maggie concluded. The fossils had been promoting the show to their friends as well, and everyone's hard work paid off. Bella's was packed, requiring the wait staff to add more tables on the floor in front of the stage.

The fossils all wondered how the two young girls would respond to the pressure of performing in public. Sammie and Maggie were clearly anxious. "I am feeling very nervous," Maggie acknowledged in her video interview with Terry Heinlein just prior to the performance. "Excited too, but pretty much all nerves right now. I'm concerned about remembering the words to 20 songs. That's a lot of words to remember."[483] Sammie also joked about Maggie's propensity to forget words. "I hope you remember the words,"[484] Sammie told Maggie before the show started. "I hope I remember the words too,"[485] Maggie responded with a big smile.

---

480   Maggie Adams in a pre-performance interview at Bella's Pizza on March 14, 2010.
481   Sammie Purcell in a pre-performance interview at Bella's Pizza on March 14, 2010.
482   Maggie Adams in a pre-performance interview at Bella's Pizza on March 14, 2010.
483   Ibid.
484   Sammie Purcell in a pre-performance interview at Bella's Pizza on March 14, 2010.
485   Maggie Adams in a pre-performance interview at Bella's Pizza on March 14, 2010.

Joking aside, Sammie also acknowledged having anxieties. "I'm really nervous," she said prior to the show. "But it's a good kind of nervous, like butterflies. But I'm really excited."[486] She expressed some concern about remembering when to come in with her parts. "We changed some things, like just some last-minute things," the 15-year-old said. "So I hope I remember the new things and not the old things that we practiced."[487] She also worried that her voice might crack. "That's the one thing I really don't want to happen because that would be pretty embarrassing,"[488] she said. With tongue in cheek, both girls predicted the show would be flawless.

Apprehensiveness was not something unique to the girls. "I'm a little nervous for her," said Ellen Adams, Maggie's mom, right before the show. "I think she's going to do great, but I'm always nervous about things so I'm probably more nervous than she is. I'm [also] excited because I think it's a great opportunity for her. [Maggie's] going to do well and improve her self-confidence even more."[489]

Tim also weighed in before he took the stage. "I'm probably more excited to be playing tonight than I've been since I was a kid," he said. "It's a big deal for me to be able to do things with my daughter that we both enjoy. And it was a thrill for me to watch her grow and have her talent come forth in such a way that it's as much a challenge for me to keep up with her as it is for her to keep up with me. And doing it with Maggie is a great deal too. One of the things that is very interesting, is the guys that I'm playing with tonight, I've known all of them for a long time and they are all amazed, to a man, that these girls are 15 and 16 years old. They're wondering if they

486 Sammie Purcell in a pre-performance interview at Bella's Pizza on March 14, 2010.
487 Ibid.
488 Ibid.
489 Ellen Adams in a pre-performance interview at Bella's on March 14, 2010.

are going to be nervous or if they're going to be forgetful, or anxious or anything. I'm sure they're anxious but both of them, in rehearsals, have acted like real pros. So, we'll see. I just want to be able to look back and know that we did the best we could. I don't want anything weird to happen. I don't want any guitar strings to break, I don't want anyone to put their capo on the wrong fret (that happened-watch Scott's face when they play America at Bella's). I don't want anybody to forget the words, or forget to come in. I just want it to be as good as we can be."[490] Tim concluded with a few words of advice for his daughter and Maggie. "Okay girls, just relax, and let yourself sit back in the warm and loving hands of these three experienced musicians and do your best."[491]

The band began their first set with perhaps the most difficult song in their repertoire, the Crosby Stills and Nash mega hit, *Suite Judy Blue Eyes.* The girls' nerves seemingly manifested themselves through their very intentional hand placement—one hand gripping the mic stand, the other gripping the mic. Though the Foxes and Fossils rendition of the song was outstanding, Darwin did, at one point, forget to return to the microphone following an excellent guitar solo, and had to be prompted by Tim. No one at Bella's probably noticed, but one of Tim's expressed fears had just come to pass and it was only the first song. It wouldn't take long for another to rear its ugly head. During the second song, *Fifteen* by Taylor Swift, Maggie forgot some of the lyrics. It was actually rather charming, and although she was embarrassed, Maggie handled the misstep like a seasoned veteran. The mistake did nothing to detract from the otherwise sterling rendition of the song—Maggie's voice was pure gold

---

490   Tim Purcell in a pre-performance interview at Bella's on March 14, 2010.
491   Ibid.

and the three-part harmonies of Maggie, Sammie and Tim, were absolutely stunning.

The band soldiered on through two sets and 20 songs with few mistakes—their first performance was officially in the books and was received by an enthusiastic audience. Tim, who wanted a keepsake of the night, had asked his friend Terry Heinlein to videotape the evening's performance. "Tim called me one day and asked if I would video a gig that he was doing,"[492] Terry said. Tim made it clear that this was not a Mustangs gig, but rather a special project. Terry agreed to do the shoot with three cameras. "I asked Maggie's dad Larry to be a camera man, and he shot the camera on the left," Terry said. "My wife, Roberta, was camera in the center, and I was the camera on the right. I had no idea what we were going to get from Larry's camera as I had not used him before. I was a little worried that all I would get was Maggie. Roberta had shot a number of venues for me, so I knew she knew what I wanted to see from her camera. Those who have seen the results of the videos from Bella's can see they both did a great job."[493]

Perhaps the one minor faux pax during the taping of the Bella's performance took place in the background. The televisions behind the stage were left on during much of the first set. The audience, who were focused on the band, might not have noticed—but Terry certainly did. "I remember thinking that the dang TVs were on and were messing up the shots," he said. "But I did not think about it being possible to ask that they be turned off."[494] Larry wasn't about to accept that, however. When the band was between songs, he approached the restaurant manager. To his and Terry's

---

492   Written comments from Terry Heinlein submitted on February 11, 2022.
493   Ibid.
494   Ibid.

amazement, management was very willing to comply, and that distraction was eliminated.

Following the performance, "Tim asked me to edit the video for him as he wanted it as a personal keepsake and to share it with family and friends on YouTube," Terry said. "[He] said if I could get him the videos of each song, he would provide the audio, rather than use the camera audio. I was thrilled to actually put together the video for each song as I had just purchased Final Cut Pro editing software."[495] Terry had a great time with the project. "When the video editing was complete, Tim provided the audio that had been recorded direct from the soundboard," he said. "Oh My Gosh…. it was amazing how alive the music came."[496]

Though they were not able to book Bella's for a second show, Tim did arrange for the band to play several additional gigs in the summer of 2010. These included an August 11 performance at the First United Methodist Church in Smyrna, appearances at Jess Lucas Park in Hapeville on August 20, and one at the Yellow Daisy Festival in Stone Mountain on September 12. The Foxes and Fossils concluded that year with another show at Jess Lucas Park on September 18.

A Familiar Face Joins The Band
2011

After the first year, Darwin decided not to stay with the group. "They weren't working very much, and he had other job opportunities including a job in the film industry,"[497] said Toby. In need of a guitar player, Tim turned to The

495   Ibid.
496   Ibid.
497   Author interview with Toby Ruckert. February 11, 2022.

Mustangs lead guitarist. "Tim said to me, 'We don't have a guitar player anymore, is it something that you'd like to do?' I said, 'Yeah, sure,'" Toby remembered. "I knew everybody in the band and liked everybody and we all got along."[498] So, in addition to his gig with The Mustangs, Toby was now officially a fossil.

Around the same time that Toby came on board, the band decided to add drums. Tim needed to look no further than Johnny Pike, who had joined The Mustangs the previous year. Johnny had no compunction about transitioning into the new band. "The Mustangs had great vocals," Johnny said. "But the dynamic with Foxes and Fossils was at a different level of good because of the combination of the vocals of Sammie and Maggie. When Tim's [voice was] added, it just created a magical sound."[499] With the addition of Johnny, "the whole scope of the band changed from being an acoustic act to being a regular band,"[500] Toby noted.

Tim continued to book the band at local shows. During the summer and fall of 2011, Foxes and Fossils played at four different venues for a total of seven performances. These included four shows on the outdoor patio of a Smyrna restaurant known as Twisted Taco, on May 29, July 3, August 21, and October 15. The group also performed at the Woodstock Music Festival in Woodstock, Georgia, on August 13; at the Jess Lucas Park in Hapeville on August 19; and at the Yellow Daisy Festival in Stone Mountain on September 11. At this point, Tim decided to film the last show of the year so that he could upload the best of them to YouTube—a prescient decision, it turns out.

---

498   Ibid.
499   Author interview with Johnny Pike, December 29, 2021.
500   Author interview with Toby Ruckert. February 11, 2022.

The Foxes Leave For College
2012 to 2014

The Foxes and Fossils now consisted of six members: vocalists Sammie and Maggie, guitarists/keyboardist Tim, Toby on lead guitar, Scott on bass, mandolin and ukulele, and Johnny on drums. The talent level was extraordinary, and the band continued their live performances with five shows in 2012. But the end of that summer marked another transition for Foxes and Fossils—Maggie set off for college at Belmont University. Because the band played mostly during the summer months, it was widely assumed that their schedule would continue largely uninterrupted. Meanwhile, The Mustangs, which included Fossils Tim, Johnny, Toby, and Scott, continued to perform year-round, albeit at a lesser rate than during the band's golden days prior to 2010.

In 2013, Maggie returned for the band's summertime gigs. They played four times at the Twisted Taco, once at the Mall of Georgia, and once at Jess Lucas Park. In August, Sammie started at Vanderbilt University. She agreed to drive home when needed to join the band for live shows, but with most Foxes and Fossils shows scheduled for the summer, Sammie didn't think her enrollment in college would be much of a problem.

Johnny remembers the year 2014 with fondness, as it was the year in which the Foxes and Fossils performed his favorite show. "One of the biggest shows, and the most fun show for me, was when we opened for Creedence Clearwater Revisited (members of Creedence Clearwater Revival without John Fogerty) at the Atlanta Botanical Gardens," Johnny said. "There was a huge crowd, and we were the opening act. Thousands of people were packed from one end to the other and there was no lack of confidence with this band.

We did a great show, as always. We were even mentioned in an article in the Atlanta Journal Constitution."[501]

In all, the band performed seven times in 2014, including their first back-to-back performances. The first of these was at the aforementioned show at the Atlanta Botanical Garden on June 6, followed by a show at the Mall of Georgia on June 7. Their other shows included the Woodstock Music Festival on June 14, Keswick Park on July 4, Ernst and Young convention at the Renaissance Hotel on July 27 and again on August 14, and Jess Lucas Park on August 15.

The Band Adds A New Fox
2015 to 2016

The seven shows of 2014 took a toll on Maggie. She spent that summer in Nashville and making the seven-hour round trip drive to Atlanta six times over 10 weeks was tough. Worse, from a practical point of view, the money she earned from most of the gigs was barely enough to cover the cost of the gas. Having a job as a hostess in a Nashville restaurant that summer further complicated matters. As much as she enjoyed being a part of the band, and as much as the band enjoyed having her, Tim felt it wasn't fair to ask her to continue to do it.

Tim thought about disbanding the group altogether. He saw no way to replace Maggie and really didn't want to. Scott, however, had a solution—Chase Truran. "Tim and Scott were waiting in the green room to start playing at a Christmas party, trying to decide F&F's future," Chase remembers. "Scott said, 'What about that girl from Amy's show? She's

---

501   Author interview with Johnny Pike, December 29, 2021

just a sophomore in high school so she will be around for a couple of years. No doubt she could do it. It would be amazing, her and Sammie!'"[502] Tim was intrigued and decided to ask Amy if she would help make the connection.

Tim's and Scott's kind support of Amy Wallace's high school chorus had resulted in a great opportunity for the band. It also had a profound impact on the course of Chase Truran's life. "In June of 2015, I was with my mom in the car when we got a call from Amy, who said Foxes and Fossils were having trouble keeping their group afloat because one of the girls was in college," Chase said. "My parents were immediately on board. I remember that my mom and I had the conversation right after the phone call and she asked, 'Do you want to do this?' and I was like, 'Heck yeah I want to do this.' I mean, I'm 15 and it was a professional paid gig. Thank God we had Amy as a liaison. It worked out really well because she knew the guys and it was just something we were really comfortable with."[503]

Chase's first two Foxes and Fossils gigs were private corporate functions with Ernst & Young, a multinational professional services network. The two events were held in the ballroom of the Renaissance Atlanta Waverly Hotel near Smyrna, Georgia, on July 19 and August 9. The first gig was very intimidating for Chase, but she was also very excited to be setting up and tearing down the equipment, as it made her feel like a real part of the band. Her mom had taken her shopping for stage clothes before the gig. "I was very nervous," Chase recalled, "But I felt pretty awesome. I was ok by the time the first gig rolled around, but at rehearsals I was so nervous. I didn't know any of these guys. I worked so hard because what Tim had given me were the soundtracks from

502   Author interview with Chase Truran, April 1, 2022.
503   Ibid.

the band's taped performances and he said to learn all these songs. I was trying to figure out which harmony he wanted me to do, so I had to just parse it out myself. I figured it was a professional gig so here we go. I did [get most of the vocal parts] but maybe botched a little bit of it."[504]

Chase has very vivid memories of her early practices. "We were all in the basement and we had headphones and live mics and we were listening to ourselves sing, trying to get a good blend," she said. "We were just going through the catalogue the first day. It was a lot of material. It had to be the whole F&F catalogue that we went through. It was like a five-hour rehearsal. I thought these guys are looking at me like I suck and was afraid I wasn't in their league. I didn't know what I was supposed to do. I was so nervous the whole time. I had my solos, and I did pretty well, but it was like throwing a kid into the water to teach him to swim."[505]

After that first practice, Chase printed out lyric sheets for every single song and put them all in a folder that she took to rehearsal. She marked each section that she had to sing with a pen. If there was a discrepancy with a harmony part, she noted it and corrected it.

"By the second practice, I was right there, and the nerves were gone," Chase said. "The night before the practice was nerve wracking. I printed out all lyrics and made notes on them indicating that I had second or third harmony."[506] By the end of the second rehearsal, she didn't need a binder. Despite the nerves and personal feelings of inadequacy, the thought of quitting the band never entered her mind. "It was intimidating and there wasn't a whole lot of information for me to work from, and I was like, how am I going to get this

---

504   Ibid.
505   Ibid.
506   Ibid.

perfect," she remembered. "I want to do this really well, but that first day we nailed down so many things that I felt a lot more comfortable."[507]

Johnny Pike described the amazing quality of Chase's voice and how it differed from those of Sammie and Maggie. "Sammie has a unique voice, almost like a kind of girl next door voice, especially when she was young," he said. "It's kind of hard to describe. It's pitch-perfect but it's very unique, almost country sounding. Maggie is different, similar to the girl next door voice, but with a little more tone to it. Chase comes in kind of in the middle of all that, with a range unlike the other two girls. All three are great, but Chase has much more range to her voice, much more depth and power. She's like this dynamo that came in. It was this perfect blend to what we already had with Maggie and Sammie, especially when they all sing together. We were able to bring in other types of songs with Chase on vocals to add to what we were already doing. Chase creates another mind-blowing experience. Here's this 15-year-old girl that comes in with a voice like Kelly Clarkson. She is incredible."[508]

Darwin agreed, noting that the girls sounded terrific whether singing solo or when harmonizing together, Chase adds that other dimension. "Finding Chase, with such a great voice—it's divine," he said, "It's the universe throwing it all our way."[509]

In 2015 the Twisted Taco, which had been a mainstay venue for the band, closed. That began a decline in the band's live performances, a trend that would continue up to and through the years of the COVID-19 Pandemic. The band had only three performances in 2015. Two were at

507   Author interview with Chase Truran. May 23, 2022.
508   Author interview with Johnny Pike. December 29, 2021.
509   Author interview with Darwin Conort. March 29, 2022.

the Renaissance Hotel Ballroom on July 19 and August 9. The final show of the year was at Jess Lucas Park on August 21. Chase did however, fill in for Amy Wallace during a Mustangs performance on October 17, giving her another opportunity to take the spotlight.

In 2016, the Foxes and Fossils schedule got even thinner, with only two performances. June 25 found the band at the Mall of Georgia for the fourth time in the past five years, while August 13 had the band testing out a new local venue at Smyrna's Crafty Hog. The band was getting tighter and tighter, and their repertoire was growing steadily even as they experienced a decline in performances.

Welcome Back Darwin
2017

In 2017—the year Sammie graduated from college—the Foxes and Fossils performed live on only three occasions. On June 10, they were at the Peachtree Corners Festival in Chamblee, Georgia. Then on July 22 they appeared at the Mall of Georgia for the fifth time, followed by a July 23 performance on the patio deck that connected two separate Smyrna businesses, St. Angelo's Pizza and Keegan's Steak House.

The temperature on July 22 and 23 was predicted to be in the upper 90s. Toby, still dealing with the after-effects of his battle with Guillain-Barre Syndrome, was unable to tolerate the hot Georgia weather. Not wanting to cancel the gigs, Tim turned to Darwin, who subbed for Toby both days. "He really came to the rescue," Tim recalls.

Although the band promoted that weekend's shows on several social media platforms, the overall crowd was rather

*Foxes and Fossils performing at the Peachtree Corners Festival
on June 10, 2017. (Photo courtesy of Terri Purcell)*

small by comparison to their past performances. Regardless, Tim was touched to see that several fans responded to the Internet postings, driving long distances to see them perform live. At that show were people from Durham, North Carolina, Orlando, Florida, Columbia, South Carolina, and Baton Rouge, Louisiana.

The Last Of The Live Performances...For Now!
2018–2021

Not only did Foxes and Fossils have no live performances in 2018, but that year also marked the official end of The

Mustangs. With Scott now living in Virginia, any thoughts of a live show by either band were a fantasy. In 2020 though, three of the fossils—Tim, Johnny, and Darwin—managed to get together for a socially distanced July 4 performance at Dearborn Plaza in Hapeville, the site of Tim's and Darwin's old high school.

Foxes and Fossils' final public appearance, at least to this point in the story, was in 2021. Tim, Darwin, Sammie, and Maggie got together to sing an a cappella version of the National Anthem at Truist Park in Smyrna, Georgia—home of the 2021 World Champion Atlanta Braves.

Chapter 11

AN AMERICAN
YOUTUBE SENSATION

aggie Adams went to Belmont with the hope of
becoming a professional singer. But by 2017, she'd
had a change of heart and switched over to the business side of the industry—in particular, marketing. "I have no
further interest in being a professional singer," she said. "I
think that ship has sort of sailed. I'm not pursuing a singing
career anymore."[510] She hadn't lost interest in Foxes and Fossils and continued to make music with them whenever the
opportunity presented itself, but singing was no longer the
main focus for her. "[Singing] feels like a separate part of my
life," she said. "It's fun and I'm glad I have it, but my career
is in marketing."[511]

She kept up with Foxes and Fossils while she worked at
Olivia Management in Nashville and especially took notice
of their YouTube statistics. "I saw the YouTube numbers
that were rising organically on the band's website," she said.
"I thought, this is not normal. The artists that I work for [at

---

510   Author interview with Maggie Adams, January 5, 2022.
511   Ibid.

Olivia Management] aren't even close to getting these numbers organically."[512]

Maggie suspected that the sudden rise in YouTube hits for the band's songs was an anomaly, but upon further investigation, she found that YouTube had recently changed its algorithm. "The algorithms used to point you to the most popular video ever," Maggie said. "In 2017, they started to switch their algorithm strategy to point people to more niche videos. That's when we saw the uptick because we had become a niche."[513]

Because she worked in the music management business, Maggie knew that the number of views that Foxes and Fossils videos were getting was not something to take lightly. "I worked for other independent artists that didn't have a label behind them, and they would be getting maybe several thousand views—maybe a hundred thousand if they were pushed by something," she said. "They definitely weren't growing at the rate that Foxes and Fossils were. This was not normal, and I knew that it shouldn't be ignored. I had the idea that we should restart the band and I went to Tim with it."[514]

After some discussion, Tim thought the anomaly interesting enough to take seriously and decided to make another video. "The first video we posted in 2019 was a video we made when Sammie, Chase, and I were all living in Nashville," Maggie said. "I asked them to get together to post a video asking people what they wanted to hear. It was the first one posted after years of not posting new stuff. Shortly thereafter, Sammie and Chase moved away from Nashville. Chase switched schools, and Sammie returned to Georgia. I regretted not doing more videos when we were together."[515]

---

512   Ibid.
513   Ibid.
514   Ibid.
515   Ibid.

Band Members React To Their Newfound Success

In response to Maggie's revelations, Tim strategized with the band members on how to take advantage of their rise in YouTube viewership. The group ultimately decided that studio recordings of the band performing new songs would work best. Tim called everyone back to his studio, and they recorded several songs. One song in particular didn't really appeal to Tim, but when Maggie suggested it, he decided to be nice. That song, *Harvest Moon*, required a key change to accommodate the shift from male (Neil Young) to female (Maggie Adams) vocals. At the time of this writing, the video has over 3,600,000 YouTube views. "The song took on a life of its own," Tim said in an interview with Ken Kojak of 60's Jukebox Review. "It was really the springboard for everything that has come since."[516]

It is rather ironic that the band reached a high level of fame after it stopped performing live. That irony wasn't lost on Darwin. "After the [2010] summer was over, the girls were back in school so there weren't that many performances," he said. "I knew we sounded good, and it was fun, but I never dreamed that it would take off like it did. We just kept following that carrot."[517]

Scott King, the man who once said that playing with The Mustangs was his dream job, also commented about the Foxes and Fossils paradox. "This band kept going and The Mustangs didn't," he said. "I would have liked it if both bands had kept on. We certainly could have done that as we were doing only six to eight Foxes and Fossils jobs a summer, so there was certainly plenty of time to do it. Though officially,

516   Kojak, Ken, 60's Jukebox Review Podcast, RememberWhenRadio.com, Interview with Tim & Chase, New York, 2021. https://foxesandfossils. com/chase-and-tim-on-60s-jukebox-revuew/

517   Author interview with Darwin Conort, March 29, 2022.

The Mustangs are still going. We never did break up, there just wasn't any more work."[518]

The Making Of The YouTube Videos

Scott was amazed by the technology that allows Foxes and Fossils to record their music remotely. "My recording studio is in my lap right now," he said. "I record into my laptop. There's a digital interface which is about the size of a pack of Twinkies, that you plug your guitar into, and you plug that into the computer. That turns everything into signals that the computer reads. I send that digitally down to [Tim in] Atlanta, and it gets on a Foxes and Fossils recording. I do most of my recording in what used to be the dining room."[519] With a hardy laugh Scott noted that no one ever uses a formal dining room anyway. "Well, okay then, mine is a recording studio!"[520] he said.

Everyone in the band uses the same equipment to record. Doug Godbold who is not only a world class sound engineer but a computer whiz as well, was able to help the sexagenarians get over their fear of computers, and make everything as easy to use as possible. Maggie records a lot of her stuff in Nashville, Sammie recorded in Boston while at grad school, and Chase in Iowa when she was in college. Everyone would send it to Tim, who would mix it all up and sync the sound with the video.

"It's a pretty amazing process," Scott said. "We never would have been able to continue to do what we're doing without it. We maybe could have gotten together once or twice a year and maybe recorded one or two songs, and maybe we'd be

---

518   Author interview with Scott King, December 17, 2021.
519   Ibid.
520   Ibid.

happy with them. But now, I usually send three of four different bass parts to Tim, because I like bits and pieces of different ones and I know he'll like bits and pieces of different ones too. He can pick the bits he likes and add them to my bits and just kind of rearrange things a little. It's amazing. With the vocals, especially when he has them there in the studio, he can get them to sing different parts until he gets what he wants."[521]

Some of the songs, Scott noted, could never be played live. "The way we record stuff is fascinating," he said. "The recordings are too intricate and there are people singing and playing multiple parts, which on the recordings overlap. I remember producing The Mustangs Christmas album, and we did one of the old traditional heavy vocal numbers—it was *I'll Be Home For Christmas*—our keyboard player had arranged a jazz version of it. It was all in five-part harmony, real close harmony, like Four Freshmen type harmony. Each part was so difficult that we would each learn and record a single line at a time, to make sure we had that right. We'd do it four or five times and make sure it was perfect before moving on to the next line. There's no way we could ever have played it live. It was simply a studio version. We probably could never do many of the Foxes and Fossils songs live [for the same reason]."[522]

It seems that all the band members were surprised by the band's sudden rise in popularity and YouTube fame. "I've struggled as a musician for 40 years, schlepping equipment in and out of hotels and seedy dives," Tim said in an interview with Bo Emerson for The Atlanta Journal-Constitution. "Then in my so-called retirement, this happens."[523]

521   Ibid.
522   Ibid.
523   Emerson, Bo, The Atlanta Journal-Constitution, Atlanta Living & Arts, Father and Daughter Lead Smyrna Cover Band to You-Tube Success, September 22, 2020. https://foxesandfossils.com/foxes-and-fossils-two-generations-make-sweet-music/

Bo Emerson contends that the "success of the band is due to Tim's skill at remote recording and to friend Terry Heinlein's willingness to shoot multi-camera videos at *Foxes and Fossils* gigs. Credit should also go to the band's flexibility," he wrote in a 2020 feature story in the Atlanta Living Arts section of the Journal Constitution. While that is true, the lion's share of the credit clearly belongs to Tim for his ability, willingness, and hard work in editing, mixing and posting all of those recordings on the Foxes and Fossils YouTube Channel.

Music Critics React

Critics have taken notice of the band and they like what they see. Jason M. Rubin is a writer for The Arts Fuse, "a curated, independent online arts magazine dedicated to publishing in-depth criticism, along with high quality previews, interviews, and commentaries"[524]. In February 2021, Rubin published a review of Foxes and Fossils in which he spoke of YouTube as a universal stage. Rubin was clearly taken with the band, noting that while he discovered their sound during the pandemic lockdown, "the real reason for their success…is that they are crazy good. Even though they are a cover band, their performances are fresh and delightful. While faithful to the originals, they are not slavish imitations."[525]

He heaps praise on the band's vocals, calling Maggie's rendition of Neil Young's *Harvest Moon* "perfectly languid," Chase's performance of Todd Rundgren's *Love is the Answer* "powerful," and Sammie's rendition of John Prine's *Angel from Montgomery* "touching."

"But there's more," Rubin continues. "Aside from being

524   The Arts Fuse Website, https://artsfuse.org/about-us/.
525   Ibid. Page 1.

talented musicians, most of the Fossils also do background vocals and, combined with the Foxes, they recreated an amazing harmony vocal stack on The Beach Boys' *Don't Worry Baby* and The Eagles' *Seven Bridges Road*. All three Foxes pay homage to the trio of Linda Ronstadt, Dolly Parton, and Emmylou Harris on the beautiful *Telling Me Lies*. Tim absolutely nails Billy Joel's *Piano Man*, and gets his Denny Doherty on in the Mamas & the Papas' *California Dreaming*. Lead guitarist Darwin Conort helps himself to a fine rendition of Gordon Lightfoot's *Early Morning Rain,* as well."[526]

A critical podcast called A Breath of Fresh Air with Sandy Kaye also offered a positive review of Foxes and Fossils. "They are definitely a band to keep your eye on,"[527] Kaye said. Speaking specifically of the band's rendition of the Crosby, Stills, & Nash hit *Suite Judy Blue Eyes*, Kaye called them an "incredible cover band whose popularity has been soaring."[528]

John E. Marshall—the host of a podcast called, Reaction Land—recently commented on the Foxes and Fossils version of *Dance With Me*, originally performed in 1975 by the American soft rock band, Orleans. "Their voices together sound like a big warm hug, ear candy,"[529] he said. "Tim Purcell and Chase on lead vocals [take] this song to a whole new level. Maggie, Sammie, Chase, and Darwin really rang the harmony dinner bell on this one. I can honestly say that they took a great song and made it even better. Having the full group ensemble also made a huge difference. Yet another musical victory for the Foxes and Fossils."[530]

526   Ibid. Page 2.
527   Kaye, Sandy, Podcast, A Breadth of Fresh Air with Sandy Kaye. https://foxesandfossils.com/a-breath-of-fresh-air/
528   Ibid.
529   Marshall, John E, Reaction Land, YouTube, April 27, 2022.
530   Ibid.

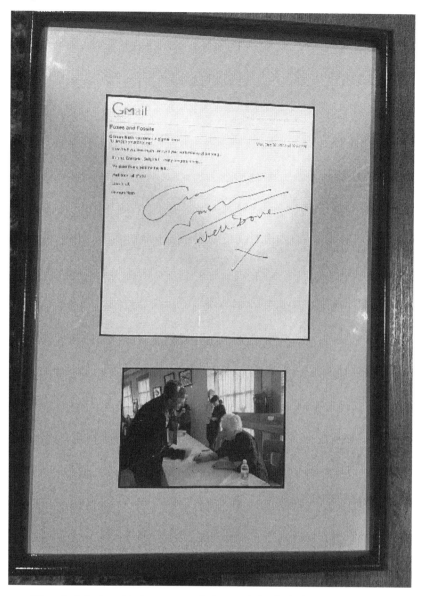

Tim asked Graham Nash to autograph the email that he had sent to Foxes and Fossils and added the photo of Nash signing it before having it framed. It is currently mounted on the wall of his studio. (Photo courtesy of Tim Purcell.)

The email reads: "I can't tell you how much I enjoyed your performance of our song. In tune, energetic, delightful…Many congratulations…. My sister Elaine sent me this link…. Well done, all of you. Love to all. Graham Nash."

On March 31, 2021, John Lange Music posted a You-Tube video evaluating various cover bands. Lange registered his opinion of the top five. He listed Foxes and Fossils as number two, just behind the touring band, The Classic Rock Show. With their many releases over the past year, and the additional 20 million YouTube views, many would say that Foxes and Fossils are clearly now in the number one position.

New York podcaster Ken Kojak hosts a program on RememberWhenRadio.com called 60's Jukebox Review. In 2021, he interviewed Tim and Chase, noting that the instrumentalists were great as were the harmonies. "You guys are fantastic," he told them. "There are harmonies and there's music...Many times the music competes with the voices, but Foxes and Fossils get this right on target. They have beautiful harmonies, beautiful voices, and the band behind them is fabulous."[531]

Mark Helpsmeet, the host of Northern Spirit Radio's Song of the Soul Podcast, spoke of Sammie's vocals in *Angel from Montgomery* describing them as "heart and beauty." Brian Player of the My Life in Music podcast featured a segment on Foxes and Fossils in 2021, noting that "their harmonies are superb and their musicians, fantastic. Their talent combined with the well-known music they cover is a can't miss YouTube."[532]

The accolades do not end with fans and music critics. The members of some of those bands that Foxes and Fossils cover have also showered their praises on the band's renditions of their songs. Graham Nash was so taken by the band's cover of *Suite Judy Blue Eyes* that he wrote Tim a congratulatory

531   Kojak, Ken, 60's Jukebox Review Podcast, RememberWhenRadio.com, Interview with Tim & Chase, New York, 2021. https://foxesandfossils.com/chase-and-tim-on-60s-jukebox-revuew/

532   Helpsmeet, Mark, Northern Spirit Radio's Song of the Soul Podcast. https://foxesandfossils.com/listen-to-sammie-on-song-of-the-soul-podcast/

Screenshot of Todd Rundgren's Facebook page showing off the Foxes and Fossils cover of his song. (Image taken from the Foxes and Fossils Fan Page)

email. "I can't tell you how much I enjoyed your performance of our song," he wrote. "In tune, energetic, delightful...Many congratulations.... My sister Elaine sent me this link.... Well done, all of you. Love to all. Graham Nash."[533]

Tim had an opportunity to meet and speak with Nash at a book signing when he headlined the 30-A Songwriter's Festival near Watercolor, Florida. Graham recognized him, chatted about the band, and autographed a copy of the email.[534] The printed and framed email now hangs on a wall in Tim's basement recording studio. Darwin also met Graham Nash at a CSN show at the Fox Theater in Atlanta.

---

533   Nash, Graham, from hand signed email sent to Tim after hearing the Foxes and Fossils rendition of Suite Judy Blue Eyes that was posted on YouTube. December 30, 2013.

534   O'Donnell, Ian, Foxes and Fossils Frequently Asked Questions, with Answers, posted on the Foxes and Fossils Facebook Fan Page May 18, 2021, and revised on April 30, 2022. (John Hazeldene also assisted with the gathering of information on this Q&A which is the basis for much of the information about other artists' reaction.)

Graham left him passes and they met backstage after the show, chatting for about an hour. Darwin described him as gracious, kind and very open.[535]

Todd Rundgren shared the Foxes and Fossils version of *We Gotta Get You A Woman* on his Facebook page and Linda Thompson, who co-wrote the song *Telling Me Lies*, joined the Foxes and Fossils Fan Group.

Both Craig Fuller and Steve Speelman of Pure Prairie League praised the Foxes and Fossils' version of the song *Aime*, while Keith Whitley's sound engineer, Gary Manasquan, was quoted as being "blown away" by the Foxes and Fossils' version of *When You Say Nothing At All*.

A short time ago, guitarist Jane Wiedlin, the co-founder of the Go-Go's, posted on the Foxes and Fossils' YouTube channel after hearing the band's version of *Our Lips Are Sealed*. "Wow! I love this,"[536] she wrote. More recently, John Hall and Brady Spencer of Orleans both took time to compliment Foxes and Fossils on their performance of *Dance With Me*. Many other original artists or those who tour with their bands have also commented favorably on the Foxes and Fossils rendition of their songs.

535   Ibid.
536   Wiedlin, Jane, reaction to the Foxes and Fossils version of the Go-Go's hit song, 'Our Lips Are Sealed'.

Part III
ODDS AND ENDS

Chapter 12

THOSE AMAZING FANS

The soulful music of Foxes and Fossils touches hundreds of thousands of fans in so many different ways. The band's harmonious sounds have become addictive to many. Once a Foxes and Fossils tune passes within hearing it is hard to turn it off and like a Lay's Potato Chip, few can have just one. All admit to going down the "rabbit hole" watching video after video sometimes for hours, others become even more involved, making statistical charts or even creating works of art for or about the band. Scott Kale hand-carved a beautiful electric guitar featuring the band's name and 'logo' (see image below) and Howard Pearlman crafted a Foxes and Fossils sign made of stained glass that hangs in Tim's studio and can be seen in many of their videos. One fan even sent his old hockey sweater!

Regardless of their depth of involvement with the band, all fans share one common characteristic. They love the music that this band produces. According to John Hazeldene, one of the group's self-appointed statisticians, the number of YouTube views increases by over one million one hundred

Darwin, pictured above, holding the guitar that was hand carved for Foxes and Fossils by Scott Kale. (Photo taken from Foxes and Fossils Fan Page)

thousand every month. That's down from a high of 2.4 million per month during the pandemic. Despite that reduction, the total number of views has now reached 80 million

In addition to the unfathomable "YouTube hit rate," the Foxes and Fossil's YouTube channel has over one hundred and sixty-five thousand subscribers. The band's Facebook fan page has some fifteen thousand followers and there are five hundred and sixty-four Patreon members who provide monthly financial support that enables the band to continue to produce music that those fans cherish.

Foxes and Fossils fans are both male and female, young and old, reside in all fifty of these United States and in about forty other countries around the world. Just what is it about Foxes and Fossils that keeps so many fans on the bandwagon (pardon the pun)? That is more than a rhetorical question and certainly warrants a response. With that in mind, we asked few fans to describe how they first stumbled upon Foxes and Fossils and what keeps them coming back. Here are some of their responses in their own words.

JAN 8, 2021

Dear Tim,
    Thought you might get a kick out of my old hockey sweater. You and the rest of Foxes a Fossils provide so much joy for so many people. Wishing you all the best in 2021!

                    Sincerely,
                    Paul Broyd

P.S. The previous owner of sweater #12 still holds the single game scoring record (8 goals) after 40 years.

Above is a photo of a hockey sweater that was sent by Paul
Broyd sent to Tim. It was accompanied by the handwritten note.
(Photos courtesy of Tim Purcell)

Bruce Johnson
California–May 10, 2022

"As the Covid-19 pandemic began around April 2020, and I was mostly at home, I happened to search the internet for The Eagles song 'Seven Bridges Road.' One of the results was a recent studio cover of the song by Foxes & Fossils. I really liked their version and started watching other You-Tube videos they had made, including those of their past live shows. I was amazed at the sound quality from those older live shows compared with most audience-recorded live shows on YouTube. Pretty soon, I somehow found the Facebook fan page and once I joined, I found out that some of the band members were also members of the fan page.

I especially noticed that the bass player, Scott King, would often comment on fan posts and I wondered if there was anything that I could contribute. With band members being scattered across the country to attend college or for some other reasons, I realized that having them all together in one place for a group photo seemed to be difficult. I noticed that there were photos of the band members in the fan page photo album, so using what was available, I attempted to digitally edit them into the same shot and posted the result. (See photo below.)

That attempt to consolidate members into one photo, needed some improvements, so I just kept my eye out for other photos of the band members and thought of how I might combine them into something visually interesting. Often, after someone posted a new photo, I'd think *Hmm... what if...* For example, the photo of Maggie (above on the left) became the photo of her (above on the right) after I mixed things together.

The idea of this photo was simple. Tim usually records Maggie, but what if Maggie was recording Tim?

The photo (below on the left) shows another room in this studio to which I added Johnny at the drums.

After about 8 hours of digital editing, I had added the rest of the band and even added me and my daughter to the far left of the image resulting in the photo on the right above.

At one point, I was thinking about the artwork of album covers and recalled the cover of Meet the Beatles, the one with the four floating heads. I turned that concept into the photo of the Foxes on the next page.

I used the images of several other album covers and posters to create a host of other photos such as the two pictured below.[537]

537   Johnson, Bruce, Written comments provided to the author. May 10, 2022.

Kevin Burns
Newburgh, Indiana—January 28, 2022

"I stumbled upon Foxes and Fossils sometime in 2019. I was looking for some classic 60's and 70's music. The first song I listened to was "California Dreaming" by one of my favorite 60's groups, The Mamas & The Papas. Tim's vocals were incredible, but it was the harmonies that got me hooked. The band has it all, terrific instrumentals, solid arrangements, but most of all, it is the group's harmonies that blow me away every time and keep me coming back for more. Their latest release, 'Carry On' by *CSNY* may be their best yet. I can only hope they keep the music coming."[538]

Mike Frey
Pennsylvania—February 6, 2022

"I discovered Foxes & Fossils in early 2019, long after they stopped performing live but before they returned to the studio to record more music. I found them the way many of their fans found them, by searching YouTube for music from my youth and stumbling onto their recording of Crosby, Stills and Nash's song 'Suite: Judy Blue Eyes'. I must confess, the first time I listened to their version of SJBE I was NOT knocked out and didn't even listen to the entire song. It was good but a band with two fifteen-year-old girls was NOT what I was looking for. Immediately after that, I watched F&F perform another CSN song, 'Helplessly Hoping'. THAT one blew me away from the very first note! Instant tears! I went BACK to SJBE and this time I listened to the entire song, and I heard

---

538   Burns, Kevin, Written comments provided to the author. January 28, 2022.

something I had not heard the first time. A band with vocalists who were GOOD, forget their age. I heard a bassist who was slaying a difficult bass line and a guitarist who was clearly channeling Stephen Stills. I decided that if they could cover CSN this well, I should check out more of their videos. I never stopped, and 3 years later I'm still listening to them every day.

What do I like about Foxes & Fossils? It starts with their vocals. Pitch-perfect and soulful with incredibly tight harmonies; harmonies on a par with bands like The Beach Boys and The Mamas & The Papas. Their vocalists don't just sing lyrics, they feel them, and they make YOU feel them too. Then there is the quality of the instrumentals. Each of the Fossils is a master of their craft. Scott on the bass. Johnny on drums, Toby and Darwin on guitar, and Tim on guitar and keyboards, and a genius at producing their videos. And then they added Chase! OMG! A clear case of the rich getting MUCH richer. And, on top of all that, they are all genuinely nice people. In the past 3 years I've come to appreciate them as people of good character as much as great musicians. What's NOT to like about this band?!

I've come to think of all of them as friends and almost family, family members I have never met! I can't explain this except to say that the band has gone above and beyond my expectations to make their fans feel like part of an extended family. My fondest wish is to meet every one of them in person so I can tell them, face-to-face, what they mean to me. My own wife and kids tolerate my support of the band even if they don't understand it entirely. My wife has become a fan as well, although not a fan of the first order like me. My kids, who are all grown and with lives of their own, know of my love for this band and are accepting of it, if not sharing in it.

Lastly, I have enjoyed my time on the F&F fan page almost

as much as my time listening to their music. Their fans are just a wonderful group of people. I'm not sure how much time I have remaining on this earth, but I refuse to leave until I have attended a live Foxes & Fossils performance. So, please tell Tim there's no hurry!"[539]

Daniel Ashton
Rio Rancho, New Mexico—February 9, 2022

"I've been watching Foxes and Fossils videos on YouTube for about five years now. I saw one of their outdoor performances pop up and clicked on it as I liked the song 'Landslide' that they were covering. Two hours later I was still watching videos and I've been hooked ever since. The harmonies of not only Maggie, Sammie, and Chase, but Tim, Darwin and (the late) Scott are some of the best out there.

Maggie has a very mellow voice where Sammie's voice has a wonderful sharpness to it. And Chase? Well Chase has an unbelievable range, and in my opinion, really nails "big band era" songs. Tim is masterful in his vocals and chooses songs well suited to his voice. Darwin is, by far, my favorite 'Fossil'. His voice has such an extraordinarily mellow sound to it and his guitar work is exceptional.

Johnny is a very talented drummer and bass player. One of the best videos, 'Early Morning Rain,' is a recent one, taken at a 4th of July event, where Johnny is playing the drums AND the bass guitar at the same time. This is one of the best assembly of musicians I've ever had the privilege of interacting with. I have purchased all their music and listen to it especially on long driving trips. It sure makes the miles pass by more quickly."[540]

---

539   Frey, Mike, Written comments, Pennsylvania, February 6, 2022.
540   Ashton, Daniel, Written comments, New Mexico, February 9, 2022.

Monique Kooij-Alphenaar
The Hague, The Netherlands—March 22, 2022

"In 2020, the year of the start of the Covid-19 pandemic, my husband, Nol Kooij, went on YouTube to amuse himself by finding cover bands who covered songs by The Mamas & The Papas. Nol was a musician who played the guitar and the bass guitar, but above all, he was a singer and arranger of voices. We own Studio 123 in The Hague, The Netherlands.

Nol was also a night owl who loved to sit in the evening and night and watch music on YouTube. I think it was in May when he discovered Foxes & Fossils. He told me about this find the next morning and said he was very moved. Never had he come across a band that made perfect music. He presented me with a sampling of their songs and cried when we listened to these covers—and so did I when I heard those perfect harmonies, great voices and wonderful music played by skillful musicians. I soon started to read about the background of these astonishing people. We ordered the CD's. It took months for them to arrive from the USA to the Netherlands during the pandemic, but they did arrive, and we loved them. I connected with the band on Facebook so we would know about any new releases.

Nol was a transplant patient who received both a kidney and a pancreas in 2004. In the summer of 2021, he fell ill. We had lived through this before so we thought it would pass. In November we ordered the Christmas CD and looked at the previews. We cried because of the beauty of the songs. On the night of December 25, Nol became extremely ill and had to be admitted to the hospital.

He was diagnosed with lymphoma and had to undergo chemotherapy. I promised him that when he was better, we would go to the USA and visit Tim and hopefully, some of the other members of the band. It was a big motivation for him to get well again.

On the day the Christmas CD arrived, we read about Scott's death. We were extremely sad about this fellow bass player and wonderful musician who died of cancer. I lit a candle, and we played the CD and cried for the sheer perfection of this music, the sadness that a wonderful musician had left this world, and for this band who would be mourning. At that moment we still thought Nol would get better....

Nol died on March 3, 2022, at the age of 64. He died knowing he would be part of this book and part of the story of Foxes & Fossils. He was very happy about that."[541]

Brad Burns
Caledonia, Michigan—February 12, 2022

"My introduction to Foxes and Fossils started when their cover of Neil Young's 'Harvest Moon' was presented to me by YouTube's analog deities during the early days of the COVID lockdowns. I began watching and listening to what I thought was a group of regular guys my age, rather informally performing and playing the music in their basement when nearly a minute later this lovely young lady appears and begins singing with a voice that was every bit as lovely as she. I was quickly enamored with Maggie's voice. She drew me into the video much like I imagine the mythical sirens would draw the sailors of ancient times into the rocky shores. If that was not enough, thirty seconds later two more young lovelies, Sammie and Chase, chimed in with their beautifully orchestrated background harmonies. I was, to say the least, an immediate fan and after listening to the song again, I wanted to hear more.

---

541   Kooij-Alphanaar, Monique, written comments provided from The Hague, Netherlands, March 22, 2022.

As I began to work my way through all the Foxes and Fossils videos, I came to realize that this was a different type of band from the norm, not just the fact that the musicians were a generation older than the vocalist, but because this is a band with not just one lead singer. This band had three absolutely marvelous female lead singers, all of whom are equally capable of performing their lead roles to perfection. And what a range of vocals! Terrific from Sammie's highs all the way down to Chases' lows. I must admit, when Chase takes her vocals down to the basement, my soul reaches seventh heaven. After listening to even more of their music videos, I discovered that, aside from the young ladies, two of those good ole boys in the band, Tim and Darwin, also provide very impressive lead vocals as well. And not just that, I realized the fossils are not just background musicians, the five of them are some of the best musicians I have ever listened to over the years.

As a 'fossil' and one-time guitarist myself, there is so much to appreciate as a fan with this group. Most of the music they cover are classics that were originally performed during my youth and every one of them brings back cherished memories. There is also the fact that the three, four, and five-part harmonies that Tim synchronizes quite masterfully, are second to none. They rival those of some of the greats they cover, such as The Mamas & Papas, Crosby, Stills & Nash, and Simon & Garfunkel. Die-hard fans like myself, who appreciate great music and who know the history of the group, also appreciate the love and affection each member of the group shows for the others. There is no jealousy or turf wars in this group. Another thing I noticed is that these highly talented fossils, each of whom could easily perform great music on their own, have gone out of their way to highlight the talents of the foxes and give them a platform to display their marvelous abilities. I am so very happy they did.

Another thing I appreciate is the fact that so many of the recordings during the first nine years or so were live and performed in bars, outside restaurants and in parking lots. To me, this makes their story even that much better. Most remarkably, all the foxes began singing with the group when they were only fifteen years old, Chase joining the group five years after the others. How Tim could find three different fifteen-year-old girls, with such marvelous voices in one little area near Atlanta seems rather remarkable.

Something I am not used to as a fan, is the fact that F&F is not above communicating with their fans from time to time. I have seen Maggie, Tim, Darwin and Johnny commenting on their YouTube channel. And Scott King, who just recently passed away after a long illness, communicated with me, as well as others, many times over the last couple years through comments on YouTube and Facebook. Because of these communications, my connection with Scott became rather strong, so much so that the news of his passing hit me quite hard. Scott will be truly missed.

So now, fans like me sit in wait each month for a new studio-recorded cover to be released. We show up early on the video chat line to talk to each other and say hello to the band members and then spend the next five minutes listening to whatever special video they have to offer. We have never been disappointed. We also wait patiently for the real possibility that someday soon there will be live performances for us to attend.

One of the members of the band, Chase Truran, is also pursuing a solo career in music and I look forward to following her career just as much as I plan to enjoy following Foxes and Fossils, hopefully for many years to come. Chase's personal YouTube channel already has a solid following and once she releases the original music she is currently producing, this guy, who considers himself to be her number one fan, hopes to have another musical dynasty to pursue. I have even started a Facebook Fan Page for Chase a couple years ago and consequently have become rather expert in her musical career."[542]

Steven Poegl
Midlothian, Virginia—March 23, 2022

"I suppose I discovered Foxes and Fossils very much the way many folks did by simply running across them while perusing YouTube for songs I wanted to hear. The first song I heard was 'Suite Judy Blue Eyes' and I was blown away by the tight vocals and spot-on musicianship of the players. My discovery came at a time when I was pretty disappointed with all the harmful noise on social media, particularly Facebook. I had learned over time that all I was interested in talking about was music, so I joined a few fan pages for other artists.

Also, I'd supported a few up-and-coming musicians and groups over the years, so when I heard and watched F&F I thought I'd like to give these folks a hand by introducing them to some of my friends in Richmond, Virginia. I decided that the best way to do that was to start a fan page. But, little did I know, the band was already trending on its own. At first, I got five or ten folks to join, followed by tens, then hundreds, and finally thousands, all very much to my surprise and delight. All this and the pandemic made for the perfect storm.

It's been a little more than two years now and the fan page is still growing. There are several folks who help maintain the page and contribute regularly to its content. The

542   Burns, Brad, written comments provided from Caledonia, Michigan, February 12, 2022.

rules are simple, and we are devoted to keeping our page clean and friendly for all, a safe harbor of sorts. The mission is to have fun, enjoy and discuss the music, make new friends, and most of all, to be kind to one another."[543]

Gary Tupholme
Bracebridge, Ontario Canada—February 11, 2022

"I am a seventy-one-year-old fossil and have played guitar (badly) since I was fifteen. I have always been a Crosby, Stills and Nash (CSN) fan and later a Crosby, Stills, Nash and Young (CSNY) fan as well. A couple of friends and I used to try to play 'Suite Judy Blue Eyes', to no avail, as it was too complicated for our abilities.

Then, one night in November or December of 2018, I was searching YouTube for 'Suite Judy Blue Eyes', expecting *CSN* to show up. Lo and behold, Foxes and Fossils popped up! My first thought was the girls looked real young prompting me to feel that this would be a pretty bad cover knowing how difficult the song is to play and sing. To my surprise, I was completely blown away at how great a job the band did on this song. I ended up listening to it about six times and then started sending it out to friends and family saying, 'You have to check out this cover band—they are incredible!'

What struck me in this song is Darwin's guitar playing because he used the same tuning as Stephen Stills, and Scott King's bass lines were phenomenal. Then you get to lead parts by Tim and Darwin and the beautiful harmonies from Maggie and Sammie and to me it sounded better than the original! I ended up viewing the rest of the songs they did at Bella's Pizzeria and every song was so well done—amazing!

---

543   Poegl, Steve, written comments provided from Midlothian, Virginia, March 23, 2022.

After that I found their later performances at the Twisted Taco and other outside venues and with every song, they did such a great job. What I also really loved was they were having fun—interacting with people in attendance at their little shows with no diva attitude or arrogance. They all seemed like real nice people. The girls were so sweet and complimentary to everyone and as this whole thing grew it was like the band, their families and fans were like one big family that became a world-wide family.

With the onset of the Covid-19 pandemic, some of the girls were away at university (that's when Chase came on-board—she has an incredible voice!) Tim started doing recordings in his basement studio. Again, their songs were incredible, the fossils are all excellent musicians and again, everyone seems to be having a lot of fun doing this.

When Maggie discovered what was happening with their songs being viewed millions of times, they really took this to the next level. She later put together the Patreon program which I joined right away to help support the band.

I love this band because they are all first-class musicians and singers, and Tim really brings out the best of each member in his production of each song. Because they cover so many different song styles and artists, I have been introduced to a lot of songs, singers and bands that I was never aware of and its great music. I purchased their CD's and listen to them all the time. One of the best things is that I have been able to "talk" with most of the band members directly through the comments sections of Patreon and Facebook. With all the lockdowns, political and Covid related "stuff" that has been going on for the past few years, it is really relaxing to sit down and either watch a bunch of their videos or listen to the CD's and feel good. I know many of the fans have said the same thing.

Lastly, I was very sad to hear about the passing of bassist

Scott King. He was one of the best bass players I've heard—he added so much to the band and thankfully I had the chance to "talk" to him about his bass guitars. He will be sorely missed."[544]

Paul Giammarco
Retired radio personality and lifelong singer/bass player.
North Providence, Rhode Island—February 10, 2022

"Whether it's the sweet soulful harmonic voicing of the Beach Boys harmonies or performing the playlist of America's pop rock songbook, Foxes and Fossils perform all their songs with the authenticity and reverence of the original. It's so gratifying to see and hear each generation within the group paying homage to the soundtracks of our lives!

I first learned of Foxes and Fossils while searching for tunes we were learning in my cover band, The CarTune Heroes. I was knocked out by the musical mastery displayed by all the members, and we were wholly inspired to reach their level of excellence."[545]

Linda and Bob LaFrenierre
Peyton, Colorado—February 17, 2022

"About two years ago Covid-19 hit and we were suddenly plunged into the 'lockdowns' that hit the world. We were somewhat prepared for this new world order, but YouTube videos helped pass many hours of education and entertainment.

544 Tupholme, Gary, written comments provided from Bracebridge, Ontario, Canada, February 11, 2022.
545 Giammarco, Paul, written comments provided from North Providence, Rhode Island, February 10, 2022.

Early into the lockdown, Bob discovered a cover band, Foxes and Fossils, performing 'Helplessly Hoping'. He watched/listened to one or two more songs then later mentioned to Linda that he had discovered a cover band who were very talented. It took only one video to bring Linda on board.

In the past two years we have watched/listened to hundreds of their performances, bought several CDs, and (Linda) followed them on Facebook. Their harmonizing abilities are equal to the best...CSN/Y. Each new release on YouTube is eagerly anticipated.

We, like thousands of others, were very sad when Scott King passed, but hope the group can continue recording for their fans and themselves. We don't go to many live concerts these days, but if they were to perform live, we would be there to enjoy!"[546]

David Weaver
Phoenixville, Pennsylvania–March 17, 2022

"I first found Foxes & Fossils late one Sunday evening in January 2019, one of those nights when you know you should try to get some sleep but keep coming up with excuses not to. I was looking up old Beatles concerts and YouTube recommended the Foxes & Fossils version of 'The Night Before'. I usually don't look up cover bands but for some reason, possibly divine intervention, I clicked on it. Of course, I quickly discovered it wasn't The Beatles song—I figured it wouldn't be. I was really impressed with everything about the video: the camera work, the sound, the editing, the musicianship and especially Sammie Purcell's performance on lead vocals. It was all really very good.

---

546   Frenierre, Linda & Bob, written comments provided from Peyton, Colorado, February 17, 2022.

Then I went to the comments section. Now the internet being what it is, I expected to read a bunch of snide comments about Sammie and Maggie. But surprisingly, all the comments were positive. The only negative thing was finding out that the band was no longer together. So just my luck, I find the greatest band in the world and they're no longer playing. But, there were these hints from Scott and Tim in comments on other videos that something might be in the works.

Then came April 29, 2019, when Maggie, Sammie and Chase released the 'What Song Will They Cover Next?' video. That was the big one because now it was clear that they would release new material. It took a while, but finally in October 2019, 'Harvest Moon' was released, along with an updated website and the band was off to the races. While nobody could have predicted seventy-two million YouTube views, a fourteen-thousand-member fan page, etc., the success of the band really doesn't surprise me.

So, it got to be the winter of 2019/2020 and I started thinking of creating a fan page for the band. Come to find out, Steve Poegl had already started one. I joined in January 2020 (I think I was member 87). It was also good fortune that some of the earliest members took it upon themselves to make posts and create content, rather than waiting for others to do it. I was asked to be a moderator in the Summer of 2020, and I still hold that position today. I think people might find it surprising that the fan page is completely FAN RUN. It was created by fans, and it is administered by fans. While members of the band and their inner circle have decided to join us, our fan page is an independent entity. We are not some "fan club" run by a publicist. Those of us who are administrators and moderators do so on an unpaid, voluntary basis. Quite frankly, I wouldn't want to be paid. Then it would just be a job.

In addition to my duties as moderator, I guess some people consider me the band's unofficial historian. That really started in earnest in the Spring of 2020. Like everybody else back then, I had a lot of time on my hands due to the Covid-19 lockdowns, so I decided to compile a list of all of Foxes & Fossils live performances. When I started, I thought the total would be about twenty to twenty-five performances. I quickly learned that the real number was considerably higher and was closer to forty! Though getting the list together was frustrating at times, learning the 'stories behind the stories' from band members (particularly Scott King) and their inner circle (particularly videographer Terry Heinlein, sound engineer Doug Godbold, and Maggie's father Larry Adams) was very interesting. It took several weeks to compile the first list and we've had a few updates since then as new dates have been discovered.

So, this is where I am now, just a regular fan who spends too much of his free time on Foxes & Fossils. Like everybody else, I look forward to the chance to see the group perform in public again, as I've never seen them perform live and have not met any of the band members in person. Until then, I just sit tight and enjoy the new videos as they are released."[547]

Terry Heinlein
Friend, fan, videographer
Mableton, Georgia—February 11, 2022

"I first met Tim in the early 90's when he became a member of our church (Smyrna First United Methodist Church). We were standing in a line (hmm, maybe for food!) and he was

---

[547]   Weaver, David, written comments provided from Phoenixville, Pennsylvania, March 17, 2022.

standing ahead of me. I introduced myself to him and after some small talk, asked him if he was a musician. Our church had a group of guys (me included as drummer) who had formed a band and one of the members had moved away. Tim said he sang and played some guitar and keyboards. I don't recollect his answer directly when I asked him if he was interested in joining us. He didn't join us initially, but he did indeed join us sometime later. It was obvious he was good and out of our league, but I believe he took us on as a project. The band's name was Mid Life Crisis, and we performed some and practiced a lot. It lasted maybe a year and the band eventually stopped playing, but Tim and I became friends.

Tim never had stopped playing music with others and I would sometimes attend his gigs. Then he started a band called Tim Purcell and the Mustangs. They would play a lot of venues that my wife and I attended. I always had an interest in what he was doing.

At church, Tim and I had some interest in videography and video editing as a hobby. We did a few multi-camera projects together, shooting events at church. In our early days of video editing, Tim taught me that one way to synchronize the cameras together was to make a loud clap with all 3 cameras pointing to the person clapping. This way, the moment of the clap could be synched in the editor easily.

In addition to Tim, I also knew Sammie and Maggie. They were teenagers in 'God's Light,' the church youth choir. This group performed multiple times during the year. In addition to church services, they performed in special events that doubled as fundraisers for the group, enabling them to travel in the summer throughout the United States. They provided music in various churches along the way. I was the drummer for that choir. Sammie and Maggie were both performers and would sing solos with the youth choir,

and also sing special music at the fundraising events. One of these events was the musical 'Cinderella' in which Sammie played the lead.

Tim called me one day and asked if I would video a gig that he was doing. He told me it was not The Mustangs, but this was a special project. He had always wanted to perform with Sammie on stage. Additionally, he had asked Maggie. The venue was Bella's Pizza on March 10, 2010. Such an odd place to perform in my mind. I decided to shoot three cameras. I asked Maggie's dad Larry to be a camera man and he shot the camera on the left. My wife, Roberta, was camera in the center, and I was the camera on the right. I had no idea what we were going to get from Larry's camera as I had not used him before. I was a little worried that all I would get was Maggie. Roberta had shot a number of venues for me, so I knew she knew what I wanted to see from her camera. (And those of you who have seen the results of the videos from Bella's, can see they both did a great job.) When I saw the group take stage, I saw Scott, so I knew the bass would be fantastic as he played for The Mustangs, but the guy playing guitar, Darwin, I did not know. Tim told me they grew up together in Hapeville, Ga, and played music together back then. When Tim introduced the group, he told the story of coming up with the name of the group. He was thinking of calling the group "The Beauties and the Beasties" but at the last moment, Scott suggested Foxes and Fossils. The music started with 'Suite: Judy Blue Eyes' and I remember I had this big smile on my face. It was an awesome sound for sure. I became a fan that day. Just a side note: I remember thinking that the dang TVs were on and were messing up the shots. But I did not think about it being possible to ask they be turned off. However, being the dad, Larry later went and asked that they be turned off!!

Tim asked me to edit the videos for him as he wanted to keep them as a keepsake and share some on YouTube. He had Toby from The Mustangs doing the sound recording. Tim said if I could get him the videos of each song, he would provide the audio, rather than use the camera audio. I was thrilled to actually put together the video for each song as I had just purchased Final Cut Pro editing software. Not only to allow me the opportunity to create a nice visual of each moment, but also to just listen to their music. Of course, in the editing process, you listen and watch over-and-over again. But it was so much fun. When the video editing was complete, Tim provided the audio that had been recorded direct from the soundboard. Oh My Gosh.... it was amazing how alive the music came.

Tim asked me again to video the group when they performed at the Twisted Taco. Again, an obscure little restaurant in Smyrna. Very small venue setup. And of course, all the cars and people in the background. I asked my friends, Claire and Jim Farmer and my wife, Roberta, to be stationary camera operators. I operated the mobile camera. This time though, Tim had decided he wanted to do the editing, so I just handed him the camera discs. This became the norm. As you can see from all the videos, Tim has become a master editor.

Tim asked me to video several more of the venues along the way. Another Twisted Taco, Crafty Hog, July 4th in Chamblee, Keegan's, and the Foxless Fossils July 4th gig in Hapeville. I also did a Mustangs event in Powder Springs. For most of these, my camera operators were the Farmers and Roberta.

I became a Fan club member in 2019. it was exciting to see the world take notice of the Foxes and Fossils. Tim approached me again and told me that he and Maggie had discussed doing some studio cover songs with the group. At the time, the members were in five different states and performing live was not going to happen. Chase was going to school in Iowa, Sammie was getting her Masters in Boston, Maggie was working in Nashville and Scott was living in Virginia. The rest of the group was in Georgia. Tim asked me to video different Fox members who came home for holidays or to see parents, in the studio. This meant doing several songs in a session. For example, Chase may be singing a lead in one song and backup in two others. Sometimes, the girls could arrange to be together in a session. Other times, Tim or Darwin would join them in backup. As far as the Fossils, I would video Johnny doing several songs in a session. When Tim played keyboards in songs, I would tape him. Both Darwin and Toby would come and do their guitar parts, either together or separate depending on their schedules. And Scott's friend, Scott Kale, did the videography and video recording of Scott which was sent electronically to Tim.

In a short period of time, I was able to participate in a number of the studio songs by virtue of doing several at a time. Then Covid hit, and Tim started borrowing my cameras to do some shoots. Eventually, Tim realized that our great iPhone cameras could get even better video, and, alas, I was no longer needed. I will always be appreciative of my opportunity to be a part of the Foxes and Fossils support team. And I still marvel that my hobby of video has helped make an impression for this group.

I am a big fan. I am connected in the fan club to a number of great people who I have become Facebook friends with. I look forward to meeting them one day at a live Foxes and Fossils Show, if that becomes a reality."[548]

548   Heinlein, Terry, written comments provided from, Mableton, Georgia, February 11, 2022.

Randy Mathews

Colby, Kansas—May 4, 2022

"Greetings! I am a 64-year-old "Fossil" who has been raving about F&F's videos to anyone who would listen for the past several years, but I only found this awesome fan page a couple weeks ago. I'm thrilled, but certainly not surprised, to discover there are so many people who love this group as much as I do. It's hard to accurately describe what this band is about. They're not really 'just' a cover band. That's too limiting. But they're not exclusively a studio band either, because they've played live gigs from time to time.

What they are, in my humble opinion, is a group of exceptionally talented singers, musicians, arrangers, producers, engineers and videographers who have blessed us with some of the finest musical tributes I've ever heard. Some of their exquisite vocal harmonies send chills up my spine, and to think the "Foxes" first demonstrated that astonishing talent when they were still teenagers! Given my age, it's probably no surprise that my favorite F&F songs (so far) are classics like 'Can't Let Go' by Linda Ronstadt, 'Let it be Me' by the Everly Brothers, 'Harvest Moon' by Neil Young, and 'Don't Worry Baby' by the Beach Boys. But I appreciate everything they do, regardless of genre or era.

I look forward to getting acquainted with my fellow *F&F* fans on this page, and to hearing more awesome music in the future. And my belated condolences on the loss of your dear friend and comrade Scott. He left a big void in the band, but his legacy will live on through all the wonderful music he shared. My best to you all!"[549]

---

549   Mathews, Randy, Comments printed on the Foxes and Fossils Facebook Fan Page, May 2, 2022.

Chapter 13

WHAT'S NEXT FOR THE BAND?

While some band members assembled at Truist Park for the a cappella version of the National Anthem before the Atlanta Braves baseball game on April 10, 2021, and three of the Fossils joined together for a socially distanced Fox-less event in Hapeville's Dearborn Plaza on July 4, 2020, the full complement of Foxes and Fossils have not performed together live since 2017.

Shortly before he passed, Scott King suggested that the advancing age of the fossils would make the likelihood of touring remote at best, but said the that band had considered the idea of doing a show that could be videoed and made available as a Pay Per View. Tim had in fact been making plans to do just that before Covid-19 arrived on the scene and put the plan on hold.

As life returned to some semblance of reality (can I say it?) post-Covid, Tim once again floated the idea of the band reuniting for a live, limited seating show in the Atlanta area. Speaking on the Artist First Radio Network Podcast, Tim told host Doug Dahlgren, "We're working on that (a show). There's been a lot of clamor from our fans. People are looking for us to do something live. I get emails everyday asking things like, 'Hey, what would you guys charge to come do my daughter's prom in Little Rock?' Someone else will say, 'I have a club in Birmingham that seats two thousand. We'd love to have you guys.' All I can say to either one is 'We're not doing anything live right now. We have no intention of 'touring' if you will, or even of doing more than a few jobs. But we know our fan base really would like to see us play live and we're working on that right now as we speak. We'd hope to announce at least a couple of shows that would take place toward the end of the year (2022). And, if all that works out, we might do something bigger later on. We have so many songs to choose from that I don't think we'll have any issues finding the right ones. We may even add a couple of players. I think everyone is into it,"[550] he said.

Maggie thinks the band is certainly capable of pulling off a live performance. "I'd love to see it happen. I've always loved performing live with the Foxes and Fossils crew, and although it's been a long time since we've done it, I know that we are capable of doing it again, just as we have in the past. It obviously won't be the same without Scott King making me laugh onstage between every other song, but I know he'd want us to carry on."[551]

Maggie credits Tim with keeping the production videos coming. With regard to future studio recordings, Maggie said, "I hope to continue that as long as we are physically able."[552]

Darwin would also like to see the band continue on, noting that he will remain a part of Foxes and Fossils "until I can't play guitar anymore. We always think of what

550   Dahlgren, Doug, Artist First Radio Network. Friday, May 13, 2022. https://www.artistfirst.com. https://media.artistfirst.com/ArtistFirst_Doug_Dahlgren_2022-05-13_Tim_Purcell.mp3.
551   Maggie Adams written response to the author's question. May 13, 2022.
552   Ibid.

happened to Scott,"[553] Darwin added. Then, after a reflective stare, he adds, "Tim thinks that even when it ends the music will live on."[554]

Statistics show that the band continues to accumulate more than a million YouTube views per month, and they are quickly approaching one hundred million total views. That incredible milestone should be reached before the end of 2023.

Pulling off a successful live performance requires a great deal of advance work. Tim is a little hesitant of putting one together for fear that it may bomb. He is particularly so in this case because of the high expectations held by the fans. "It would be a lot easier if we were all in the same place," Tim explained, "and we could do six weekends in a row where the girls and I got together and made sure we can still sing the songs. I'm a lot older than I was when we started and there are some notes I just can't hit anymore," he said. "We want to be sure that we're not biting off more than we can chew."[555] Tim had similar doubts when they were preparing for the National Anthem, but it worked out fine. Still, you have to be able to get together and rehearse, and with Maggie being out of state, there is a question of how often that could happen.

There are also aspects of a live show that Tim hasn't dealt with in a long time. "It's different than just setting up in a parking lot during the day and playing. We'll have to have lighting, stage direction (blocking), planned instrument changes, and all of this takes planning,"[556] he said.

As of this writing, Tim's thinking is to do something in

553   Author interview with Darwin Conort, March 29, 2022.
554   Ibid.
555   Author interview with Tim Purcell, May 23, 2022.
556   Ibid.

a small theater with a seating capacity of around one hundred and thirty. "We would do two nights," Tim said as if planning out loud. "We'll film it for potential pay-per-view. We'll have to figure out the ticket cost so we'll have enough funds to hire a bassist and potentially an extra keyboard player. I don't think fans will want to hear the stuff we did before, I think they want to see us do some of the new stuff live, and a lot of that has multiple keyboard parts that I would not be able to do and sing at the same time. We'll probably ask Greg, the last keyboard player from *The Mustangs* to join us. Richard Meeder has agreed to play bass. We need to pay the theater, the videographer, someone to do the lights and Doug Godbold to do the sound. We'll also need to rent a lot of gear to allow the guitar players to be wireless so they can move about and change positions and guitars quickly without being tethered to a cord. We'll need more in-ear monitors, etc. This is not a matter of just saying, 'hey, let's go play,'"[557] Tim said.

Health of the band members, particularly the fossils, is also a consideration. Toby, for example, deals with the effects of Parkinson's disease and the long-term effects of Gillian Barre syndrome and if he is having a bad day on the day of the show, that will certainly have an impact. Tim deals with his own issues of hearing loss with severe hearing loss in his right ear and profound hearing loss in his left ear.

If the small event is successful and the two shows go well, then "We'll begin to plan something much bigger," Tim said. "Perhaps a destination show that would be held on a weekend at a resort. We'd have arrival on Friday and a 9:00 acoustic show that night. Golf, the beach or something else on Saturday followed by dinner and a big concert, maybe

---

557   Ibid.

F&F videos potentially reaching one million total YouTube views in 2022/early 2023 (7)							
Video title	#	Date published	17/05/2022 views (k)	Current monthly views (k)	Days to 1M views	Month	
1	Telling Me Lies	26	19/11/2020			445	01/02/2022	
2	American Girl	27	26/09/2011	987.4	9	42	Jul-22	
3	Thinking Out Loud	28	21/12/2016	951.1	10	147	Oct-22	
4	Mr Sandman	29	24/12/2020	924.1	14	163	Oct-22	
5	The Night Before (Life Goes On)	30	24/09/2012	940.2	8	224	Dec-22	
6	Carry On	31	03/11/2021	588.6	45	274	Feb-23	
7	Let It Be Me	32	14/02/2021	844.1	17	275	Feb-23	

The chart above depicts the length of time it might take for the next seven songs to reach 1 million views on YouTube. (Courtesy of John Hazeldene)

outdoors. Then breakfast with the band on Sunday morning before departure. A cruise is another possibility. There are a lot of things we could potentially do," Tim noted. "The real question is do we have enough of a following to pull something like that off."[558] The number of YouTube views would indicate they do, but large events like the ones described would require fans to travel and outlay some significant cash. "It is uncharted water," Tim says.

To this end, the band has come up with a preliminary set list of twenty-three songs which will be just shy of a two-hour concert. Making up the list is no small task. It has to include songs where, for example, Tim is on keyboards for a few consecutive songs to avoid down time involved in moving from one instrument to another. Consideration must also be given to the style of song to ensure that there aren't eight ballads in a row, but rather a good mix of music. There needs to be up tempo songs at the beginning and end.

The discussion of *Foxes and Fossils* performing live shows

---

558   Ibid.

at any of these venues is enough to get most fans rather excited, but these are only plans and they are very preliminary plans at that. It is possible that none of it will ever happen. It is also possible that at the time you are reading this, it has happened already. Regardless, one thing is certain. Foxes and Fossils popularity continues to grow, and the love and devotion shown by fans all over the world is showing no sign of waning any time soon.

APPENDICES

Appendix A | Live Performances
Provided by Christopher Ketchum[559]

YT = YouTube video | A = Audience video | P = Private event

All live performances in Georgia

2010
03/14/10 Bella's—Smyrna—YT
08/11/10 First United Methodist Church—Smyrna
08/20/10 Jess Lucas Park—Hapeville
09/04/10 House Party—Smyrna—The Mustangs w/ Maggie
          & Sammie—P
09/12/10 Yellow Daisy Festival—Stone Mountain
09/18/10 Jess Lucas Park—Hapeville

2011
05/29/11 Twisted Taco—Smyrna
07/03/11 Twisted Taco—Smyrna
08/13/11 Woodstock Music Festival—Woodstock—A
08/19/11 Jess Lucas Park—Hapeville—A

---

559 Ketchum, Christopher, Chart of Foxes and Fossils live performances, pro-
     vided to author on May 3, 2022.

08/21/11 Twisted Taco—Smyrna—YT
09/11/11 Yellow Daisy Festival—Stone Mountain
10/15/11 Twisted Taco—Smyrna

2012
04/29/12 Twisted Taco—Smyrna
07/13/12 Twisted Taco—Smyrna—Foxless Fossils—YT
07/14/12 Mall of Georgia—Buford
08/05/12 Twisted Taco—Smyrna—YT
09/09/12 Yellow Daisy Festival—Stone Mountain
11/17/12 Wedding Reception—Cairo—The Mustangs w/
Maggie & Sammie—P

2013
05/18/13 Twisted Taco—Smyrna
06/16/13 Twisted Taco—Smyrna
06/29/13 Mall of Georgia—Buford
07/13/13 Twisted Taco—Smyrna
07/19/13 Jess Lucas Park—Hapeville—A
08/02/13 Twisted Taco—Smyrna—YT

2014
06/06/14 Atlanta Botanical Garden—Atlanta
06/07/14 Mall of Georgia—Buford
06/14/14 Woodstock Music Festival—Woodstock—A
07/04/14 Keswick Park—Chamblee—YT
07/27/14 Renaissance Hotel—Smyrna—P
08/14/14 Renaissance Hotel—Smyrna—P
08/15/14 Jess Lucas Park—Hapeville

2015
07/19/15 Renaissance Hotel Ballroom—Smyrna—P
08/09/15 Renaissance Hotel Ballroom—Smyrna—P

08/21/15   Jess Lucas Park—Hapeville—YT
10/17/15   PC&E—Atlanta—The Mustangs w/ Chase

2016
06/25/16   Mall of Georgia—Buford—A
08/13/16   Crafty Hog—Smyrna—YT / A

2017
06/10/17   Peachtree Corners Festival—Peachtree Corners
07/22/17   Mall of Georgia—Buford
07/23/17   St. Angelo's/Keegan's Patio Deck—Smyrna—YT

2020
07/04/20   Dearborn Plaza—Hapeville—Foxless Fossils—YT/A

2021
04/10/21   Truist Park—Atlanta (National Anthem)—YT/A

Appendix B | Audio/Video
Prepared by Christopher Ketchum560

Updated 5/25/22

CD1=A Curious Mix (11 songs)

CD2=Foxes and Fossils Live (18 songs)

CD3=Songs from the Basement (14 songs)

CD4=Have Yourself A Very Mellow Christmas (10 songs)

CD5=Carry On (13 songs)

DD=Digital download

DVD=Live at Bella's (20 songs + interviews)

YT=YouTube video

A=Audience video

*=Bonus studio track

All CDs are also available as full album digital downloads

A Day in the Life—CD3 / DD / YT

A Hazy Shade of Winter—CD5 / DD / YT

Ain't it Fun—CD2 / DD / YT

All Right Now—A

America—CD2* / DD / DVD / YT

American Girl—CD1 / DD / YT

American Honey—CD1 / DD / DVD / YT

Amie—YT

Angel from Montgomery—CD3 / DD / YT

Barton Hollow—CD2 / DD / YT

Black Water—DVD / YT

Boondocks—DD / DVD / YT

Bring it on Home—DVD / YT

California Dreamin'—CD3 / DD / YT

---

560   Ketchum, Christopher, Listing of Foxes and Fossils audio and video recordings, provided to author on May 3, 2022 and updated May 25, 2022.

Carry On—CD5 / DD / YT
Chicken Fried—YT / A
City Of New Orleans—YT
Crazy—YT
Cruel To Be Kind—DVD
Dance With Me—CD5 / DD / YT
Dedicated To the One I Love—CD3 / DD / YT
Destination—CD5 / DD / YT
Doctor My Eyes—CD2 / DD / YT
Don't Worry Baby—CD3 / DD / YT
Early Morning Rain—CD3 / DD / YT
Fairytale—CD2 / DD / YT
Fallin' For You—CD1 / DD / YT
Famous in a Small Town—CD1 / DD / DVD
Fifteen—DVD / YT
Good Kisser—CD3 / DD / YT
Goodbye Yellow Brick Road—CD5 / DD / YT
Harvest Moon—CD3 / DD / YT
Helplessly Hoping—YT
Here and Now—CD2 / DD / YT
Hip to My Heart—CD1 / DD / YT / A
Ho Hey—YT / A
I Can't Let Go—CD2 / DD / YT
I'm With the Band—YT / A
It Wouldn't Have Made Any Difference—CD5 / DD / YT
Landslide—CD2 / DD / YT
Let It Be Me—CD5 / DD / YT
Let the Rain—CD1 / DD / YT
Lottery—CD5 / DD / YT
Love is the Answer—CD3 / DD / YT
Mama's Broken Heart—A
Man of Constant Sorrow—DVD
Mayberry—CD1 / DD

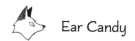

Monday Monday—CD1 / DD / DVD / YT
Mr. Sandman—CD5 / DD / YT
My Church—CD5 / DD / YT
Neon Moon—CD3 / DD / YT
Nobody Love—CD2 / DD / YT
One Sweet Love—CD2 / DD / DVD / YT
Our Lips Are Sealed—YT
Peace Train—CD5
Piano Man—CD3 / DD / YT
Rolling in the Deep—YT
Royals—CD2 / DD / YT
Runaway—DVD / YT
Senses Working Overtime—YT
Seven Bridges Road—CD3 / DD / YT
Strawberry Wine—DVD / YT
Suite: Judy Blue Eyes—CD2* / DD / DVD / YT / A
Sweet Nothings—CD2 / DD / YT
Telling Me Lies—CD3 / DD / YT
The First Cut is the Deepest—DVD / YT
The Night Before—CD2 / DD / YT
The Only Exception—CD1 / DD / DVD / YT
The Road to Forever—CD3 / DD
The Shoop Shoop Song / It's In His Kiss—DVD
The Star-Spangled Banner—DD / YT / A
The Things We Do For Love—CD5 / DD / YT
Thinking of You—CD1 / DD / DVD / YT
Thinking Out Loud—YT
To Sir with Love—CD2 / DD
Vacation—YT
Walk On By—CD5
We Gotta Get You a Woman—CD2 / DD / YT
We Run—DVD / YT
When You Say Nothing at All—CD2 / DD / YT

Why Should I Care—CD1 / DD
World News Polka—YT
You Can't Hurry Love—CD2 / DD / YT
Angels We Have Heard On High—CD4 / YT
What Are You Doing New Year's Eve?—CD4
Have Yourself a Merry Little Christmas—CD4
Christmas Bells (I Heard The Bells On Christmas Day)—
CD4 / YT
Christmas Time Is Here—CD4 / YT
Silver Bells—CD4 / YT
In The Bleak Midwinter—CD4
Christmas Don't Be Late—CD4
O Holy Night—CD4 / YT
Greensleeves (What Child Is This?)—CD4*
Acoustic guitar instrumental

Appendix C | Song List
(Alphabetical Listing with Original Artist)
Prepared by Christopher Ketchum[561]
Updated 5/25/22

A Day in the Life—The Beatles
A Hazy Shade of Winter—Simon & Garfunkel (The Bangles)
Ain't it Fun—Paramore
All Right Now—Free
America—Simon & Garfunkel
American Girl—Tom Petty & the Heartbreakers
American Honey—Lady A
Amie—Pure Prairie League
Angel from Montgomery—John Prine
Barton Hollow—Civil Wars
Black Horse and the Cherry Tree—KT Tunstall
Black Water—Doobie Brothers
Boondocks—Little Big Town
Bring it on Home—Little Big Town
California Dreamin'—The Mamas & the Papas
Carry On—Crosby, Stills, Nash & Young
Chicken Fried—Zac Brown Band
Crazy—Gnarls Barkley
Cruel To Be Kind—Nick Lowe
Dance With Me—Orleans
Dedicated To the One I Love—The Mamas & the Papas
Destination—Nickel Creek
Doctor My Eyes—Jackson Browne
Don't Worry Baby—Beach Boys
Drive South—John Hiatt
Drops of Jupiter—Train

---

561   Ketchum, Christopher, Alphabetical listing of Foxes and Fossils songs
with original artist, provided to author on May 3, 2022.

Early Morning Rain—Gordon Lightfoot
Every River—Kim Richey
Fairytale—Sara Bareilles
Fallin' For You—Colbie Caillat
Famous in a Small Town—Miranda Lambert
Fifteen—Taylor Swift
Follow Your Arrow—Kasey Musgraves
Getting Better—The Beatles
Good Kisser—Lake Street Dive
Goodbye Yellow Brick Road—Elton John (Sara Bareilles)
Harvest Moon—Neil Young
Helplessly Hoping—Crosby, Stills & Nash
Here and Now—Letters To Cleo
Hip to My Heart—The Band Perry
Ho Hey—Lumineers
How Do I Make You—Linda Ronstadt
I Can't Let Go—Evie Sands (Linda Ronstadt)
I Want You to Want Me—Cheap Trick
I'm With the Band—Little Big Town
It Wouldn't Have Made Any Difference—Todd Rundgren
Landslide—Fleetwood Mac (The Chicks)
Let It Be Me—Everly Brothers
Let the Rain—Sara Bareilles
Lottery—Jade Bird
Love is the Answer—Todd Rundgren
Mama's Broken Heart—Miranda Lambert
Man of Constant Sorrow—*Dan Tyminski*
Mayberry—Rascal Flatts
Mexico—James Taylor
Monday Monday—The Mamas & the Papas
Mr. Sandman—The Chordettes
My Church—Maren Morris
Neon Moon—Brooks & Dunn

Nobody Love—Tori Kelly
Nothin' Better to Do—LeAnn Rimes
On a Bad Day—Kasey Chambers
One Sweet Love—Sara Bareilles
Only Prettier—Miranda Lambert
Our Lips Are Sealed—The Go Go's
Piano Man—Billy Joel
Rolling in the Deep—Adele
Royals—Lorde
Rumor Has It—Adele
Runaway—Love & Theft
Senses Working Overtime—XTC
Seven Bridges Road—Steve Young (Eagles)
Strawberry Wine—Deana Carter
Suite: Judy Blue Eyes—Crosby, Stills & Nash
Sweet Nothings—Brenda Lee
Teenage Dream—Katy Perry
Telling Me Lies—Linda Thompson (Parton, Ronstadt, Harris)
The First Cut Is the Deepest—Cat Stevens
The Night Before—Carrie Underwood
The Only Exception—Paramore
The Road to Forever—Foxes & Fossils
The Shoop Shoop Song (It's In His Kiss)—Betty Everett
The Star Spangled Banner—Francis Scott Key
The Things We Do For Love—10cc
Thinking of You—Katy Perry
Thinking Out Loud—Ed Sheeran
365 Days—ZZ Ward
Timber, I'm Falling In Love—Patty Loveless
To Sir with Love—Lulu
Vacation—The Go Go's
We Gotta Get You a Woman—Todd Rundgren
We Run—Sugarland

When You Say Nothing at All—Keith Whitley (Alison Krauss)
Why Should I Care—Sara Evans
World News Polka—Barry Mitchell
Wouldn't It Be Nice—Beach Boys
You Can't Hurry Love—Supremes

Appendix D | Bands/solo artists covered from A to Z

Prepared by Christopher Ketchum[562]–Updated 5/25/22

Adele x2	Gordon Lightfoot	Nick Lowe
Band Perry	Jackson Brown	Nickel Creek
Barry Mitchell	Jade Bird	Orleans
Beach Boys x2	James Taylor	Paramore
Beatles x2	John Hiatt	Patty Loveless
Betty Everett	John Prine	Pure Prairie League
Billy Joel	Kasey Chambers	Rascal Flatts
Brenda Lee	Kasey Musgraves	Sara Bareilles x3
Brooks & Dunn	Katy Perry x2	Sara Evans
Carrie Underwood	Keith Whitley	Simon & Garfunkel x2
Cheap Trick	Kim Richey	Steve Goodman
Chordettes	KT Tunstall	Steve Young
Civil Wars	Lady A	Sugarland
Colbie Cailliat	Lake Street Dive	Supremes
Crosby, Stills, Nash &	LeAnn Rimes	Taylor Swift
Young x2	Letters To Cleo	10cc
Dan Tyminski	Linda Ronstadt	Todd Rundgren x3
Deana Carter	Linda Thompson	Tom Petty & the
Doobie Brothers	Little Big Town x3	Heartbreakers
Ed Sheeran	Lorde	Tori Kelly
Elton John	Love and Theft	Train
Everly Brothers	Lulu	XTC
Evie Sands	Lumineers	Yusuf Islam/Cat Ste-
Fleetwood Mac	Mamas & the Papas x3	vens x2
Free	Maren Morris	Zack Brown Band
Gnarls Barkley	Miranda Lambert x3	ZZ Ward
Go Go's x2	Neil Young	

---

562   Ketchum, Christopher, Bands/solo artists covered by Foxes and Fossils from A to Z, provided to author on May 3, 2022.

Appendix E | Photo List
Prepared by David Weaver[563]

+=Onstage and Offstage Photos
-=Offstage photos only
*Photos of the audience without band members

03/14/10 Bella's+
05/29/11 Twisted Taco+
07/03/11 Twisted Taco+
08/13/11 Woodstock Music Festival+*
08/19/11 Jess Lucas Park
08/21/11 Twisted Taco+
09/11/11 Yellow Daisy Festival+
10/15/11 Twisted Taco
07/13/12 Twisted Taco (with David Purcell)
07/14/12 Mall of Georgia
08/05/12 Twisted Taco
06/16/13 Twisted Taco
06/29/13 Mall of Georgia
08/02/13 Twisted Taco*
06/06/14 Atlanta Botanical Gardens-*
06/07/14 Mall of Georgia*
06/14/14 Woodstock Music Festival*
07/04/14 Keswick Park*
07/19/13 Jess Lucas Park
07/27/14 Renaissance Hotel
08/14/14 Renaissance Hotel
08/15/14 Jess Lucas Park*
07/19/15 Renaissance Hotel Ballroom
08/09/15 Renaissance Hotel Ballroom

---

563   Weaver, David, Foxes and Fossils photo list, provided to the author December 1, 2021.

08/21/15 Jess Lucas Park
06/25/16 Mall of Georgia
08/13/16 Crafty Hog
06/10/17 Peachtree Groves Festival
07/22/17 Mall of Georgia–
07/23/17 St. Angelo's/Keegan's Deck

ALSO

Wedding; Cairo, GA 11/17/2012. (Mustangs show with Sammie and Maggie on vocals)+
Tim, Johnny & Darwin, Hapeville, GA 7/4/20—"Foxless Fossils" show

**Some photos are video captures.
Any show that has video is considered photographed.

Appendix F | Official Live Performance YouTube Videos:

Prepared by David Weaver564

(posted to the Foxes & Fossils YouTube Channel)

03/14/10 **Bella's;** 14 Videos (Suite: Judy Blue Eyes, Boondocks, etc)

08/21/11 **Twisted Taco;** 6 Videos (Our Lips Are Sealed, American Girl, etc)

07/13/12 **Twisted Taco;** 3 Videos (Pride and Joy, Key To The Highway, etc)—with David Purcell

08/05/12 **Twisted Taco;** 6 Videos (The Night Before, Sweet Nothings, etc)

08/02/13 **Twisted Taco;** 10 Videos (Landslide, Helplessly Hoping, etc)

07/04/14 **Keswick Park;** 2 Videos (Hip To My Heart, Can't Hurry Love)

08/21/15 **Jess Lucas Park;** 4 Videos (Royals, Fairytale, etc)

08/13/16 **The Crafty Hog;** 1 Video (Thinking Out Loud)

07/23/17 **St. Angelo's/Keegan's Patio Deck;** 2 Videos (Amie, Crazy)

07/04/20 **Hapeville, GA;** 3 Videos (Early Morning Rain, Piano Man, etc)—"Foxless Fossils" Concert

Crowd Shot Excerpts

(posted in the VIDEO section of our fan page)

08/13/11 **Woodstock, Georgia;** "Hip to My Heart"

06/14/14 **Woodstock, Georgia;** "I'm With The Band/Suite: Judy Blue Eyes/Chicken Fried"

06/25/16 **Mall of Georgia;** "Chicken Fried"

---

564   Weaver, David, Official Foxes and Fossils Live Performance YouTube Videos, posted to Foxes and Fossils YouTube Channel.

08/13/16 **The Crafty Hog**; "Ho Hey"
07/04/20 **Hapeville, GA;** "Get Together" & "The Boxer"
—"Foxless Fossils" Concert
07/04/20 **Hapeville, GA;** "Wooden Ships"& "Get Together"
(full songs)—"Foxless Fossils" Concert

(These can all be found by searching
CROWD EXCERPTS on our fan page)

Others

The F&F YouTube Channel also has 6 Videos of Sammie's pro debut with the Mustangs at the Yellow Daisy Festival; September, 2009 (Mercy, Chain of Fools, etc)

There are 6 songs from the "Live at Bella's" DVD that have not been published to YouTube.

There are low quality cell phone videos of "All Right Now" (8/19/2011) and "Momma's Broken Heart" (7/19/13, both in Hapeville) kicking around the internet.

BIBLIOGRAPHY

Author Interviews:

1. Sammie Purcell interview #1, July 14, 2021
2. Toby Ruckert interview #1, September 28, 2021
3. Tim Purcell interview #1, October 4, 2021
4. Scott King interview #1, October 12, 2021
5. Scott King interview #2, October 26, 2021.
6. Toby Ruckert interview #2, November 2, 2021.
7. Tim Purcell interview #2, November 29, 2021.
8. Darwin Conort interview #1, November 30, 2021.
9. Tim Purcell interview #3, December 13, 2021.
10. Scott King interview #3, December 17, 2021.
11. Johnny Pike interview #1, December 29, 2021.
12. Tim Purcell interview #4, December 30, 2021.
13. Tim Purcell interview #5, December 31, 2021.
14. Maggie Adams interview #1, January 5, 2022.
15. Larry Adams interview #1, January 6, 2022.
16. Tim Purcell interview #6, January 7, 2022.
17. Tim Purcell interview #7, January 10, 2021.
18. Mary & Michael Thomas interview #1, January 28, 2022.
19. Tim Purcell interview #8, January 28, 2022.
20. Sammie Purcell interview #2, February 8, 2022.

21. Darwin Conort interview #2, February 10, 2022.
22. Toby Ruckert interview #3, February 11, 2022.
23. Larry & Ellen Adams interview #2, March 3, 2022.
24. Scott & Karon Truran interview #1, March 17, 2022.
25. Larry & Ellen Adams interview #3, March 29, 2022.
26. Darwin Conort & Jill Ewing interview #3, March 29, 2022.
27. Scott & Karon Truran interview #2 and Chase Truran interview #1, March 29, 2022.
28. Chase Truran interview #2, April 1, 2022.
29. Christopher Ketchum interview #1, May 2, 2022.
30. Bruce Johnson interview #1, May 5, 2022.
31. Chase Truran interview #3, May 23, 2022.
32. Tim Purcell interview #9, May 23, 2022.
33. Tim Purcell interview #10, July 26, 2022.

Written Comments Provided to the Author:

1. Tim Purcell, July 19, 2021.
2. Tim Purcell, July 20, 2021.
3. Terri Purcell, August 16, 2021.
4. Johnny Pike, August 20, 2021.
5. Johnny Pike, October 20, 2021.
6. Toby Ruckert, October 27, 2021.
7. Tim Purcell, October 28, 2021.
8. Sammie Purcell, October 29, 2021.
9. Darwin Conort, November 8, 2021.
10. Christopher Ketchum, December 2, 2021.
11. Johnny Pike, December 30, 2021.
12. Johnny Pike, January 3, 2022.
13. Larry Adams, January 6, 2022.
14. Maggie Adams, January 9, 2022.

15. Mary Thomas, January 23, 2022.
16. Mary Thomas, January 24, 2022.
17. Maggie Adams, January 24, 2022.
18. Mary Thomas, January 28, 2022.
19. Duncan James, January 28, 2022.
20. Billy Parks, January 30, 2022.
21. Billy Parks, February 3, 2022.
22. Mike Frey, February 6, 2022.
23. Billy Parks, February 9, 2022.
24. Paul Giammarco, February 10, 2022.
25. Terry Heinlein, February 11, 2022.
26. Gary Topholme, February 11, 2022.
27. Terry Heinlein, February 12, 2022.
28. Brad Burns, February 12, 2022.
29. Toby Ruckert, February 12, 2022.
30. Ross King, January 14, 2022.
31. Bob & Linda LaFrenierre, February 17, 2022.
32. Sammie Purcell, February 23, 2022.
33. Jill Ewing, March 7, 2022.
34. Ian O'Donnell, March 9, 2022.
35. Jill Ewing, March 12, 2022.
36. Jill Ewing, March 14, 2022.
37. David Weaver, March 17, 2022.
38. Toby Ruckert, April 23, 2022.
39. Toby Ruckert, April 17, 2022
40. Toby Ruckert, April 18, 2022.
41. Monique Kooij-Alphenaar, March 22, 2022.
42. Steven Poegl, March 23, 2022.
43. Darwin Conort, May 2, 2022.
44. Christopher Ketchum, May 2, 2022.
45. Bruce Johnson, May 4, 2022
46. Randy Mathews, May 11, 2022.
47. Darwin Conort, May 11, 2022.

48. Darwin Conort, May 12, 2022.
49. Maggie Adams, May 13, 2022.
50. Darwin Conort, May 15, 2022.
51. Scott Kale, May 18, 2022.

Internet Sources:

1. A Breath of Fresh Air with Sandy Kaye Podcast, An Interview with Tim Purcell. September 26, 2020. https://foxesandfossils.com/a-breath-of-fresh-air/.
2. ALLMUSIC, Biography Mark Wills. https://www.allmusic.com/artist/mark-wills-mn0000334041/biography.
3. American Air Museum in Britain, Capt. Donald Eugene Purcell, Pilot B24-H #418 8th AF, 2nd AD, 96th CBW, 466th BG, 784th BS RAF Attlebridge, Sta 120. http://www.americanairmuseum.com/terms-conditions.
4. Beauchamp, Charlie C., Tampa Bay Times, St. Petersburg, Florida, Obituary, April 6, 1967. From Newspapers by Ancestry.com. https://www.news-papers.com/image/320286044.
5. Beauchamp, Charlie, Boca Ciega High School— BCHS Class of 1967. https://bogieclassof67.com/ [age.php?groupingID=miscellaneous14.
6. Chitchat with Chuck, Podcast, March 30, 2021. Interview with Sammie and Maggie. https://foxesandfossils.com/sammie-and-maggie-on-chitchat-with-chuck/.
7. Classmates, School Yearbooks. https://mail.google.com/mail/u/0?ik=b0d90baeea&view=pt&search=.
8. Conort, Dorothy E, Obituary. Lewis Funeral Home

December 12, 2009. https://www.legacy.com/
obituaries/atlanta/obituary.aspx?n=dorothy-conor-
t&pid=137183757&fhid=5035.

9. Dahlgren, Doug, Artist First Radio Network. May 13,
    2022. https://media.artistfirst.com/ArtistFirst_Doug_
    https://www.artistfirst.com. Dahlgren_2022-05-13_
    Tim_Purcell.mp3.

10. Dyer, Candice, ArtsATL, Music 'Put A Lid On It',
    Singer Charts Hopeful Direction: Diane Durrett's
    Soulful New Album Aims To Cheer Us Up.
    December 3, 2021. https://www.artsatl.org/diane-
    durretts-latest-album-put-a-lid-on-it-charts-a-
    hopeful-soulful-direction/.

11. Emerson, Bo, The Atlanta Journal-Constitution,
    Atlanta Living & Arts. Father and Daughter Lead
    Smyrna Cover Band to YouTube Success.

12. Foxes and Fossils Facebook Fan Page, https://www.
    facebook.com/groups/1632462426895484.

13. Foxes and Fossils website, https://duckduckgo.
    com/?t=ffab&q=foxes+and+fossils+website&ia=web.

14. Foxes and Fossils YouTube Channel, https://duck-
    duckgo.com/?t=ffab&q=foxes+and+fossills+you-
    tube+channel&ia=web

15. FineArtAmerica, Gary Limuti Art, https://fin-
    eartamerica.com/profiles/garry-limuti.

16. Harris, Art, The Washington Post, Memories of
    Chapman, December 12, 1980. https://www.
    washingtonpost.com/archive/lifestyle/1980/12/12/
    memories-of-chapman/798581a0-8440-46ee-859f-
    fc7d8bbcafd7/.

17. Hudak, Joseph, Rolling Stone, How the Base-
    ment East Built Back: A Deadly Tornado and
    a Global Pandemic Haven't Been Enough to

Stop One of East Nashville's Favorite Live Venues for Long. September 20, 2021. https://www.rollingstone.com/music/music-country/basement-east-nashville-1224623/.

18. Kojak, Ken, 60's Jukebox Review Podcast, RememberWhenRadio.com, Interview with Tim & Chase, New York, May 29, 2021. https://foxesandfossils.com/chase-and-tim-on-60s-jukebox-revuew/

19. Kale, Scott, The Grey Riders. https://youtu.be/nlBXrIPDVQU.

20. Lemlick, Jeff, Jeffers 66, Real Teen Tragedies Behind 2 Moody Garage 45s. https://savagelost.com/the-real-teen-tragedies-behind-two-moody-garage-45s. September 26, 2015.

21. Levs, Josh; Anderson, Emily; Nicolaidis, Virginia; and Bash, Dana. Big Three Auto CEOs Flew Private Jets to Ask for Taxpayer Money. CNN, November 19, 2008. http://www.cnn.com/2008/us/11/19/autos.ceo.jets/.

22. Northern Spirit Radio—Song of the Soul Podcast, Uncovered Music of Tim Purcell, December 5, 2020. https://foxesandfossils.com/uncovered-music-of-tim-purcell/.

23. Northern Spirit Radio—Song of the Soul Podcast, Mark Helpsmeet Interview with Sammie Purcell. September 26, 2020. https://foxesandfossils.com/listen-to-sammie-on-song-of-the-soul-podcast/.

24. Old Farmers Almanac, The, For The Atlanta Harsfield, 1 GA USA Weather Station. https://www.almanac.com/weather/history/GA/Atlanta/1956-02-22.

25. Olivia Management Website, Maggie Adams/Tour Marketing Coordinator and Director

of Content. October 11, 2016. https://www.
oliviamanagement.com/blogfull/2016/10/11/
meet-the-team-maggie-adams.

26. Perdue, Sonny Gov. Schedule of Inaugural Events.
January 4, 2003. https://sonnyperdue.georgia.
gov/00/press/detail/0,2668,78006749_91290006_912
90042,00.html.

27. Player, Brian, Folk & Acoustic Interview—with
Sammie & Scott, March 8, 2021. https://foxesand-
fossils.com/our-lives-and-music-interview/.

28. Rixstep, It Was Eight Years Ago Today, 2018, https//
rixstep.com/1/1/1/20180321.shtml.

29. Rubin, Jason M., The Arts Fuse. Music Review/Inter-
view: Foxes & Fossils—50 Million YouTube Views
Can't Be Wrong, February 5, 2021. https://artsfuse.
org/221384/music-review-interview-foxes-fossils-
50-million-youtube-views-cant-be-wrong/.

30. SHEDOOBEE with StonesDoug. May 13, 2010.
https://www.tapatalk.com/groups/shidoobee-
withstonesdoug/keith-talks-about-when-his-gui-
tars-were-stolen-t23485.html. Tapatalk, Inc. 202
Bicknell Avenue, First Floor, Santa Monica, CA
90405

31. Simply Cremation, Obituary for Scott Moncure King.
January 13, 2022. https://csofhr.com/obituaries/
scott-moncure-king/.

32. Vanderbilt University Website. Commencement Traditions, posted by Melina Prentakis on
May 14, 2018. https://admissions.vanderbilt.edu/
vandybloggers/2018/05/commencement-traditions/.

33. Wikipedia Encyclopedia, Turner, Ted. https://
en.wikipedia.org/wiki/Ted_Turner.

34. Wikipedia Encyclopedia, America (Simon

and Garfunkel song), Recorded in Colum-
bia Studio, New York City on February 1,
1968. Release on April 3, 1968, from the
album *Bookends*. https://en.wikipedia.org/wiki/
America_(Simon_%26_Garfunkel_song).

35. Wikipedia Encyclopedia, Hayes, Michael (wrestler), Wikipedia https://en.wikipedia.org/wiki/
michael_hayes_(wrestler).

ABOUT THE AUTHORS

Paul F. Caranci

Paul F. Caranci is a third-generation res-
ident of North Providence and has been
a student of history for many years. Paul
served as Rhode Island's Deputy Secretary
of State from 2007 to 2015 and was elected
to the North Providence Town Council
where he served from 1994 to 2010. He
has a BA in political science from Providence College and is working toward an
MPA from Roger Williams University.

Together with his wife Margie he founded the Munici-
pal Heritage Group in 2009. He is an incorporating member
of the Association of Rhode Island Authors (ARIA) and a
member of the board of the RI Publications Society. He also
served on the Board of Directors of the Heritage Harbor
Museum and the Rhode Island Heritage Hall of Fame. He is
past Chairman of the Diabetes Foundation of Rhode Island
(formerly the American Diabetes Association, Rhode Island
Affiliate) where he served on the Board for over 15 years.

During his tenure on the North Providence Town Council Paul's efforts earned him several awards. For his legislative

work in the prevention of youth addiction to tobacco Paul was recognized with the James Carney Public Health Award from the RI Department of Health and an Advocacy Award from the American Cancer Society. Paul's legislation to expand health care coverage to include the equipment, supplies and education necessary for the home management of diabetes and his work toward the elimination of the pre-existing condition clause from health insurance policies written in Rhode Island were recognized with an Advocate of the Year Award from the Diabetes Foundation of RI and an Advocacy Award from the American Diabetes Association. Those new laws also made Rhode Island the first state in the nation to both eliminate the pre-existing condition clause and expand coverage for diabetes care. His efforts in exposing political corruption in his hometown earned him the Margaret Chase Smith Award for Political Courage from the National Association of Secretaries of State, the group's highest honor.

Paul is the author of fourteen published books including four award winning books. *The Hanging & Redemption of John Gordon: The True Story of Rhode Island's Last Execution* (The History Press, 2013) was voted one of the top five non-fiction books of 2013 by the Providence Journal. *Scoundrels: Defining Corruption Through Tales of Political Intrigue in Rhode Island* (Stillwater River Publications, 2016) was the winner of the 2016 Dorry Award as the non-fiction book of the year. *The Promise of Fatima: One Hundred Years of History, Mystery, and Faith* (Stillwater River Publications, 2017) earned Paul a spot as a finalist in the International Book Awards, and *I Am The Immaculate Conception: The Story of Bernadette of Lourdes*, (Stillwater River Publications, 2019) landed Paul the same honor. Paul's memoir, *Wired: A Shocking True Story of Political Corruption and the FBI Informant Who Risked Everything to Expose It* (Stillwater River Publications, 2017) tells his own story of courage in the face of the political corruption that surrounded him.

Paul and his wife Margie recently celebrated their 45th wedding anniversary. The couple have two adult children, Heather and Matthew; and four grandchildren, Matthew, Jacob, Vincent and Casey. They continue to make residence in the Town of North Providence.

Sammie Purcell

Sammie Purcell is an Atlanta native and a member of Foxes and Fossils. She is a graduate of Vanderbilt University and holds a masters in journalism from Boston University. She currently works as a journalist for a local paper in the metro Atlanta area, writing about city politics and the occasional movie review. She lives with her dog, Willie Nelson. This is her first book.

Also By Paul F. Caranci

The History Press
2012

The History Press
2012
*Named one of top 5
non-fiction books
of the year*

Stillwater River Publications
2014

Stillwater River Publications
2014

Stillwater River Publications
2015

Stillwater River Publications
2016
*Dicey Award
Non-fiction Book*

Stillwater River Publications
2017

Stillwater River Publications
2017
*Finalist in the 2018
International Book
Awards*

Stillwater River Publications
2019
*Finalist in the 2019
International
Book Awards*

Stillwater River Publications
2019

Stillwater River Publications
2020

Stillwater River Publications
2020

Stillwater River Publications
2021

ORDER FORM
Please use the following to order additional copies of:

1. Heavenly Portrait: The Miraculous Image of Our Lady of Guadalupe ($20.00)
2. I Am the Immaculate Conception: The Story of St. Bernadette And Her Apparitions At Lourdes ($20.00)
3. The Promise of Fatima: One Hundred Years of History, Mystery & Faith ($20.00)
4. Wired: A Shocking True Story of Political Corruption and the FBI Informant Who Risked Everything to Expose It ($23.00)
5. Scoundrels: Defining Political Corruption Through Tales of Political Intrigue in Rhode Island ($20.00)
6. Monumental Providence: Legends of History in Sculpture, Statuary, Monuments and Memorials ($20.00)
7. The Essential Guide to Running for Local Office ($15.00)
8. The Hanging & Redemption of John Gordon: The True Story of Rhode Island's Last Execution ($20.00)
9. North Providence: A History & The People Who Shaped It ($20.00)
10. Award Winning Real Estate in a Depressed or Declining Market ($10.00)
11. Terror in Wichita: A True Story of One Woman's Courage and Her Will to Live ($12.95)
12. Darkness at Dachau: The True Story of Father Jean Bernard ($20.00)
13. Before the End of the Age ($20.00)

____(QTY)_____(Title) X _____ (Price) = $ _____

____(QTY)_____(Title) X _____ (Price) = $ _____

____(QTY)_____(Title) X _____ (Price) = $ _____

____(QTY)_____(Title) X _____ (Price) = $ _____

____(QTY)_____(Title) X _____ (Price) = $ _____

Total for books $_____ + Postage** $_____ = TOTAL COST $_____

**Postage: Please add $3.00 for the first book and $1.50 for each additional book ordered.

Payment Method:

____Personal Check Enclosed (Payable to **M. Caranci Books**)

____Charge my Credit Card

    Name:_____BILLING ZIP CODE:_____

    Visa____Master Card_____

    Card Number:_____EXP:___/__CSC (3 digit code) _____

    Signature:_____

(Order form continues on next page)

Ship My Book To:

Name _____

Street _____

City_____State:_____Zip:_____

Phone_____Email:_____

Special Signing Instructions: i.e. To Whom do you want the book signed? Do you want me to include a message? Just sign my name? Etc.

_____

_____

_____

MAIL YOUR COMPLETED FORM TO:

Paul F. Caranci

26 East Avenue

North Providence, RI 02911

You may also order using my Email address at municipalheritage@gmail.com

or by calling me at 401-639-4502

Please visit my Website at www.paulcaranci.com